Implementing Multiage Education: A Practical Guide to a Promising Future

Implementing Multiage Education: A Practical Guide to a Promising Future

Wendy C. Kasten

Elizabeth Monce Lolli

Christopher-Gordon Publishers, Inc.
Norwood, MA

Credits

Every effort has been made to contact copyright holders for permission to reproduce borrowed material where necessary. We apologize for any oversights and would be happy to rectify them in future printings.

All interviews used with permission.

Excerpts from *Curriculum and Evaluation Standards for School Mathematics* are reprinted with permission from *Curriculum and Evaluation Standards for School Mathematics,* copyright © 1989 by the National Council of Teachers of Mathematics. All rights reserved.

Excerpts of standards from *National Science Education Standards* reprinted with permission from *National Science Education Standards.* Copyright © 1996 by the National Academy of Sciences. Courtesy of the National Academy Press, Washington, DC.

Standards for the English Language Arts by the International Reading Association and the National Council of Teachers of English. Copyright © 1996 by the International Reading Association and the National Council of Teachers of English. Reprinted with permission.

The *National Council for Social Studies Standards* is reprinted with permission from the National Council for Social Studies.

Muldoon *Elementary School Report Card Goals* used with permission of Muldoon Elementary School and its principal.

Copyright © 1998 by Christopher-Gordon Publishers, Inc.

Christopher-Gordon Publishers, Inc.
1502 Providence Highway, Suite #12
Norwood, MA 02062

Printed in the United States of America
10 9 8 7 6 5 4 3 2 1

02 01 00 99 98

Library of Congress Catalog Card Number: 97-78326
ISBN: 0-926842-78-1

To my parents, Mary Kasten Overeem and Henry Overeem, who have always been loving and encouraging in all my pursuits but especially my education. Thank you.

—W.C.K.

To Matthew and Benjamin, my sons, who have taught me so much more than books or college courses! To my husband, Eugene, the "wind beneath my wings."

—E.M.L.

Contents

Appendixes

Foreword

Multiage education is continuing to receive a great deal of interest as educators, legislators, and parents seek to find ways to improve educational experiences for all children. Every fall as the school year begins, newspapers and magazines feature schools or classes that either are disastrous or highlight promising, supposedly, new practices. For the past few years, multiage classes have been receiving such publicity. More often than not, these "new" practices are either new to the journalist or have been publicized in the past under a different name. This is the case with multiage classes that have been in existence for nearly 40 years under the labels of nongraded or ungraded classes. Credible comparative research studies conducted during this period of time find that students in nongraded or multiage schools are more likely to have higher academic achievement, stronger self-concepts, and more positive attitudes toward school than those in graded schools with single-age classrooms. Many of the schools now being organized under the choice, charter, or voucher umbrella are in essence multiage schools.

Teachers embarking upon a journey to implement multiaging in their classrooms and principals facilitating such change in their schools are in for a treat as they read *Implementing Multiage Education: A Practical Guide to a Promising Future* by Wendy Kasten and Elizabeth Lolli. Not only do Wendy and Libbie provide written guideposts, they write as if they were speaking directly to the readers and even offer to continue the conversation by giving their e-mail addresses to you. These authors care about their readers and their efforts to implement multiaging.

The authors take their readers by the hand and guide them as they move from exploring the concept of multiage to the actual stages of implementation. As is consistent with the philosophy of multiage, they do not suggest that there is only one right way to put multiage into practice but present many possible avenues to beginning multiage classes. Clipboards and memos at the end of each chapter provide summaries or discussion questions for the faculty to ponder as they decide if and how to implement multiaging in their school. Practices are described that have been gathered from many different locations in the country. Readers are encouraged to identify the context of their particular situation as they make decisions. Yet the readers are not left to struggle, as Libbie and Wendy suggest what their experience and observations have indicated is an effective way to begin.

Many of you may already know Wendy Kasten because you have read her previous book, *The Multicultural Classroom: A Family of Learners*, coauthored with Barbara "Kitty" Clarke. Through vignettes, her short book introduced you to the teacher and school in Florida in which she has spent extensive periods of time beginning in 1988. Here, in this longer and more detailed book, Wendy expands on the experiences in this and other Florida schools with which she is involved. Her expertise in literacy instruction in the early childhood years is evident throughout this book. In fact, the reader wishing to learn about the practice of reading-writing workshop will find detailed descriptions of the elements of this process along with information on the types of materials needed. I would encourage such readers also to read carefully the information on math instruction using the same workshop format. Elementary teachers so often do not feel confident about the teaching of math (note the quote in one of the boxes here). This treatment of math instruction would be a good place for a faculty already engaged in multiage teaching to expand their horizons by reviewing their own practices.

I met Libbie Lolli when she attended the first weeklong Phi Delta Kappa Gabbard Institute on Implementing Nongraded Schools, held at Indiana University in Bloomington in July 1991, which Bob Anderson and I conducted. As noted in this book, Libbie came because she had been appointed the principal of a new magnet school that was to open that fall as a nongraded school. In 1993 Bob and I began asking Libbie to the Nongraded Institute to share her experiences with others. Libbie invited us to her school after three years of implementation to provide both written and verbal feedback to the staff and the school district on the progress of the school, so I have firsthand knowledge of many of the practices described in this book. Right now she is working in her present school district to implement multiage classrooms, so she continues to be actively engaged in the subject of this book. Her work on change, consensus building and school organization is invaluable for school principals and others assuming leadership functions in multiage schools. Readers should know that her enthusiasm is contagious.

Most educators like to read about how others implemented a program that they themselves are now considering. It helps them to visualize how their own program might look. Additionally, they hope that such reading will help them avoid as many problems as possible. This book not only provides a variety of such stories, which tell how others have implemented multiage education, but includes implementation guidelines for the readers. Besides explaining how to implement various aspects of multiaging in the text, a number of boxes include quotes and stories from teachers and principals, and clipboards at the end of each chapter are reviews and summaries given on one page that might be copied and circulated. Other ready-to-use materials are included for school usage or staff development handouts.

The book structure moves from the general to the school to the individual classroom. Part I, Before Multiage Happens, provides background on the multiage concept and the change process to enable readers to make their decisions on implementation of multiage. Part II, Inside the School, describes the elements for designing the multiage structure and a process for school governance that involves both school personnel and parents. Part III, Inside the Classroom, is the largest section, and it addresses curriculum and instruction in the multiage school. Specific implementation strategies for literacy, math, science, and social studies plus the topic of student assessment are addressed here. Moving from the usage of topics to thematic instruction that is inquiry-based is thoroughly examined along with the need for addressing district curriculum mandates. The material from the last section would be useful both for schoolwide implementation of multiaging and for individual or small groups of teachers developing multiage classrooms.

This book was a team effort. One author would take primary responsibility for the first draft of a particular chapter. Then they would meet, read the chapter aloud together and discuss changes that needed to be made. The researcher role, as might be expected of a university faculty member, was held by Wendy. The practitioner role was held by Libbie as a former multiage school principal, present school district director of curriculum and instruction, and trainer for multiage implementation. These were not exclusive roles, as Libbie is also a researcher and Wendy is a teacher and has spent much time observing in multiage classrooms. However, this is a good mix; research and theory inform the reader along with an understanding of the practical issues of mandated curriculum and testing and the realities of life in the schools.

Implementing Multiage Education: A Practical Guide to a Promising Future by Wendy Kasten and Elizabeth Lolli should be read, studied, and discussed as a decision is made to implement multiage instruction. It will then become a reference guide as multiaging is implemented. School principals will find the book of value both to understand the multiage classroom and to understand their role in facilitating this change. Parents would find the book useful to understand this innovation. This book contains not only many "how we did it" stories but also guidelines in the form of reproducible material that the readers may use as they implement multiage education.

—Barbara Nelson Pavan

Acknowledgments

Many people have contributed to thinking about and writing this book. We hope we don't forget anyone here.

Thanks to the many schools we have either worked in or visited in the last 10 years that were multiage, partly multiage, or in the process of becoming multiage. These schools span the United States as well as New Zealand, Australia, and Canada.

Several very special schools deserve additional mention. The teachers and principals in Elizabeth's current school district in Northfield, Ohio, deserve a tremendous thank you. They are Nancy, Lisa, Barb, Noelle, Rima, Kristen, Lana, and Gail; Treva, Goksu, Gennell, Jan, and Ron; Cindy, April, Robin, and, last but never least, Neil. Central Academy in Middletown, Ohio, is the school where Libbie was a principal for three years. Its implementation and success story is very important.

Moody Elementary School in Manatee County, Florida, has had a special role as well. Moody became a professional development school for the University of South Florida during the time in which multiage classes were being implemented. Wendy spent lots of time there doing inservice and teaching college courses on site. It was a wonderful place to be and in which to mentor preservice teachers. To all the Moody staff and to the Manatee County School Board, who let Wendy and colleague Barbara Clarke do their original research, a big thank you.

We also wish to acknowledge the contribution made by Wendy's first coauthor, Barbara "Kitty" Clarke, with whom a previous book on multiage education was written.

Joni Ramer is a talented teacher in Manatee County, Florida. In her classroom, four years of research on multiage education was done (with B.K. Clarke). Ramer's practices, and the anecdotes and insights learned there as her classroom community flourished, are an inspiration.

Teachers and principals we have met along the way graciously agreed to be interviewed for this book. They include: SueBeth Arnold, Beth Biery, Beth Bonner, Barbara Kidwell, Jodi Kinner, Diane Kittelberger, Gloria Morrison, Nancy Norman, Marybeth Phelps, Jackie Robbie, and Franki Sibberson— multiage teachers extraordinaire! Stephanie Acri, Dr. M. Ruth Davenport, Judy Joachim, Dr. Virginia Juettner, Dr. Brenda Keefe, Dr. Myna Matlin, and David Rossman are principals with whom we wish we worked!

We are grateful to Kathy Doberstyn and Dawn Ochocki for all their technological know-how. Without their help, the process would have been much more difficult and much less fun!

Karen Brothers assisted with some of the figures in the book. Thanks!

Introduction

● ●

"Those who still live in the past confidently set the norms for educating those who will live in the future." John Goodlad (1984) noted this irony of educational change more than a decade ago (p. 245).

Can you name three inventions in your home or school that did not exist when you were in elementary school? There's the fax machine, laser discs, personal computers, pagers, cellular phones, the Internet, microwave ovens, videocassette recorders, and so on. With the rapid pace of change that has occurred around the world in the last few decades, the schools that many of us remember, sometimes nostalgically, are no longer acceptable. They were the institutions of another time and of a simpler life.

We as educators have not been quick to explore or reinvent classrooms to suit a rapidly changing society. In fact, we have held on to traditions long after knowledge has suggested their obsolescence. People have lived through and accepted changes in every other aspect of their lives but have generally wanted education to remain the same. For example, no one wants to drive a car that was made 30 years ago (unless it's for fun). No one wants a house that hasn't had any maintenance or updating for decades. No one hires a physician whose knowledge is 40 years old. Education, however, should be as it was when "we" went to school.

If you bought or borrowed this book, you are probably among a growing number of educators who recognize an urgent need to change schools and classrooms. Whether it is because of frustration in not meeting the needs of all learners, a feeling of discontent with the lack of professional dialogue among colleagues about change, or the school's governing structures being out of touch with the needs and issues of today's classrooms, you sense a definite need to do things differently.

This book can be used by teachers and administrators together. The best-case scenario is that they are working on change together. There are several other assumptions that we make in writing this book. Since multiage education is not a program but rather a grouping pattern, we assume that other changes involving authentic and relevant curriculum have already taken place or are happening concurrently. Within the slow and deliberate process of change, classrooms are becoming places with a sense of both joy and rigor. Classroom practice is becoming more constructivist and developmentally appropriate. In other words, teachers are no longer standing before the class equating teaching with telling. Instructional methodologies vary as situations dictate. Teachers are the decision makers in their classrooms, using materials and guides as resources rather than as prescriptions for learning.

Teachers are learners just like their students, and each one changes and develops at his or her own unique pace. We do not advocate mandating this or any other school change, but rather encouraging ample professional development to help teachers feel rejuvenated, recharged, and eager to move forward in their own personal and professional development.

Teaching has historically been a passive profession—taking directions and mandates from a variety of stakeholders who, while concerned with educational issues, are inadequately informed to make classroom-based decisions. Although it is the job of every professional to maintain an attitude of lifelong learning, it is equally crucial that as a profession we educate the constituency we serve about our own changes and the growing knowledge base that informs our practice. We cannot expect good community support unless we have made adequate efforts to continually educate the public about the best practices. Educational outreach and community education is just as much a part of our job as responsibility for the students we teach.

We hope that this book guides the reader through a successful and exciting change process at the community, school, and classroom levels. Consequently, we have divided the book along these lines.

Part I, Before Multiage Happens, lays some groundwork. The two chapters in this section will educate or further educate the reader in two ways. First of all, we hope to make you knowledgeable and articulate about the research on and rationale behind multiage education. We hope that you find the various kinds of evidence as stimulating and exciting as we do.

Second, we know that educators have been inundated with the word *change*. Some of it has probably gone well, and some has not. We want your desired changes to be successful. Understanding more about the process, and the mistakes and wisdom of others who have been through it, can assist your process in going as smoothly as possible. Like most of you, we've lived through many educational changes and have been around long enough to see them come and go. We don't really think that this subject falls into the category of things that will eventually "go away." As professionals, we know too much now about teaching and learning to just sit back and not take action.

Part II, Inside the School, addresses implementation at the school level. This will include creating schoolwide democratic leadership, community involvement, and practical decisions—such as how to get started, who should start, how many classes, and how classes should look. Here we share stories from schools that have paved the way in multiage education. This section should answer many of your "how-to" questions for getting started.

Part III, Inside the Classroom, addresses teaching in a multiage setting. It covers the issues of reconsidering and possibly designing curriculum, building the classroom climate, using strategies that work in diverse settings, teaching math, and assessment. No one can teach anyone else exactly how to run his or her classroom; there are no simplistic recipes. But models and experiences of others can provide guidance and ideas from which to draw. Like all advice, teachers must take it and make it their own!

This book is written from a holistic, constructivist perspective. We believe in integrated learning and curriculum experiences. As a result, you'll notice all traditional subjects are integrated in chapters 5, 6, and 7. Chapter 8 deals separately with math, however, not because we believe it's truly separate but because of the multitude of questions we are continually asked about math in the multiage classroom.

We've put some features at the end of each chapter that we thought you'd find helpful. Each chapter has one *clipboard*, which is generally summative in nature and can be reproduced for teacher meetings and inservices. Each chapter also has at least one *memo*. These augment our discussions in different ways and can also be reproduced when needed.

We have added some information at the end that we'd want to have handy as we implement multiage classrooms. These include sample surveys, curriculum guidelines from the learned societies that govern our profession, a sample brochure, forms for making class rolls and lists, and samples of home-school communication.

At the end you'll also find a glossary. We hope this clears up the sometimes vague and occasional misuse of terms in the field.

We'd like to help you through this and celebrate your victories as well as guide you through some possible rough spots. If you have questions that we didn't answer in this book, contact us by e-mail (wkasten@phoenix.educ.kent.edu; lolli@nordonia.summit.k12.oh.us). If we can't help to solve your problem, then we'll try to find someone who can.

PART I

Before Multiage Happens

● ●

This portion of the book provides the foundation for the decision on becoming multiage. Chapter 1 provides a thorough discussion on what multiage is as well as what it is not. The chapter further describes the factory model of teaching and reasons to consider multiage grouping. Comparative research studies are also discussed. Chatper 2 is dedicated to issues surrounding change. Stories of school change as well as types of change are given. The chapter concludes with ideas for assuring that change happens. Both chapters provide a solid foundation for those exploring multiage.

CHAPTER 1

Why Become Multiage

● ●

In this chapter, we explore why you and your school may want to learn about becoming multiage, either completely or partially. In addition to defining *multiage*, we discuss how multiage classes may be more compatible with long-term goals for our children, revisit the Frankenstein we have created called "grade levels," share how research supports the multiage setting as a more humane environment, and explore other areas of research that support this grouping plan. We end the chapter by trying to rethink and shed the time-worn industrial model of education.

When Is a Classroom *Multiage?*

A classroom is *multiage* when it has been deliberately grouped across age levels instead of by chronological age. The classroom must also be a single learning community that meets the academic, social, emotional, physical, and aesthetic needs of its members. Membership may take different forms and sizes, just as a family does. Sometimes a cluster (the equivalent) of two traditional grade levels makes a multiage class. A class of 5- to 7-year-olds (a K–1 in traditional terms) is popular, but so are classes of 6- to 8-year-olds (grades 1–2, traditionally), 8- to 10-year-olds (grades 3–4), and 9- to 12-year-olds (grades 4–6). Some teachers even think that you might as well have a complete spectrum, with 5- to 12-year-olds.

The shape and form of the classes may also vary. "Self-contained" classes are common (one teacher, 18–28 kids), but so are two-teacher teams (with 45–

3

50 kids, all in one big room). We've also met teachers from a school where four-teacher teams and 100 children share a "pod" of four classroom spaces with flexible walls. In their unique setting it's highly successful, but it does present a challenge for four teachers to find time to plan together and keep in constant communication.

What models are *not* multiage? First of all, if classes located near each other in the same building often get together for activities, and they happen to be of different "grade levels," they aren't "doing some multiage stuff." It's wonderful when classes get together to do things, but that's not a multiage model.

Another trend, coming from special education, is the concept of *inclusion* (Harris & Hodges, 1995, p. 114). Where appropriate, students with very special needs—whether learning needs (e.g., learning disabilities) or physical needs (e.g., hearing impaired)—are integrated into regular classrooms rather than segregated. Sometimes the "special" kids included in such a classroom are older or younger than the other kids. This configuration does not, however, make the class multiage.

Multiage classes are not the same as *split classes* or *combination classes*. Those groupings are created because there aren't enough kids of each category to make an entire class of either one. So we get a split fifth and sixth grade or second and third grade. In these circumstances, there are separate curricula. This grouping pattern is not usually viewed as a strength; it has more to do with leftover numbers. However, a split or combination class can easily be turned into a multiage one with a little change in attitude and curriculum.

"What's different, of course, in the multiage [classroom] is that it allows them [students] to do more exploration, more independent study. If they've got an interest, it allows them to evolve with that, do research about it. You're not trying to turn out 29 little peas in a pod. It really looks at individuals and let's them go with their strengths and helps them out with their weaknesses."

—Parent of a multiage student

Box 1-1

In a multiage class, the kids don't have different curricula based on their "grade level," nor are they grouped for instruction by "grade level." They may often be grouped for many reasons, such as need for special attention, interests, cooperative teams or families, particular projects, or even independent studies, but "grade level" within the multiage class is not the criterion for this grouping, with the possible exception of reviewing for upcoming tests (which are, unfortunately, administered by "grade level"). Figure 1-1 summarizes the criteria for a multiage classroom.

A classroom is multiage when

- it's deliberately grouped across "grade levels"

- it's a single learning community

- diversity is celebrated and seen as an asset

- grouping within the class is rarely on the basis of the "grade level" designation on paper

- the class has the same profile as the rest of the school in terms of gender, ability, ethnicity, and achievement

- students forget what "grade level" they are in

Figure 1-1

What Are Our Long-Term Goals?

Every school, parent-teacher organization, and district need to have conversations about schoolwide goals. This does not mean test scores or "outcome-based education" but refers to more lofty, long-term goals for our children.

It's really pretty simple. Raise these questions: At the end of K–12 schooling, what would we like for our children? What kind of people do we want to turn out? What kinds of learners do we want to produce? What are our hopes and dreams for those we educate?

We've each had this conversation many times with schools and community groups. It's amazing how universal these goals are. Both parents and teachers say they want their kids to grow up to be good citizens, productive, happy, curious, and able to earn a living. To do that, they need to have good communication skills, life skills, social skills, and the desire to continue to grow and learn. These goals should be displayed in obvious, public places. Parents and even casual visitors should see these goals posted in classrooms, offices, and teacher lounges.

The next logical question examines our everyday practices. Look at the daily schedules, activities, tests, lessons, content, and methodologies. Put them on a list, and for each item on the list ask yourself two questions: Is this consistent with our long-term goals? Is this going to help us reach those goals?

If each of these questions doesn't get a *yea* vote, then it's very possible that you have discovered something that doesn't belong in your school; most likely it isn't a good use of your time. There is so much to do for our children, and so little time, that we shouldn't be wasting it with activities that don't count. That may mean fighting for change, locally or more widely.

What's Wrong With Grade Levels, Anyway?

We have all lived with the term *grade level* for a long time (a century and a half, to be precise). Most of us grew up with it and thought of our progress through our childhood years according to our grade-level assignments. While grade leveling is undoubtedly an ingrained tradition, have you ever wondered why we use this term and where it came from? You may not like the answer, for the story is not flattering to education.

What "Grade Level" Really Means

The term *grade level* is actually a mathematical average of some test scores. In other words, someone made up a test that was administered to a bunch of children who all attended the same "grade level." There was a range of performance on the test, so the mean (or average) score was determined, and that number was designated as the "grade level." In other words, about half the students who took the test did better than that "grade level" score, and about half the kids did worse.

Another important fact to understand is that every time students as a group do better on the tests, the tests are "renormed," and so a higher number becomes the "grade level." Too often, these scores are taken very seriously by educators, parents, and the wider community. This seriousness seems unaffected by the grave concerns of educators as to the appropriateness, fairness, and validity of the tests. Vito Perrone (1990) tells us that he "wonders about those who believe that testing young children and then making placement, promotion, or retention decisions on the basis of such testing leads to any constructive ends" (p. 1) and that the assumptions concerning such uses "defy almost everything we have come to understand about children's growth as well as their response to educational encounters" (p. 2). An administrator or community leader who states that he or she wants all the kids to be "on grade level" is lacking in knowledge of the concept of arithmetic average that we have just discussed.

Eisner (1994) has analyzed the commonly used SAT (Scholastic Aptitude Test) and its familiar multiple-choice format, which is used by nearly all achievement tests. He notes that it takes only six missed items to account for a drop from 466 to 424 in the verbal section, and only four missed items to explain a drop from 492 to 474 in the math. He further notes that such a drop may result from a more diverse population taking the test. That sort of information is rarely provided to the public when a drop of a few points makes a sensational news headline. These things contribute greatly to the foundation of "grade levels," which underlies much of what we have been doing in education and what will require rethinking as we move to more multiage models. The tradition and practice of grade levels is also strongly perpetuated by grade-level materials prepared by various publishers who followed the example of Massachusetts. Too often, these materials are looked upon as curriculum instead of being utilized as *tools* for a curriculum, of which they are only a part.

Why We Group Students by Grade Levels

Here's the second part of the not-so-flattering truth about grade levels. Imagine, for a moment, early 19th-century North America (and other places as well) when most kids attended one-room schoolhouses. These were not deliberate groupings. Sparse populations necessitated a place where kids of all ages were taught by one teacher for all their elementary school years (and sometimes longer). Compulsory education is not as old as grade levels; many children stayed home to help on farms, in family businesses, and in factories (often under unsafe conditions). Let's not make the mistake of referring to this as the "good old days."

The event precipitating change occurred just prior to 1848, when a Boston educator, generally assumed to be Horace Mann, visited Prussia (now Germany), where more and more structuring of educational experiences was taking place, including segregating students by age and grade level (Anderson & Pavan, 1993; Goodlad & Anderson, 1987; Pratt, 1986). Because the popular idea of the time was industrialization with its enormous and exciting advances, this model was applied to education. Separating children and giving them common educational experiences provided a direct link to the factory assembly line. Teachers and school administrators ran and monitored the school assembly line for quality control, measured by grades, tests, and, in cases where uniform quality was defective, nonpromotion of pupils.

The reasons, then, for making the change to grade levels from previous nongraded structures were as follows. First of all, early educators thought that graded systems would be efficient and more cost-effective, like the factories of the times. Second, they thought that it would ensure some uniformity of experiences (like an assembly line). Third, they thought it would be easier for administrators to monitor.

Has anyone noticed what is conspicuously absent in their reasoning?

The sad truth is that we still live with this industrialized model of education in many places. Grade levels, grade-level tests, promotion criteria, and "getting kids ready for" the next grade are all industrial thinking and the antithesis of developmentally appropriate practice (Bredekamp, 1987; see Appendix A). Moving to multiage models is one step toward shedding the industrial model.

Sometimes people ask, "What is the research that shows that multiage models are a good idea?" This is a good question and will be addressed later in this chapter. The more important question, however, is "What is the research that supports grade-level structures?" There isn't any! Grade levels are a tradition, not a practice grounded in research. Furthermore, the practice of grade levels defies everything we know about learning and child development.

We told you this was going to be embarrassing!

Birth Order in the Classroom

Imagine, for a moment, a little boy who is socially more immature than many of his age-mates. Perhaps you have known such a youngster, taught such a child, or maybe you were that kind of child yourself. Let's say that he started school on the early side because his birth date was just prior to the cutoff date of the local school for starting kindergarten.

Let's also assume that this boy is very smart. Although younger than his classmates, he performs adequately and is promoted to first grade, second grade, third grade, and so on. Each year that he is in school, he remains in the same relative position to his peers. That is, he is still the youngest, or among the youngest, and less socially mature as well. He proceeds through the structures of schooling in this omega position by luck of the draw. As he proceeds, he notices more of what he *can't* do than what he *can*, because he does not have the opportunity to see how far he has come. How will this affect his aspirations in life? Will he aspire to be all that he can be?

Now let's say that this same student was young and immature in a multiage primary class (K–2 equivalent). Even if he is in the omega position during the first year, in the second year new students will enter the class who will be less mature and less knowledgeable, especially about schooling in that classroom. No matter what this boy's strengths or weaknesses, he will now be in a position to view himself along the continuum of learning instead of always only looking forward. He will begin to understand how far he has come when he compares his learning to those younger and less experienced.

Which situation is more realistic and likely to help him form a positive self-concept?

As educators, we do not control birth order in the home. Birth order in the family is an important fact of life. It has been researched and written about extensively. There does not seem to be any dispute that, in most cases, the oldest child in a family has a considerable intellectual advantage, for two reasons. The firstborn not only receives increased attention and responsibility but also has the opportunity to teach someone else (Zajonc & Markus, 1975). This effect becomes diminished when children are spaced more than four years apart.

Historically, firstborn *sons* have been favored. Until recently, the eldest son has been the inheritor of the family fortune, property, title (in aristocracies), and business. Great novels have been written about rivalries between brothers because the older one got everything and the younger ones received little or nothing. Unlike parents of earlier times who made no pretense of being fair or equitable to all their children, parents of today work harder to somewhat temper the effects of birth order. In spite of that, differences persist that are difficult to avoid.

Being the oldest child in a group confers status and privilege as well as certain responsibilities and expectations. In a classroom, the principle still applies: The most advantageous position is the oldest. Older students are admired by younger ones; older students can do more and have more responsibilities; older students feel their position. In interviews of adults who were educated in one-room schoolhouses, the most common report is how they waited with anticipation to take on this high-status role and get to help the younger or less advanced students.

The single most commonly asked question about multiage grouping is this: How does an older child benefit? Won't older children be less well served, becoming bored or being used as tutors for the younger students? There are several responses to this question. First of all, should we assume that older or more advanced students in grade-level classrooms are always well served now? After all, even in a grade-level classroom there can be a variation of up to two chronological years, and abilities run the gamut from least advanced to most advanced. It is up to the capabilities of the teacher to challenge all students and meet their individual needs. Naturally, some teachers are better at this than others, but it is part of the job.

Second, why should we assume that we can meet the needs of a group of learners better when they are more similar in age? Most families have children of various ages, not children of an identical age. Which is more desirable, a family of four children of different ages or of quadruplets? Which is better for the parents? Which is better for the children? The implications for the classroom are not so different from the implications for a family.

"I was concerned as to how there would be enough time to accommodate her [parent's daughter] learning. . . . and would she be held back by having younger students in there as well. I found that not to be the case, especially because the multiage classroom allows them to go as far as they want in whatever subject. They're not restricted by anyone else."

—Parent of a multiage student

Box 1-2

In a family setting, responsibilities are assigned based on needs. Older or younger family members each do what they can in a family activity. Oldest children may take on more complex tasks or mentor less advanced siblings. In that role of teaching and mentoring, a great deal of learning takes place. The ones being helped benefit, but the teaching sibling learns the most. Hence, their role is to their advantage.

The best-case scenario for classrooms is that at different times, each child has an opportunity to be a younger child, a middle child, and an older child. In this manner, all students can experience the relative advantages and roles that different positions afford and can benefit from each. No one is the youngest or oldest all the time. This aspect of a multiage classroom cannot be duplicated or contrived even in the best grade-level environment.

The Promotion Dilemma

One of the really sticky problems with grade levels is that with them come expectations of achievement. This assembly-line thinking is right out of the factory, where at the end of the conveyor there's an expectation of a state of completion for the merchandise. The problem, however, is that schools deal with human beings, not merchandise. Human beings, especially youthful ones, vary a great deal. You can "cook" them all the same, but they aren't all done at the end. Nor should they be.

So, then, at the end of the grade or the year, what do you *do* with them? They haven't all learned everything that was taught. They all can't read. They all can't write. Some of them still can't add. The reality of the missing pieces has always been the promotion dilemma. Sometimes we have decided to retain students in the same grade. That seemed like a logical idea: If they're not finished, put them back on the assembly line and start over, do the same thing again, and hope it works the second time.

The dismal track record for nonpromotion will not likely surprise our readers. The promotion debate has resulted in a large body of literature concluding that a second time around does nothing to remedy a problem; in fact, it creates some new ones. Not only does achievement not improve, it worsens. Furthermore, nonpromotion is linked to a high drop-out rate (Goodlad, 1966; Goodlad & Anderson, 1987; Anderson & Pavan, 1993). Why do we keep having this dilemma?

The promotion dilemma is caused by our graded structure. If we didn't artificially segregate students by grade levels like an assembly line, then we would not have to wonder at the end of each academic year what to do with them! Every parent and every teacher knows that children develop differently. Even twins don't necessarily develop the same. Why did we think we could devise structures based on sameness that would be educationally sound?

Imagine a different scenario, one in which children of the future may live and be educated. Perhaps they will enter school at a primary level. They might start at age 5 or so and stay until they are intermediate learners, at which time they might move to an intermediate level. Some of them may move when they are 8 years old, but others will be 9 or 10.

Primary and intermediate houses are not as common as composite, multiage grades (K–1, 1–2, 2–3, 3–4, 4–5) that encompass two of the traditional levels. Still, in this setting, where most students will remain for two years, it is relatively easy to have some children stay longer if needed, even making movements at midyear. Once this practice becomes common and is communicated to families as an accepted practice, there will be no stigma attached to staying a little longer.

How does this differ from retention in a grade level? One of the problems with retention is that little or nothing new happens the second year. The curriculum is repeated to the retained student while most of the class consists of new students. The repeating student has no peer group from before and sometimes sticks out like a sore thumb. In a composite or other multiage setting, on the other hand, the curriculum is not repeated. Students who are veterans from previous years (and there will be more than one or two) have the status and responsibility that go with age. They have the opportunity to become more comfortable with concepts they previously found difficult, to teach things to newer students, to act as role models for classroom procedures, and to continue to excel in their best subjects. They remain members of the same community of learners, but their roles in the community will change.

Doing away with grade levels and the resulting promotion dilemma means that students can be treated as individuals, with experiences that are developmentally appropriate for them based on their current ability and not their placement.

More Reasons to Consider Multiage Classrooms

This section is especially important for schools that are considering multiage classrooms for the first time. We present here the research that compares multiage classrooms with other classrooms as well as the research that speaks to multiage classrooms in other ways. These include arguments for a more humane environment, the interrelationship between academic and social development, cross-age tutoring, the specific issues of promotion and retention, developmentally appropriate practice, whole language, and continuous progress.

A Case for Humanity

Throughout history, human beings have lived in family groupings, whether those families lived in caves, huts, tents, or other dwellings. Family groups were arranged in clusters or small communities known as clans, tribes, or villages. The family structure has persisted because it works well.

Humans have also traditionally reared their young in clusters. This pattern still persists in the 180 hunting and gathering societies that have survived to the 20th century, including the Inuit, Australian native peoples, and the !Kung San of the Kalahari desert. All these groups rear their young in play groups composed of clusters of ages, and in which children are expected to caretake and nurture those younger than themselves (Pratt, 1986).

Today, in activities outside school, children participate as members of age clusters, often grouped by approximately three chronological years. Scouting, sports, dance, and countless other activities have traditionally been grouped around clusters made up of younger children, middle children, early teens, or late teens. These groupings are so popular and successful that they have been used since the beginning of our species, except for the last century and a half in schools.

A cluster of children under adult supervision is a humane model by which to raise children. Such an environment can easily develop nurturing among members when, for example, older members look after younger members and older members provide models for learning and development. The major aspects of this humane environment are stability and predictability—a feeling of safety and acceptance. These environments also stimulate altruistic behavior rather than competitive and aggressive acts.

Safe and Stable Environments   Certain educators have come to strongly believe that the environment in which we function affects our ability to think, learn, and perform (Forester & Reinhard, 1989; Hart, 1983). The human mind, including that of a child, functions best when the individual feels safe and accepted. Feeling comfortable emotionally helps prevent the mind from "freezing" (Hart, 1983, p. 109). Similarly, in an atmosphere of acceptance, where members have a feeling of status and ownership and there is a focus on positive achievements, risk-free learning is supported along with children's natural curiosity (Forester & Reinhard, 1989).

In order to understand this better, try to imagine a time when you were in a situation that was truly frightening. It may have been during a fire, during a marital dispute, following the news of an accident or the death of a loved one, or in any life crisis. What was it like trying to think clearly, decide what to do first, or merely cope during such a trauma? It is usually difficult to think and act clearly and logically.

A less extreme example might occur in the workplace. Some people have work situations that are extremely stressful and in which they begin to feel burnout. Supervisors may be displeased, harassment may be taking place, or extreme discomfort from confrontations or disputes between workers may be present. How often, in such cases, does one go home, reflect on what has happened, and think of all the things one *wishes* one had said or done? This occurs because the conditions at the time were not conducive to optimal thinking.

These feelings also occur in the context of a classroom. Surely the reader can remember some classrooms that were more pleasant experiences than others. While recalling the unpleasant ones, frustrations may come to mind regarding the ability to work and learn well, receiving positive feedback, and feeling encouraged to continue. Thus, we can all understand how the environment is influential.

We certainly prefer the school environment to be positive, safe, and accepting. In a study of 27,000 teachers, students, and parents, John Goodlad (1984) asked what kind of environment people want in their schools. He discovered that most people want more from schools than "intellectual development." They also want some attention paid to social, vocational, and personal issues and for school to be a "nurturing, caring place" (p. 61). In fact, two mottos emerged from his study: "Teach my child with tender loving care" and "Knowledge sets the human spirit free." Another insight from this study is that when schools are measured or rated to determine their success or effectiveness, these issues are almost never considered.

Parents of students placed in multiage classrooms have helped us to understand this. These parents have reported that they observe their children feeling more accepted and secure. This comfort level is most noticeable when school changes are imminent (such as the start of a new school year) or when the family life is in crisis. In the first scenario, parents noticed that children preparing to reenter the same classroom had no anxiety during the summer about starting school. Oddly, the parents had never really noticed how much anxiety school changes inflicted on their kids until it was gone.

During family crises, such as a death, divorce, or loss of employment, parents noticed that school had a calming, stabilizing influence on their children. Thus, the home was unpredictable and in flux, but school was not. School was, in fact, a haven because of the family-like nature of the multiage setting.

Aggression and Competition in Schools   There is understandably a great concern about the alarming statistics of youth and violence—both the "culture of violence" in which our children are being raised (Sherblom, Tchascha, & Szulc, 1995) and the rise of violence in schools since the 1960s (Noguera, 1995).

Some researchers have noted that there are differences in how members of a group treat each other when the group is age-stratified versus mixed-age. In age-stratified groups of youngsters, observers have noted more incidents of aggression and competition. Conversely, acts of nurturing and altruism are more frequently observed in settings with mixed ages. This phenomenon has been observed in studies of preschool children (Bizman, Yinon, Mivtzari, & Shavit, 1978; Goldman, 1981; Hammack, 1974), school-age children (Hartup, 1976, 1977, 1979; Pratt, 1986; Wakefield, 1979), and nonhuman primates (Pratt, 1986).

Why is this so? In the unusual setting of being with people who are only like themselves (such as world-class athletes, most talented pianists, or 7-year-olds), there is a tendency and a need for individuals to discover their relative place and worthiness. One way this is accomplished is through competitive and aggressive behavior that begins to establish a hierarchy. This behavior is frequently associated with the animal kingdom. (Wolves, for example, establish a hierarchy of status, and only the alpha male and female are able to mate. Their positions are regularly challenged by maturing younger wolves through aggressive and competitive acts.)

We are not suggesting that human behavior is identical to that of higher order animals, but there are some similarities. Human beings have a need to know and understand their place within a group. While this need may diminish somewhat with maturity, the family structure seems most suitable for minimizing it.

Creating a Humane Place   We know a little boy (and many of you probably know youngsters like him) who has an "unstable home life." This topic is often discussed in the teachers' lounge, as we ache for the children we teach and the life to which they may go home. By an "unstable home life," we mean that Sean lives with his divorced mother and feels rejected by his biological father, who seldom sees him and frequently misses scheduled visits, leaving Sean waiting at a window in tears. Sean's two subsequent stepfathers have left his life due to failed marriages with his mother. Sean also sees a before-school caretaker because his mother must leave for work earlier than his school bus arrives. He attends after-school programs because his mother does not get out of work until after school lets out. Sean's only other consistent caretaker, his grandmother, recently died. His life has therefore been characterized by frequent changes and loss of adults.

What happens to Sean in school? Even during the primary years, Sean's school had children changing classes for each subject, as students typically do in secondary school. In addition to four regular teachers per day, Sean had a different teacher for physical education, music, art, library, and computers. After nine months of school, his cast of characters had changed so much that by the time he entered middle school, he had encountered a minimum of 24 teachers and a maximum of 48, depending on the stability of the personnel. In addition, other caregivers supervised him at lunch and at recess on the playground. The school principal changed three times in one school, and he attended two different schools during these years.

Does this sound like a stable school life? Who, of the myriad of teachers who see Sean daily, will be the most responsible for him? Who will notice when something is wrong?

If we recognize the need for consistent caregivers in home life, doesn't it follow that some consistency and stability would also be beneficial in a child's school life? None of us would advocate the regular change of parents and grandparents, and yet we routinely change their teachers. Does this make sense? As educators, we lack control over the home lives of the students we teach, but we have a great deal of control over the environment we create in schools. School can be, as John Goodlad (1984) advocates, a nurturing, caring place, but there's positively no way to accomplish that when we keep changing the children's teachers.

Understanding Academic and Social Development (Why Basics Are Not Enough)

Because the structure of schooling with grade levels defies everything we have come to understand about teaching and learning, in this section we address some of the research and theoretical support for multiage settings, including the relationship between academic and social development, developmentally appropriate practices, whole language, continuous progess, and cross-age tutoring (children teaching other children of different ages).

How Academic and Social Development Are Related   We used to think of academic and social development as different arenas. Academic development was certainly the job of the school, but social development was viewed as a more peripheral part of school life. Certainly school affected social development, but many parents and educators thought of it as beyond the basics. The development of values and responsibilities was considered the domain of parents, religion, and community-based organizations.

Consider the image that many adults have of schools, rooted in their memories of the classrooms of the 1940s, 1950s, and even the 1960s. They picture a stark room, student desks in neat rows, a teacher's desk at the front, an orderly procedure of teachers directing instruction, and students quietly working and listening except when their hands are raised to respond or ask a question. When television commercials want to use a classroom setting as part of their ads, they generally look like this because this is the classroom in the memories of the adult writers, who have had no reason to visit a classroom since.

In these old classrooms, students did "their own work." Talking out of turn was forbidden, and report card grades of "deportment" were based largely on this concept of quiet obedience. Fortunately, the classrooms of today are messier and noisier, and furniture is moved around if necessary. Today, more is known about the nature of interaction and the relationship of interaction to learning.

Long ago, Jean Piaget noted that "social life is a necessary condition for the development of logic" (1928/1977, p. 239). Lev Vygotsky observed that "development does not proceed toward socialization, but toward the conversion of social relations into mental functions" (1981, p. 165). What does this mean for classroom teaching?

> "In a multiage setting, the learning by osmosis is significantly greater. The students' motivation for and knowledge of growth and advancement is higher because of the experienced role models. The zone of proximal development is engaged more regularly."
>
> —Beth Biery
> Mechanicsburg, PA

Box 1-3

It means that academic, or cognitive development and social development are not separate. In fact, they are as interrelated as reading and writing. Bornstein and Bruner (1989) lament that this relationship has not been studied and given more press among psychologists. Yet they feel certain that "development is intrinsically bound up with interaction" (p. 13). Academic development impacts social development, and social development impacts academic development. The two build on each other in a spiraling fashion that increases gradually over time. Through this process, students gain in sophistication and maturity because learning does not take place in a vacuum;

it takes place in the highly social context of the world and the environments of living and learning (Bornstein & Bruner, 1989; Bruner 1979, 1990; Doise & Mugny, 1984; Hooper, 1968; Trudge & Rogoff, 1989; Valletutti & Dummett, 1992; Webb, 1977; Wood, 1988, 1989).

The bottom line is that educators cannot pretend that school goals and missions are limited to "basics" like reading, writing, and arithmetic, as we once did. Classrooms of today are, as they should be, noisier places where students interact, cooperate, and solve learning problems together, much as they will do later in their careers.

In multiage classrooms, the potential to learn and grow from naturally occurring interactions is enhanced by the diverse environment. The presence of different ages as well as abilities in the class capitalizes on the availability of diverse models, even if all the models are not perfect. The mere presence of multiple models spurs cognitive dissonance, critical thinking, problem solving, and the consideration of various perspectives that a more sterile, homogeneous environment cannot supply (Doise & Mugny, 1984; Hooper, 1968; Trudge & Rogoff, 1989; Valletutti & Dummett, 1992; Vygotsky, 1978; Webb, 1977; Wood, 1988, 1989).

Cross-Age Tutoring   Another way to capitalize on the naturally occurring interactions is through cross-age tutoring. One common form of help is the 30-second review of directions, expectations, or other clarifications. Initially, these dynamics begin with younger students needing guidance from older ones, but soon younger ones become helpers, too. The group comes to know each individual's strengths. For example, in a multiage primary class we visited, a younger autistic boy became known as the most gifted class speller. Students of all ages took their tough spelling concerns to him, and he was generally able to help. Before long, students learn who is best at working with computer difficulties, helping with math problems, working the class VCR, and other such skills, and age is generally no longer an issue.

Sometimes cross-age tutoring is more explicit and formally set up by the teacher(s). A younger member of the multiage community might need help with learning letter names or counting, and it might behoove a slightly older child to be his or her teacher. Wise teachers will select children to do tutoring who will be helpful to others but also benefit from the tutoring themselves. The more experienced learner might need a review of the material or concept, opportunities to talk about the information, or the esteem that comes from helping.

One of us once taught sixth grade. A second-grade teacher requested some older students to visit weekly and assist the second graders with editing their writing. The first impulse in such a situation might be to select the best writers in the class for this opportunity. A better plan, however, would be to send some struggling authors. Students who are struggling with writing in the sixth grade still know a lot more about editing than most second graders. Having to present and explain the editing process to younger students will most likely help the tutor's own personal progress more than lessons or games done in the name of instruction.

Studies have been done on partnerships similar to the one described for spelling. Drake (1993), Juel (1991), Leland and Fitzpatrick (1994), and Teale and Labbo (1990) have studied cross-age tutoring and its effects. Sometimes the ages were just a few years apart, and at other times they were more disparate. All these reading-related studies found positive attitude changes and skill advancement in the tutors in addition to the learning that took place for the tutored. These often dramatic outcomes gave a boost to the tutors, who in some cases had been turned off to school and to learning.

Hedin (1987) offers a cogent explanation of why tutors benefit so greatly. Grounded in "role theory," Hedin contends that placing youngsters in the tutoring role offers them a new and more responsible role than they may have previously played. The result of this role is a heightened sense of competence. She further argues that people tend to live up to the role that others expect of them, even if the others are children. Tutors receive respect, and sometimes even admiration, from their charges. For some, this may be a new position to be in, and it has some newfound status attached to it.

The benefits don't stop there, however. Hedin also digs into cognitive theory to explain the multiple benefits to the tutor. Teaching is a complex job (as the readers of this book already know). Presenting material and verbally explaining something requires several embedded tasks, such as deciding what to begin with (sequencing), how to proceed, and what examples might prove helpful (application). The combined effect of these processes is higher order thinking skills and more mature psychological development (Hedin, 1987).

The benefits to the tutored are perhaps more obvious. They receive personalized and individualized instruction, which are difficult to deliver in a regular classroom setting with 20–30 pupils. Perhaps many of our readers have noticed, as we have, that kid-to-kid explanations can be better than our own. One of us remembers when an attempt to explain improper fractions to 11-year-olds wasn't going well. The explanations and language offered in the teacher's manual, as well as the ones invented on the spot, were falling on confused-looking faces. Suddenly, a classmate turned around to his peers and said to them, "Just remember they're *top heavy*," after which sighs were heard, and heads nodded in that "Oh, I get it" mode.

One of the most common concerns of parents of older children in a multiage classroom is that their children will be "used" for tutoring, often in place of their own studies. The teacher may be accused of "using" the more advanced students to do the teaching "that we're paying the teachers to do."

"My son was rather impatient with other children, and I think one thing he profited from last year was in learning how to help other children and also being rewarded for being a leader in the class-room—for being an educator himself."

—Parent of a multiage student

Box 1-4

Parents need to understand that teaching a class is far more complex than teachers doing all the teaching to students who do all the learning. All youngsters can and should be made to feel like teachers at times, because the act of teaching is the most powerful learning tool known. In a learning community, as in a family, everyone needs to feel membership, and having responsibilities is part of that membership, just as it is in a well-functioning household. Parents know that doing jobs for the family is part of how children learn to be grown-ups. The same concept applies to classrooms.

A story will illustrate the importance of cross-age tutoring and the powerful act of teaching. A graduate teaching assistant was hired to teach physics, which wasn't his best subject. Like all new teachers, he studied his lessons diligently to keep ahead of his students—reading, taking notes, and preparing presentations of the material. One day he had to teach a lesson with which he was still uncomfortable. Although he could repeat the explanations in the text and deliver it to the college class, he was worried that he didn't actually understand the material. "What if someone asks a question I can't answer?" he thought nervously.

Because he really had no choice (the material had to be presented), he rehearsed his presentation and prayed in earnest that no one would question his explanation. The class session began, and he gave his presentation flawlessly. When someone raised a hand to say, "I don't get it, could you please explain it further," he drew a deep breath and repeated his explanation again.

After the second explanation, the same hand went up. Nervously but politely, he called upon the individual, who again said that he did not understand the concept and would the teacher please perhaps explain it differently? The teaching assistant began his rehearsed explanation for the third time; however, while giving the monologue again, a light bulb went on in his head, and he suddenly understood it.

Developmentally Appropriate Practice (DAP)   The field of early childhood education has promoted the notion that learning experiences and play experiences for children should be appropriate both to their level of development and to them as individuals. The specific recommendations have extensive research supporting them that is extremely well documented (Bredekamp, 1987). The key points are outlined in Appendix A for easy reference during curriculum planning. In addition to knowing these recommendations, putting them into use implies teaching in a way that is best for the children and not treating them like items on the education assembly line. In other words, the idea of developmentally appropriate practice (DAP) is more suited to multiage teaching than to grade-level structures.

The notion of DAP further implies a child-centered curriculum, contructivist teaching, and a great deal of experiential learning. The older transmission model of teaching (the teacher does the telling, the students listen and absorb knowledge) is simply inadequate; hence, the need for staff development is critical in many cases.

Whole Language   *Whole language* is a term that is commonly used but frequently misused and misunderstood by both educators and the public. Frequently mistaken for a methodology, whole language is actually a body of literature on teaching, especially literacy teaching, that somehow got this name because the beliefs and principles resulting from numerous bodies of research have a common element of wholeness. Originating from the field of literacy, whole language began as a way of looking at reading that included understanding print through the use of the structure, semantics, and orthography of a language (Goodman, 1986; Goodman, Watson, & Burke, 1987). In other words, readers were taught to use context, prediction, decoding, picture clues, and anything else available to them to make sense of what they were reading. Whole language has always included phonics as part of the whole, but not separately for its own sake.

Extensive research on reading, writing, and language learning has been assembled into a group of principles that are meant to guide decisions about methodology. Some of this research that forms the root of whole language theory includes miscue analysis (learning to read and struggling readers), transactional theory (readers reponding to and understanding texts), oral language, how children learn to write, contructivist learning (Piaget and others), and classroom ethnographies. These principles are outlined similarly in a number of resources (Cazden, 1992; Cordeiro, 1992; Crafton, 1991; Edelsky, Altwerger, & Flores, 1991; Goodman, 1986; Goodman, Goodman, & Bird, 1991; Goodman, Hood, & Goodman, 1991; Heald-Taylor, 1989; Manning & Manning, 1989; Raines, 1995; Raines & Canaday, 1990; Weaver, 1990). These guiding principles, as outlined by the Whole Language Umbrella (WLU), an international teacher's confederation, are listed in Appendix B. There is a high degree of overlap between the principles of whole language and those of DAP as well as those of continuous progress.

Continuous Progress (CP)   Another extensive body of data that has grown out of the educational leadership field is continuous progress (CP). Like DAP and whole language, CP principles speak to theoretically grounded practices for schools and include honoring individual differences, taking learners from where they are and allowing them to progress at their own pace as far as they can go (Anderson & Pavan, 1993). CP also implies that learning should be interesting, pleasurable, and geared to capitalize on student interests; that the whole child should be educated, including his or her social, emotional, cognitive, physical, and aesthetic needs; that students should interact with and learn from others of diverse backgrounds; that arrangements should be made for flexibility in progressing through schooling structures; that expectations for learning are commensurate with the development level of individuals; that assessment is holistic; and that teachers are empowered.

CP describes the total schooling structure, just as whole language and DAP describe the classroom philosophy and practice. These three components are the features and goals to work toward in multiage classrooms.

Comparative Research: Multiage and Nonmultiage Classrooms

A substantial body of research exists that compares students in multiage classes and nonmultiage classes, using quantitative considerations such as test scores. (Remember, there are no tests that have suggested that grade levels are a good idea.) Taking into consideration that quantitative results are not qualitative, the results are nevertheless interesting.

Kasten and Clarke (1993) reviewed more than 20 studies on various ages and educational settings that compared achievement and affective factors such as self-esteem in multiage and same-age classrooms. Their conclusions were that students in multiage classes did the same or better in academic areas but were consistently better in the affective areas such as confidence, self-esteem, and attitudes (Bizman, Yinon, Mitzari, & Shavit, 1978; Buffie, 1963; Bunting, 1974; Carbone, 1961; Day & Hunt, 1975; DiLorenzo & Salter, 1965; Ford, 1977; Gajadharsingh, 1991; Goldman, 1981; Graziano, French, Brownell, & Hartup, 1976; Halliwell, 1963; Hammack, 1974; Hartup, 1976; Hillson, Jones, Moore, & Van Devender, 1965; Lougee, Grueneich, & Hartup, 1977; McLoughlin, 1969; Milburn, 1981; Morris, Proger, & Morrell, 1971; Papay, Costello, Hedl, & Speilberger, 1975; Pavan, 1973; Steere, 1972; Way, 1979). Anderson and Pavan (1993) did a very similar review of the research and came up with the same conclusions. They added that the research also shows that the longer students are placed in multiage education, the more likely that the results worked in their favor.

Subsequent to these reviews, Veenman (1995), a Dutch researcher, coordinated a meta-analysis of more than 80 studies involving an evaluation of multiage or multigrade educational settings, including many published only in languages other than English. Veenman's overall conclusion is that no one need be concerned that students in multiage environments will be at any disadvantage. We concur but would note that neither his review nor anyone else's controlled for or took into account other aspects of the classroom, such as curriculum and instruction.

We have done our own research comparing multiage and nonmultiage models in order to add to this body of knowledge. Libbie tracked the progress of socioeconomically diverse, mostly White students in a multiage school in southwestern Ohio for 3 years using standardized tests scores (the California Achievement Test), who were compared with matched students in nonmultiage schools in the same district (Lolli, 1994). The students who were in the multiage setting were there for 3 years and were compared on variables including gender, age, ability range, socioeconomic status, and number of parents in the home.

Like the other studies we have cited, these results showed that no one in a multiage class ever suffered and, in fact, they sometimes scored better than students in nonmultiage classes. Lolli concurred with Anderson and Pavan's conclusion that the longer students remained in multiage classrooms, the better the results. Children who were behind their peers when they entered the multiage class caught up to those peers by the third year of testing.

Wendy, along with another colleague (Kasten & Clarke, 1993), followed one group of children from a low socioeconomic school with a high minority population in southwest Florida for 4 years. These children began as kindergartners together in 1988 and were followed until they completed the equivalent of "grade 3" in the same multiage whole language classroom. For the purpose of comparison, children elsewhere in the school in grade-level classes were matched for ability, age, and ethnicity. Children in both groups were tested at the close of their "first grade," "second grade," and "third grade" school years with the National Achievement Test and the Stanford Achievement Test.

As in Lolli's study, children in multiage settings in the Kasten and Clarke study had actual mean scores higher than their counterparts on all subtests, but only those in *thinking skills, math computation, math concepts*, and *using information* on the Stanford Achievement Tests were significantly higher. The National Achievement Test was only used for literacy-related subtests, and although actual mean scores were almost always higher, they were not statistically significant.

The Florida study included some qualitative measures. There were noteworthy results in reading attitudes and writing. Among younger subjects (grades "K" and "1"), all multiage students had healthy attitudes toward "school reading," and most of the students in grade-level classes did, too. The area of difference was in "recreational reading," where multiage students scored considerably higher than those in the grade-level classes (instrument by McKenna & Kear, 1990). No statistical tests of significance were applied due to the small sample size.

Among the older children ("grade 2" and "grade 3") who had been in the settings either 2 or 3 years, interesting differences were found that are relevant to creating lifelong readers. Students in the multiage class were more articulate about books and more able to name favorite authors, illustrators, and titles of recently read books, favorite books, and books their teacher read to them. These findings should not be generalized, however, since the multiage teacher taught from a literature-based approach to reading, whereas the other classes used traditional basal readers. Although the multiage aspect of the class may have contributed to the enthusiasm for reading, because older students frequently read to younger ones and socializing about reading habits was encouraged, there were no literature-based grade-level classes available for comparison.

Writing results were also interesting. "Slice-of-time" writing samples were collected at three different points throughout the study, in which students from both groups were asked to write on the same prompt. Students in the multiage class wrote with 30% more different words and generally wrote longer pieces with more syntactic complexity. Again, generalizing warrants some caution. Although students in the multiage classes regularly helped each other in writing, shared their writing, and responded to each other (all of which could support writing growth), they also wrote more often than students in the grade-level classes because of the teacher's commitment to journaling and the writing process.

In spite of its interesting results, the Kasten and Clarke study points out all the areas of multiage education that have not been studied and warrant further investigation concerning academic results. Clearly, test scores have shown differences, but not in consistent ways, between multiage and nonmultiage groups. More authentic assessments still need to be used in order to illuminate other interesting differences.

However, if teachers, parents, or administrators have any reservations about changing to multiage classrooms because of a fear that test scores might be negatively influenced, we can assure them *with confidence* that there is no need for concern. In fact, there is a possibility that test scores would improve with this change (but that should not be the reason for doing it).

Figure 1-2 summarizes the information described in this chapter.

A Summary of Features of Multiage Classrooms and Their Research Support

Features of Multiage Classrooms	Theory	Theorists—References	Can Feature Be Replicated in Unit Grade?
Children are placed longer with same teacher & group, creating a stable, nurturing, accepting environment.	People learn & perform better in safe, accepting settings; the brain works best under these circumstances.	Bruner, 1979; Forester & Reinhard, 1989; Hart, 1983; Ridgway & Lawton, 1965; Wakefield, 1979.	"Looping" or "cycling" Scandinavian model
Interaction with diverse ages stretches learners; they in turn respond to their roles as both helpers & recipients.	Learners in interaction, or the "zone of proximal development," problem solve better; people live up to expectations of others.	Bornstein & Bruner, 1989; DiLorenzo & Salter, 1965; Piaget, 1928/1977; Trudge & Rogoff, 1989; Vygotsky, 1978, 1981; Webb, 1977.	Only in limited sense; less continuous; less likely to be truly diverse.
Students have multiple encounters with concepts, even before it is "taught" to them, creating a schema for future learning; academic & social development are both influenced.	Having a schema for something prior to actually meeting it academically makes the learning more smooth; academic and social development are interrelated, each positively influencing the other.	Bunting, 1974; Doise & Mugny, 1984; Hooper, 1968; Piaget, 1928/1977; Pontecorvo & Zucchermaglio, 1990; Resnick & Klopfer, 1989; Vygotsky, 1978; Webb, 1977; Wood, 1988.	Only with frequent interactions with learners of different ages; models less powerful when not consistently present.
Cross-age tutoring happens both implicitly & explicitly.	Teaching is the most powerful learning tool known. It solidifies learned concepts while learners benefit from individual instruction. Payoff is academic & self-esteem for both.	Drake, 1993; Hedin, 1987; Juel, 1991; Leland & Fitzpatrick, 1994; Lougee, Grueneich, & Hartup, 1977; Teale & Labbo, 1990; Valletutti & Dummett, 1992.	Would have to be contrived between classes of different ages. Would be less consistent.

Figure 1-2

Learning is well suited to constructivist theory, as individual paces are accepted & accommodated, including developmentally appropriate practices.	Children learn & develop at their own pace and have to make their own sense of learning.	Brooks & Brooks, 1993; Cushman, 1990; Gartner, Kohler & Riessmon, 1971; Goodlad & Anderson, 1987; Resnick, 1987; Weber, 1971.	With difficulty, in child-centered class; grade-level expectations omnipresent.
There's a decrease in competitive & aggressive behaviors and an increase in nurturing, altruistic ones.	Mixed-age settings decrease competitive and aggressive acts in school or at play in humans & other primates.	Bizman, et al., 1978; Carbone, 1961; Goldman, 1981; Hammack, 1974; Muir, 1970; Piaget, 1928/1977; Pontecorvo & Zucchermaglio, 1990; Pratt, 1986; Schrankler, 1976; Wolfson, 1967	No.
Birth-order effect in classrooms is diminished when students have opportunity to be younger & older in different years.	Each position has different benefits; eldest is most privileged & admired by classmates.	Wolfson, 1966; Zajonc & Markus, 1975.	No.
Social development & self-esteem are enhanced.	Repeated effects in studies favor multiage/nongraded structures in these areas. Seeing oneself on a continuum of development & opportunities to be a helper enhance this feature.	Bizman, et al., 1978; Carbone, 1961; Goldman, 1981; Hammack, 1974; Piaget, 1928/1977; Pontecorvo & Zucchermaglio, 1990; Pratt, 1986.	No.
Promotion can be flexible or decisions delayed because of the absence of more frequent grade-level benchmarks.	Effects of promotion in long-term studies are dismal. Promotion/retention is the assembly line of factory-model schooling.	Goodlad & Anderson, 1987.	No.

Figure 1-2, continued

Shedding the Factory Model of Schooling

One day, one of us was reading a book about a relatively unknown Japanese educator who was actively trying to improve education in his country just prior to World War II. At that time, a controversy was raging in his homeland about the overall purpose of education. One faction, of which he was a part, argued that the purpose of education was to *create good citizens*. Another faction, which was stronger because it had tradition and the establishment on its side, argued that the purpose of education in Japan was to *create good subjects*.

Unfortunately, the purpose was established to foster good subjects—a thought that sends chills down the spines of members of a democracy. Fortunately, the war changed all that.

Most people in English-speaking countries cannot fathom having such an argument. Yet Howard Gardner (1991b) writes that he sees education even in America at a turning point. He describes two overall factions: One cries for *uniformity* and the other for *individuality*. Those who call for uniformity want basic competencies, a core body of knowledge, every individual mastering certain minimums, and an efficient education system. The factory model of education, on which much of our system is built, espouses similar notions. Gardner contends that this view is rooted in a faulty view of human learning. Hester (1994) explains it differently:

> the effort in America today to mass produce education has already yielded some negative results. Using the assembly line metaphor, the business and industrial communities are calling for quality educational production to increase, as if to say that teaching and learning are but a series of inputs and outputs. Those who control the economic purse strings of America have failed to find quality for which they have paid, and like in their factories, have demanded teaching conformity and quality control through measurable evaluations of teaching and learning. The effort to mass produce education from a common mold remains a cultural result of the industrial revolution, one whose day has certainly passed. (p. 41)

Although Hester is talking specifically about American education, the idea applies to other countries as well. Some people feel that an emphasis on individuality may sacrifice some assured minimums. Others, however, view learners as individuals who cannot be treated like industrial merchandise. When we talk about equal education for all, what we mean is not that everyone should get the same dose of mediocrity but that every student should have an equal opportunity to develop individual abilities and talents to their fullest, to be nurtured to go as far as one can in one's education.

Figure 1-3 lays out the dilemma as we see it. The side that advocates uniformity would have us produce cookie-cutter products, at least in theory. Uniformity is a notion borrowed from the industrialized model of education. Grade levels are the structure of the assembly line; standardized tests and promotion are all part of quality control. Teachers and administrators are the supervisors or overseers to ensure the uniformity in the final product.

The other side has individuality as a goal. Various educational terms are associated with educating individuals to become participants in a democratic way of life. These include developmentally appropriate practice, nongradedness or multiage education, whole language, integrated instruction, and authentic assessments. Although these ideas are highly related to each other, they spring from different traditions and overlap greatly in their meanings. All share values that honor learner differences, see diversity as a strength, and empower those closest to the classroom to make many crucial decisions. Unlike the factory model, no uniformity is anticipated, only structures that are geared to the success of individuals.

Learning facts and information is not at the heart of education. The heart of rational learning is solving problems, especially the yet unborn problems of the world, so we must give our students the tools to deal with change and with a world we will not see. Such skills will require critical thinking, judging, and collaboration, which a factory model simply cannot provide. We have high expectations for the role of education and plan to do our part in making it happen.

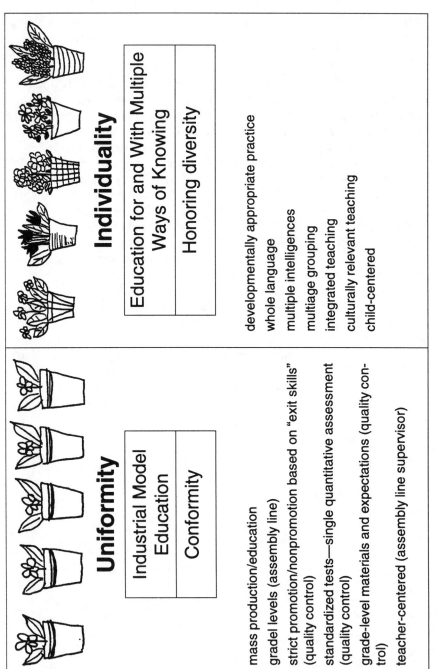

Figure 1-3

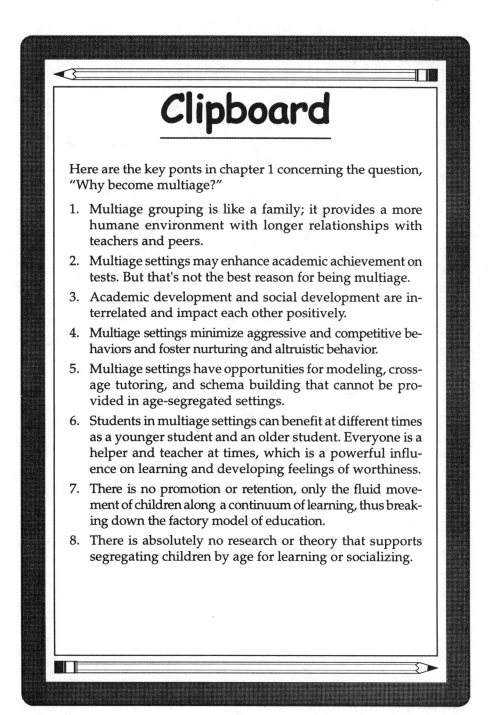

Clipboard

Here are the key ponts in chapter 1 concerning the question, "Why become multiage?"

1. Multiage grouping is like a family; it provides a more humane environment with longer relationships with teachers and peers.

2. Multiage settings may enhance academic achievement on tests. But that's not the best reason for being multiage.

3. Academic development and social development are interrelated and impact each other positively.

4. Multiage settings minimize aggressive and competitive behaviors and foster nurturing and altruistic behavior.

5. Multiage settings have opportunities for modeling, cross-age tutoring, and schema building that cannot be provided in age-segregated settings.

6. Students in multiage settings can benefit at different times as a younger student and an older student. Everyone is a helper and teacher at times, which is a powerful influence on learning and developing feelings of worthiness.

7. There is no promotion or retention, only the fluid movement of children along a continuum of learning, thus breaking down the factory model of education.

8. There is absolutely no research or theory that supports segregating children by age for learning or socializing.

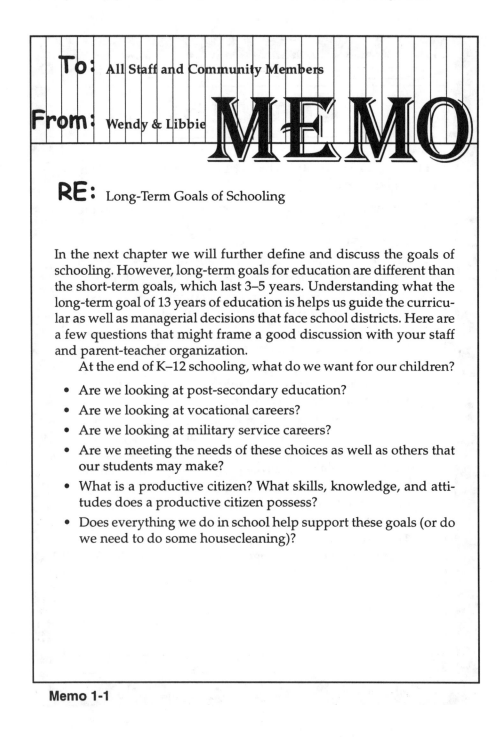

To: All Staff and Community Members

From: Wendy & Libbie

MEMO

RE: Long-Term Goals of Schooling

In the next chapter we will further define and discuss the goals of schooling. However, long-term goals for education are different than the short-term goals, which last 3–5 years. Understanding what the long-term goal of 13 years of education is helps us guide the curricular as well as managerial decisions that face school districts. Here are a few questions that might frame a good discussion with your staff and parent-teacher organization.

At the end of K–12 schooling, what do we want for our children?

- Are we looking at post-secondary education?
- Are we looking at vocational careers?
- Are we looking at military service careers?
- Are we meeting the needs of these choices as well as others that our students may make?
- What is a productive citizen? What skills, knowledge, and attitudes does a productive citizen possess?
- Does everything we do in school help support these goals (or do we need to do some housecleaning)?

Memo 1-1

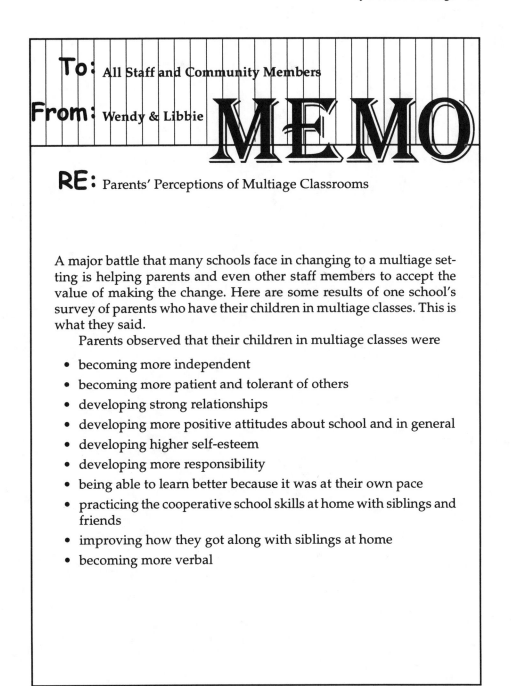

To: All Staff and Community Members

From: Wendy & Libbie

MEMO

RE: Parents' Perceptions of Multiage Classrooms

A major battle that many schools face in changing to a multiage setting is helping parents and even other staff members to accept the value of making the change. Here are some results of one school's survey of parents who have their children in multiage classes. This is what they said.

Parents observed that their children in multiage classes were

- becoming more independent
- becoming more patient and tolerant of others
- developing strong relationships
- developing more positive attitudes about school and in general
- developing higher self-esteem
- developing more responsibility
- being able to learn better because it was at their own pace
- practicing the cooperative school skills at home with siblings and friends
- improving how they got along with siblings at home
- becoming more verbal

Memo 1-2

CHAPTER 2

Changing the Face of Education— Successfully

● ●

How many times in your career have you seen "innovations" and "panaceas" come and go with promises that they will change education for the better? We have lived through new math, individually guided instruction, open classrooms, and even the nongraded education of the 1960s. This chapter will describe schools that have changed, the nature of change, how to lead change, and how to avoid those bandwagons of the past.

Stories of School Change

The Madison City Schools (names are pseudonyms) was an urban district that had a student population of around 10,000. This district, though labeled urban, also had some suburban and rural areas within its boundaries. The district's primary staff had been moving purposefully toward DAP for the past several years. However, even with quality, ongoing staff development and money to purchase the necessary materials, several people (including the superintendent) believed that something more was needed.

The superintendent's recommendation was to open a building that had been closed earlier, leading to the creation of a model nongraded, multiage school that would service any district child who chose to attend. This school maintained a waiting list of children from the other 12 elementary schools.

The teachers who chose to move to this building felt a sense of urgency to do something more for children. In their previous schools, DAP was effective but was tied to graded courses of study and existing progress reports that *rated* children rather than reported progress. Parents who wanted more from education for their children chose to have them attend this unique school. Because of a commitment to children, staff members and parents together created a multiage school for ages 5–13 that was developmentally appropriate and totally nongraded.

United Local Schools, in the western United States, began exploring multiage classrooms as a means of reducing their retention rate, which had grown from 10% to 25% of their kindergarten-age children in only 2 years. This trend indicated to the superintendent, the administration, the staff, and the community that something was definitely wrong.

The staff decided that multiage grouping might allow children more time to learn the kindergarten curriculum and consequently reduce retentions. However, the need to retain students resurfaced when the students still did not progress through the existing curriculum. The initial solution had not been properly understood or implemented, so the problem still existed. In other words, multiage grouping without attention to DAP was not an easy answer.

After close scrutiny and much dialogue, United found that its curriculum and teaching methodologies were not appropriate for kindergarten-age children. They proceeded to redesign their kindergarten curriculum at the same time that teachers were receiving ongoing staff development in DAP. As the kindergarten teachers progressed through both experiences, they realized that the entire K–12 curriculum needed to be examined for appropriateness and content. They led the movement to have others understand child development and current research on teaching and learning. The results were K–1 and 2–3 multiage classrooms with a curriculum that allowed for CP and meeting students' needs.

Jackson School, in the southwestern United States, is a third example of schools that have sensed the need to change. This school was rural and, until about 5 years ago, had a relatively stable population. Then Jackson School suddenly found itself in the midst of a population boom. Not only was there a need for a larger facility, there was also a need to reorganize the schooling structure from a K–6, essentially one-room school to a school that could house one and a half classes of each "grade level."

The community and the school joined together to explore solutions to the sudden and somewhat unexpected growth. They decided to continue with the one-room schoolhouse concept, but they redesigned it to fit student needs. The result was a 3-year plan to implement multiage classrooms housing two "grade levels" (composite multiage) in each, beginning with first-grade-age students. Half-day kindergarten remained separate except in planning units and school activities.

The Many Faces of Change

Change has been a topic of interest and concern for thousands of years. In fact, wariness about change was believed to be the subject of the first known book in human civilization, the Chinese *I Ching*, or *Book of Changes* (Wing, 1979). Ancient peoples used this book, it is believed, to address changes concerning farming, fishing, hunting, and social life. The prospect or reality of change isn't always a popular notion, and it causes concern in many people. If we understand it better, change can be a smoother and somewhat more comfortable process.

Our concern here is organizational change, and that of schools especially. Cuban (1988) describes two types of change. *First-order change* consists of "reforms that assume that the existing organizational goals and structures are basically adequate and what needs to be done is correction of deficiencies in policies and practices" (p. 228). Correcting policies and practices implies that the learning environment will consequently be improved.

For example, many times in schools we try to fix problems that have little or nothing to do with teaching and learning. We might develop a strategic plan that could truly change the structure of education, yet in the implementation phase we concentrate on new landscaping for the school grounds, school uniforms, year-round calendars, or controlling the cafeteria noise level by installing a huge traffic light that turns red when students talk too loudly. Often schools concentrate on procedural change because it seems to make life smoother, but it fails to improve *learning*.

In the above stories of change, United's first attempt at solving their retention problem was a first-order change. The staff tried to change procedures and routines by using multiage grouping patterns. The real problem, the lack of a CP curriculum, did not surface until the initial solution failed. First-order changes are superficial and may solve the problem for a short time, but in the long term they generally fail.

Cuban (1988) then describes *second-order changes* as those that "aim at altering the fundamental ways of achieving organizational goals" and "introduce new goals and interventions that transform the familiar ways of doing things" (p. 229). Second-order changes fundamentally affect the way that education is done in classrooms and entire schools. When site-based decision making is implemented correctly, second-order change usually occurs. Consensus teams that include parents, students, and staff members usually effect second-order changes as well. The changes that result from these types of processes are second order because, as Cuban says, they alter the *fundamental* way that the school works to achieve its goals.

Both Madison and Jackson effected second-order changes, because they didn't just worry about routines or procedures but addressed more important issues. The buildings were redesigned with different philosophical foundations and therefore required a different means of reaching the goals of schooling.

Implementing multiage classrooms mandates second-order change because this type of classroom goes against tradition in every way, including the materials used, the assessments given, and even the types of testing that may be done. This also becomes a second-order change because the fundamental philosophy of how children are educated shifts to one that is truly child-centered. Even the organizational structure of the school may be affected. Later in this chapter and in Part II, we suggest that the implementation of multiage classrooms comes about through shared decision making, which may be a new type of leadership for some schools. When we put the needs of children at the center of all our decisions and goals, then we have also implemented a very fundamental belief that education is for *all* our children, not just those who can survive our archaic structures. In this system, children grow by age, not grade levels. These differences are not about procedures, routines, and policies but about changing the structure of teaching and learning; hence they are second-order changes.

Changing to a multiage classroom, or any other second-order change, requires several preliminary steps. The first, described by Lewin (1947), is becoming *unfrozen* or open to change. Teachers who have successfully made changes in their classrooms, such as using manipulatives, implementing the writing process, or abandoning texts in favor of thematic teaching, have done so because they realized that the environment or the instruction was not truly the best that it could be for children. For whatever reasons, they were still not totally satisfied with their teaching. One could say they felt a sense of urgency.

"The concept that each child could learn at his or her own pace really was important to me, but I was never able to do that as well as I wanted in a self-contained, traditional classroom. I know that I tried my best to help each child individually, but there was never enough time or hands."

—Barbara Kidwell
Findlay, OH

Box 2-1

Many times this urgency is created because teachers think they are not meeting students' needs as well as possible, or they may see that a particular student is not responding to current instruction. Some have concluded that the system is not working for students. Whatever the cause, an urgency to change is the natural result, and it helps to unfreeze each of us so that we become open to solutions. Teachers who have become unfrozen and open to options are enabled to move into an innovation and remain there until they are once again ready for another change.

During the second phase of the change process, in which implementation actually occurs, teachers progress in their own professional development. Lewin views this as desirable. He describes this higher level as a productive one that includes action. These changes might be toward using DAP, math manipulatives, or literature-based reading. In this second phase, the fruits of change are evident; the classroom is operating differently.

"Our approach to the multiage was from the same vantage point as full-day kindergarten, which began one year earlier. We worked to meet individual needs through developmentally appropriate practices, including centers, contracts, and hands-on experiences."

—Beth Biery
Mechanicsburg, PA

Box 2-2

After a while, what was once a change becomes a natural, everyday occurrence. In other words, the teachers involved were sufficiently supported to continue to use the innovation until it became their own. Support may have taken the form of continued staff development, peer coaching or mentoring, observations of other innovative teachers, and additional time for planning and discussion provided through the use of retreats or substitute teachers.

Sometimes teachers who receive little or no support will revert to old practices. Feeling frustration or disappointment, they once again become stuck in the past and unopen to change. This is the legacy of the failed bandwagon at its best, with the automatic hopping on, no support for continued growth and understanding, and ultimate failure. Obviously, for successful change to occur, this likelihood must be minimized through careful planning.

One might say that change comes in many shapes with many faces. Just as a sense of urgency causes some teachers to change, for others change occurs as an *accident*. Imagine teaching a lesson one day and suddenly realizing that the way something was taught was particularly effective for the students. In such a case, the teacher would decide to continue to use the method or strategy because of the success.

Miles (1964) states that accidental changes are unplanned, occurring by chance or unexpectedly. Sometimes larger issues cause such an accident, and a change is upon us, such as a natural disaster. In Jackson's case, the change was caused by unexpected population growth—a complete surprise!

Another type of change is created by *drifting*. Owens (1981) claims that change by drifting is unplanned "adaptation to the overwhelming forces of change that permeate the environment in which the school functions" (p. 22). In many schools the initial change to combined classrooms began as the result of financial hardship, and these combined classrooms became multiage ones. Or perhaps the district or province had to release a teacher from a contract because of a deficit. Mitchell (1991) wrote about her experience with this when, after a reduction in school population, she had the choice of a multiage K–1 or fifth-grade math, and the former seemed the lesser of two evils!

A third type of change that we all need to experience is *planned*. The sense of urgency felt by a group results in systematic problem solving. In planned change, a definite time line is established, with lists of tasks and responsibilities, benchmarks to indicate success, and a means of continued support and growth. Madison experienced planned change through the careful work of the staff and the administration of the school district. Because of the lengthy, thorough process, this school and others have experienced marked success with their efforts.

By keeping this change information in mind, multiage as a bandwagon can be avoided. Jumping into a change because it seems to be the right thing to do will not allow for the type of lasting change that is needed in schools today. We hope that this change can be smooth, planned, and second order to fully realize success. Gaining an understanding of how a change can affect the organizational structure of a school and ultimately influence learning is the most powerful form of educational change. Multiage must be approached in this manner to improve learning for all children.

In Figure 2-1, change is illustrated as a positive and a negative depending upon the actions of those in control. The positive side of change occurs when urgency is felt and discussion results, identifying the real problem and implementing a chosen solution. The negative side occurs when urgency is felt and only procedural or superficial changes are made or no action is taken at all. In both negative cases, the problem continues.

Helping Change to Happen

Educators interested in change can learn a few things from the experience of the business community. In *Leading Change*, Kotter (1996) describes ideas for

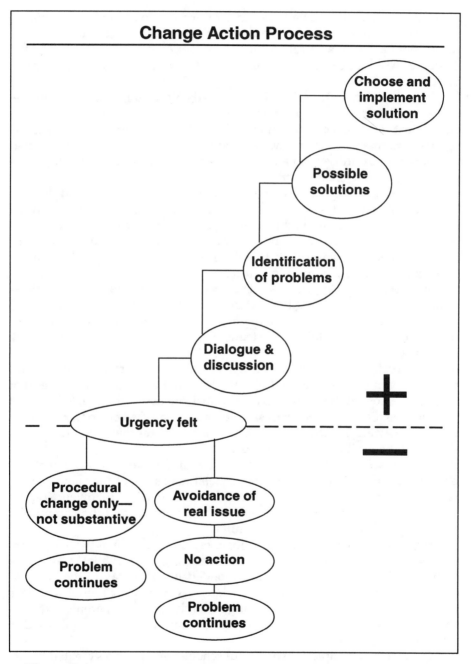

Figure 2-1

businesses to actually increase the sense of urgency to change. To do this, he suggests several strategies: (a) setting extremely high standards and goals, (b) creating a crisis, and (c) continual dialogue and discussion with the customer. We will discuss strategies 1 and 3, which are both relevant to educators.

In conjunction with setting high standards, Kotter suggests, for example, that instead of having everyone be responsible for their own area or specialty, create a system of interdependence that makes everyone accountable. In such circumstances, everyone has a larger stake in the success of the organization, not just those who are working on a particular aspect of the business. The idea is to create a *community*.

In schools, setting extremely high standards should go beyond the limited information on test scores, which qualify as "narrowly defined functions." Broader measures might include opening the decision-making process to all involved, creating a true partnership with parents and the community, and making students and their families feel a real part of the school by including them in setting goals for learning.

In education, we typically are expected to be accountable for our classrooms. We are rarely asked to be accountable for the rest of the school, the district, or the state! What would happen if, instead, we were all accountable for the success of *all* children? The teamwork required to perform such a task is rarely seen.

Some of the broader measures might be ascertained through Kotter's third strategy, continual dialogue and discussion with the customer. He states that business personnel should talk to the unsatisfied customer more, for without constructive feedback from both satisfied *and* unsatisfied customers, growth and creativity are limited. Feedback results in changes that increase productivity and the market for the business.

What would a classroom or school look like if we raised the need for change because we recognized that societal needs aren't the same as they once were? How can we gather that information? If we followed Kotter's advice, we would regularly survey parents, students, and the community and consider responding to those results.

What would happen if we actually asked parents once or twice a year to honestly evaluate what type of job we were doing in the school? What if we actually analyzed the results and responded in some way to the parents? Think about what would come of such a survey in your school. Would a sense of urgency be created for change from hearing the parents' expectations and desires for their children? (Sample survey forms are included in Appendixes C and D.)

In the three examples of successful schools, urgency was created before the changes occurred. For Madison, the superintendent and others believed that "something more was needed," while the teachers thought that not enough was being done for their students. At United, the staff felt a sense of urgency twice: First when the retention rate rose sharply and then when the first solution (multiage without any other changes) failed. Jackson felt a sense of urgency when the school became too small for all the new children. Without these senses of urgency, would these schools have changed so dramatically?

Issues That Create a Sense of Urgency

1. Money problems

2. Need to raise test scores mandated by higher authority

3. Innovations occurring all around except in your school or classroom

4. Parent dissatisfaction

5. Community dissatisfaction

6. Bold new leadership with new expectations

7. Honest assessment, internal or external, on the state of the schools

8. Intrinsic need to make classrooms better for children

Figure 2-2

Making a Commitment

We don't recommend jumping into any change, much less converting your classrooms to multiage, if you think the change will be painless, less time consuming, or if you aren't willing to commit to the process, which will likely take several years. Easy answers simply don't exist.

Fullan (1993) states that you cannot *make* people change, think differently, or force them to develop new skills (p. 23). Change has often taken the form of a mandate, whether from a central office, a district, a state or province, or just at the school level. Changes of this sort do not endure because they lack the commitment of those who are closest to the classroom. According to Klein (1985), "Change consists not of an event, but of a process or series of events occurring over a period of time, usually involving a more or less orderly and somewhat predictable sequence of interactions" (p. 98).

Change requires a genuine interest in the topic and an immersion in the implementation process. Interest in the topic generates the commitment to see the change through. The bandwagon is avoided because the change becomes a reality, accomplished by those interested, who are supported through staff development, given choice and time, and in turn show a commitment to success.

One of us worked with some teachers who needed to make a change because their state had implemented proficiency tests in writing for grades 4, 8, and 12. Although the teachers believed that they were teaching writing, they were actually providing very little true writing instruction and opportunities for students to practice. In considering their plight, they went to a catalog to see what curricular materials they could purchase that would help them to teach writing. What's wrong with this picture?

Once a problem has been identified, the next step is to educate or immerse yourself in information about the problem area from worthwhile sources. These might be conferences, professional books and journals, or local inservice offerings. Solutions to problems are not found in catalogs. The outcome of these teachers' endeavors was that they purchased a very expensive set of materials about writing. While the materials may have had some value, they did not educate them about the theory and practice of teaching writing. Hence, they were unable to use the materials to the best advantage for their students. True commitment to change, no matter what sort of change, takes more than browsing through a catalog. It takes the knowledge that change is a process, involving education, risk taking, and time. There are no shortcuts!

Schools need to examine the commitment to and reasons for change. The capacity for change is built within an environment that allows for constructive risk taking. The environment supports appropriate experimentation and failure as a means for growth and understanding. Through this growth and understanding, a clear vision of what changes need to occur can be generated, thereby allowing well-planned, second-order change to be facilitated. Encouragement of continued risk taking increases the capacity for change and increases the commitment to the change. By building the capacity to understand and accept change, school personnel will no longer wonder why new innovations sometimes fail.

The People Versus Change

Knowing what reactions to expect can help ease growing pains. First of all, while we would all like to believe that everyone wants the same changes to occur, this isn't always the case. Several different types of people are involved in schools, so you can expect several kinds of reactions to proposed changes.

The Risk Taker

The first and most desirable reaction is full cooperation and buy-in. In such a case, the teachers, administrators, parents, and community have described the type of school that they want for the children, and it's just a matter of achieving the vision. The people who react in this way are usually the risk takers. They have probably stayed current with the trends in education as well as the changing needs of the world. These people work cooperatively toward the set goal. Life is good.

One example of this type of reaction occurred in Libbie's former school district. The school community united to decide what the school's function and purpose would be. Parents nicknamed the school the "family." The staff was committed to doing whatever was necessary to meet the children's needs. Two outside consultants, Barbara Nelson Pavan and Robert Anderson, developed the acronym CAN for the school, based not only on the initials of the school's name but also on the "we can" attitude that permeated the building.

This type of environment might be just as trying as other, more resistant types of environments. The focus must continually be on the *children* and the *vision* that was created to serve them. Outside as well as inside influences can sometimes distract everyone from the real reason that the school operates. Working in this type of situation requires a delicate balance between constructive, open dialogue and movement toward the vision. The school community cannot be so sure that they alone have all the answers. The staff must continue to analyze the results of the work toward the vision.

The Watcher

The second type of expected reaction comes from a group that is not opposed to change but is hesitant about the proposed change and its outcome. Such reactions can enable the group to make sure that the ideas are not merely an effort to jump on a bandwagon. People who are slower to change because they analyze the situation and continually evaluate the change results are valuable within a changing organization. While they may not jump immediately into the change, they will support others' efforts to change as they positively assess the situation.

Julie, a second-grade teacher, does very creative things in her classroom. However, she will not jump on any bandwagon. She wants facts, places to visit, research about effects on children, and dialogue. Even though Julie does not immediately move forward, she continues to support her colleagues who do. She will slowly begin to implement the necessary changes if she believes that they will enhance the learning of her students. Most of us are like Julie when it comes to change.

Working with the "Julies" of the staff is usually fairly pleasant. In a trusting atmosphere, Julie can help the principal or other teachers see a different viewpoint. She needs time and support from those around her—time to continue her research and support as she moves slowly toward the change. Julie will use articles, books, tapes, visitations, and coursework for her own journey. She will, in turn, provide support and a platform for dialogue and debate about the proposed changes.

The Heel Digger

This type of person will react by digging in one's heels and not budging. He or she hopes that if a few people resist very loudly, others will be intimidated. These people typically react out of fear of the change. Occasionally, the root of their reaction is a dislike of the profession or even a dislike of children. However, most of these adamant resisters can usually be offered a job elsewhere (perhaps a fast food restaurant?).

Suzette is a person that most of us don't want to encounter. The principal usually spends a great deal of time in meetings trying to gain her support through eye contact or direct conversation. Suzette rarely has a legitimate reason to oppose the change. However, she can and does talk very loudly about her rights and her workload. When she is confronted by others she tends to insult or embarrass them, usually causing them to retreat and work quietly in their own rooms. Suzette seems to be more concerned with procedures and routines that favor her power base than with children and teaching and learning. She usually asks questions such as, "When the superintendent leaves, won't this fad go with him?"

Most faculties and parents find the "Suzettes" of the staff to be unapproachable and unbending. However, humanity demands that Suzette not be isolated. It is important to include her without permitting her to dominate or intimidate others. The principal needs to be strong in this effort and not reduce meetings to compromising sessions with Suzette or others like her. If the risk taker and the watcher unite with a common goal, the Suzettes won't be able to disrupt the change. In other words, power lies in numbers, not in loudness of protests.

The Saboteur

This category reacts to change by sabotaging the effort. Sabotage can take many forms, including rumors, false information, anonymous letters of complaint, and even demonstrations. The saboteur may be internal or external. We have come across both types in our experiences.

One external example, and perhaps the most difficult to battle, was the pediatrician who had never visited the multiage school yet recommended to others that they not send their children there because it was "so unstructured" that the children would not succeed. Upon receiving an invitation to visit the school, the person stopped the sabotage. The fact that other multiage parents, who either used this pediatrician for their children or were doctors themselves, talked with him about his incorrect assumptions and obvious dislike of the school seemed to help as well. Generally, saboteurs need to be confronted by inviting them into the process instead of shutting them out and hoping the problem will go away. It almost never does.

A case of internal sabotage occurred when the principal in the district's wealthiest school told parents that the multiage school was for "special needs" children. Her goal was to possibly eliminate special needs children from her building so that she would only have to deal with the wealthier, "smarter" children. At the opposite end of town, in an area with a high minority population and lower socioeconomic level, another principal told his parents that the multiage school was for "doctors' and lawyers' kids." Would you want your child to attend the multiage school if it was a either a "special needs" school or an elitist one?

Fortunately, the public relations effort by the multiage parents cleared up some of these misunderstandings. In these situations both the staff and the parents of the multiage school refused to join in a "mudslinging" contest. Instead, positive articles about school activities, as well as pictures, were placed in the local newspapers, open inservice meetings for community members were arranged, a booklet discussing the multiage grouping pattern and nongraded philosophy was distributed, and a pamphlet describing the school was created and sent. As the school continued to win recognition from local, state, and national arenas, much of the obvious sabotage subsided.

In creating a multiage classroom or school, we must remember that knowledge about multiage is power. Creating the type of atmosphere that will best serve children is a goal of the majority of stakeholders, including parents, staff, and the broader community. The effort to create a lasting change is not easy. The change agents need knowledge and information on the "how to" of creating a multiage situation. Those slower to change need knowledge to enable a thoughtful decision. The people who refuse to change need to have the knowledge so that they cannot be excused when they spread incorrect information in an effort to block the change. The saboteurs obviously need information, but more importantly, stakeholders need information in order to fight the sabotage. Parents, the community, grandparents, school personnel, and colleagues need information to combat rumors and possible hysteria that may be caused by the saboteurs. Without knowledge and correct information, no one is empowered except the saboteurs and the heel diggers. Successful change will not occur in this situation.

Is creating a lasting change possible with the four types of people mentioned here? It is, but life becomes a little more interesting when the heel diggers and the saboteurs are thrown into the mix. The most important advice that we have to offer about change can be found in Figure 2-3. These ideas can be used in either staff or parent meetings to organize the change process.

Strategies for Successful Change

- Research community needs, especially seeking information from parents and students.

- Brainstorm solutions with an open mind, not a hidden agenda.

- Educate the stakeholders on all possible solutions and the substance of those solutions, not just the "buzz words."

- Request input from all stakeholders about the possible solutions.

- Analyze and explore all the input with an open mind.

- Determine the best possible solution for all involved.

- Plan the change thoughtfully and carefully, sharing information.

- Continually assess the plan, both long-range and short-range goals.

- Educate the stakeholders along the way.

- Seek and use stakeholder perceptions and assessments of the change.

Figure 2-3

Getting to the Dream

Schools today, as in our one-room schoolhouses of the past, are closed organizations. Teachers, secretaries, custodians, cooks, and administrators arrive to work each day and immediately report to their individual work areas. Many staff members don't see another staff member until lunch or planning time. If you think about it, the only time the entire teaching staff is together is at periodic meetings. Under these circumstances, how can we expect to have a common vision for the school, much less work toward that vision?

Schools today function better when they become communities that are dependent in some way on each person in the school. Several steps are required to break down the walls of isolation in schools. These are *communication, unification, implementation,* and ongoing *self-renewal.* We will now outline each of these steps.

Communication

The first step is communication—open, honest dialogue that leads to discussion and, hopefully, agreement. We are often unclear about what our colleagues believe about teaching and learning. We don't have the time in our current schedules to discuss issues and concerns, much less philosophies and beliefs. We think we know what others believe, but we can't always be certain.

Designing a change requires knowing what the common beliefs are in a school. Only through an open, honest dialogue can people's beliefs emerge. The environment must allow freedom of expression yet protect speakers from attack by others. Several "do you believe" questions can begin this dialogue in a faculty meeting or during a team-building staff development session. Memo 2-1 gives only a few examples; several other questions can be used based upon your school's particular needs.

With dialogue may come discomfort and some sense of distrust. Facilitators of the discussions can work toward several goals, such as holding discussions that are honest. Everyone should have an opportunity to speak; confidentiality should be ensured; personal attacks should be forbidden; agreement should be sought at the conclusion of the session; and no side conversations or retaliation should be tolerated. Through professional dialogue, the ability to come to a point where true discussion can occur will begin to take shape.

After such dialogues, the beliefs that have emerged can be outlined by the staff, and commonly held beliefs about the school can be identified. This may be achieved in several ways.

First, a survey might be sent to both parents and the community at large. Sending surveys home in report cards, or even as a memo from the school to parents, might be helpful. For the community at large, surveys could be placed in fast food restaurants or printed in the local newspaper. The results would then have to be compiled and analyzed for commonly held beliefs. Discovering what the community has in common with the school can be very exciting and illuminating!

Another means of determining community beliefs is through a forum. Perhaps the staff's beliefs can be listed for the audience, with dialogue and discussion of each one. Another way is to ask those in attendance to begin to think about schools in terms of what they believe about children, teachers, leaders, parents, community, teaching, and learning. These dialogues can be recorded on chart paper or even by videotaping the discussions. Small groups rather than large groups may be used to facilitate this type of forum.

In addition, input can be gained by selecting a representative body of parents and community members to work with the staff on defining or refining beliefs about the school. In this case, a preliminary dialogue and discussion might be held with the staff to avoid controversial or divisive debates between staff members or between parents and staff members. For example, in one school the faculty itself could not agree on whether to continue using an honor roll. Many of the faculty felt that rating children was unnecessary and counterproductive, whereas others felt that without it standards would be compromised. Before discussing this issue in a community forum, the administrator had to ensure some consensus among the staff members.

Unification

·The process of unifying our beliefs into a vision is the next step. After the development of core beliefs about education, specifics are needed about the school's vision and goals. Kotter (1996) explains:

> Vision plays a key role in producing useful change by helping to direct, align, and inspire actions on the part of large numbers of people. Without an appropriate vision, a transformation effort can easily dissolve into a list of confusing, incompatible, and time-consuming projects that go in the wrong direction or nowhere at all. (p. 7)

Kotter's statement about the power of a vision cannot be taken lightly. Many schools have statements hanging on the walls of their offices, but how many use the vision to lead their everyday activities? The vision is the guiding force for change. Once we have identified, sometimes painfully, what we as a staff agree on about education, then we need to identify the guiding principles for our actions. The vision provides everyone with an understanding of what road the school is taking (see Memo 2-2).

According to Nanus (1992), a vision leads to a realistic, credible, attractive future for the organization. He describes it as something that you are willing to work hard to achieve. This believable future for the organization will energize everyone. Nanus cautions that a vision is not a prophecy or prediction; it is not static or a constraint on action (unless the action is inconsistent with the vision). The vision is not a mission (which is a purpose); rather, it is a statement of direction. A vision is, in the words of the proverbial song, "the unreachable star."

The vision leads to specific goals for moving toward it. Formulating goals that express both the core beliefs and the vision can be achieved with a process that has been used in many schools. Here are some steps that may help.

- Everyone on the staff—as well as parents, students, and community members who are interested in the process and willing to spend some quality time developing the goals—is invited. If many people attend, small groups can be used to generate goals that can then be filtered through by the whole group.
- After reviewing the vision and core beliefs, the question is posed, "Where will we be as a school community in 5 years?" Suggested answers are listed. The items on the list are then clarified if necessary and are either highlighted if they pertain directly to the vision and beliefs or removed if they do not.
- The members of the group then narrow the list to about 12 goal statements. These should indicate what the end result will look like and not be just a lofty ideal.
- Each goal is checked for appropriateness by asking, "Does this goal serve children first?" If the answer is truly "yes," then the goal becomes accepted.

The final step of unification includes displaying and talking about the beliefs, vision, and goals. Each area of the school should have the same poster, chart, or sign stating the vision and the goals. Every time a newsletter or memo is sent home, the vision should be included. The school letterhead and outdoor sign can also state the vision or a shortened version of it. Everything that is printed for public relations purposes should identify the vision and the goals, including such things as sweatshirts and gym bags that children and parents purchase. Ownership of these goals becomes imperative for their success.

Implementation

Once unification is under way, the process of implementation of the vision and goals can begin. A time line begins to take shape. Most schools begin with the goal, for example, of multiaging with two "grade levels" first, and after the fifth year having all or most grade levels multiaged in the appropriate age spans. Time lines are created for all the goals that were agreed upon. Every goal cannot possibly be achieved in the first year, so reasonable time lines allow everyone to know the expectations for progress in the process of change.

Implementation is the second most difficult phase (after communication). Implementation requires a slow, steady process toward each of the identified goals. When the road becomes bumpy, reverting to the "old" way is tempting.

For example, a goal that was designed by Libbie's former staff described an individualized approach to discipline that relied heavily on the children becoming responsible for their own behavior. With some of the older children in the school, who had already experienced at least 3 years of a more "assertive" form of discipline, this new style seemed to be relatively easy— no consequences, no punishment. "Let's test it to the limit" became their motto.

The multiage teachers, who were also master teachers, spent more than a few minutes in the office trying to convince others of the need to move back to the old form of discipline. However, with perseverance and continual support, these teachers survived the change along with the children who had tested the system so energetically. By the end of the third year, the teachers determined that the results were well worth the struggle.

A case in point is that of a young man who had been retained twice before reaching third grade (in another school). Rick lived with his grandmother, never really knowing his mother or father. One day he came to Libbie's office for what was probably the thousandth time. When Libbie asked him the purpose of the visit (since he was already on a behavior contract signed by grandma, the teachers, and Libbie), he stated that he wanted to negotiate his "rewards" for successful completion of the contract. When asked what that reward should be, Rick stated that he wanted to do a 10-minute karate demonstration in the gymnasium for his class. He was a brown belt and believed that this experience would be valuable to his classmates. This turnaround of a lost, streetwise young man into one who wanted to do something worthwhile for his school indicated that the new discipline, and the other changes in the schooling structure were worth the effort.

Implementation requires a great deal of energy and support for everyone involved. Sometimes even teachers who were instrumental in designing the new school will ask if it is really the way to go. Perhaps the principal will wonder why the school isn't moving faster or why the school is moving so quickly. These same fears will be voiced by parents, even those who were great supporters of the change. Everyone will be concerned about assessment results and the periodic reports that are sent to the parents. Will the children be successful? What if we really didn't make the right decision? Doubting is a natural part of change.

We facetiously joke that when stress is high in a multiage school, eat chocolate! Aside from the humor, the message is to reconnect with everyone for a "stress reduction" time. Meet to socialize or address your fears and concerns. Whatever the flavor of the meeting, remember to focus on the vision you created together. Ask yourself if you want to return to the way it was. You'll find strength in numbers, and you'll realize the answer is no.

Self-Renewal

"In self-renewing organizations, educators in all positions in the system create a better learning environment for themselves and students by studying education and how to improve it" (Joyce, Wolf, & Calhoun, 1993, p. 29). Self-renewing schools continually assess their purpose and vision. Goals are achieved, and new goals are formulated, thereby avoiding the stagnation that is often found in a once-successful organization.

Self-study by self-renewing schools creates the necessary data for determining successes and needs. Self-studies can be achieved by requesting student and parent feedback through survey instruments or even interviews (see Appendixes C and D for samples). It is not uncommon for self-renewing schools to send out parent surveys twice a year. Student and staff surveys are also very common in this type of school. People's perceptions and concerns can help the staff to understand what the results look like to their "customers" as well as to themselves.

The ongoing success of a multiage school or classroom depends on careful scrutiny of the implementation and results. If goals are to be achieved and new goals set, this information is necessary. Feedback may be difficult to accept because insiders sometimes see things differently than parents do.

One example of this occurred after a set of parent survey results was returned. The parents in this school frequently commented that they did not know what was really happening in the classrooms on a day-to-day basis. The teachers and principal could not understand this concern because all the children had individual goal sheets that parents helped determine quarterly, narrative report cards without any grades, quarterly thematic unit updates, and wonderful student-developed portfolios. How, then, could the parents not know what happened at school? It seemed incredulous to the staff!

The staff's first reaction was anger: How dare those parents question our hard work and long hours! After the initial reaction subsided, the staff realized that they knew what happened daily. They knew the miniskills lessons that were taught, they knew the discussions that were held between children, and they knew that the children were progressing. The staff was looking at the constructive criticism from the view of insiders. Of course, the parents didn't see that instruction on a daily basis. The result of this constructive feedback and subsequent dialogue by the staff was a weekly schoolwide newsletter that outlined the miniskills lessons and the extra projects within the thematic unit. Parents reacted positively to the bulletins.

Another avenue for gathering data on the school's progress toward its goals is to use outside experts to "audit" the school. Knowledgeable multiage experts can visit and observe your school. They can interview staff, parents, and students to gather further documentation for the school. A final report can be written for distribution to chosen sources. This type of outside help often provides an objectivity that enables additional growth.

Self-renewing schools must be open to constructive criticism if they are to continue the growth cycle. Criticism that is unfounded or only hurtful is not given the careful attention that constructive criticism deserves. Unfounded criticism is usually voiced by one person who thinks that the school or classroom does not individualize enough or that the school is mediocre compared to another school. That parent would probably never discuss this issue openly so that it could be resolved. Usually this type of criticism is unwarranted and shouldn't be taken too seriously.

Constructive criticism is seen in several surveys or interviews. The voices may be requesting additional information or change in a positive manner, often including suggestions to alleviate the issue. Through careful analysis of the criticism, the comments and concerns can be successfully sorted and addressed.

Seeing Change Through: Getting the Community Aboard

With the implementation cycle started, continued staff development and parent-community education is needed to sustain the process. Many times schools forget the ongoing support and learning that is needed by those in the midst of change.

Staff development in various theoretically grounded methodologies and philosophies has probably occurred prior to implementing multiage classrooms. These sessions might include whole language philosophy, DAP, and manipulative-based math and science. We have found that once these are in place, additional development is still needed.

The multiage classroom requires more individualization of student learning to be effective. Actual implementation requires a greater understanding of assessing different student needs and accountability for the CP curriculum. Staff development opportunities for these types of skills are not as readily available as the earlier mentioned ones. Specifics about staff development are addressed in Part II.

Sometimes a district's internal resources are overlooked in staff development, but they may help meet many staff development needs. For example, any outstanding special education teacher readily knows how to individualize learning for students; the speech pathologist, school counselor, or selected classroom teacher is probably adept at assessments; and curriculum management is probably a breeze for at least one of your staff members. These internal resources are frequently undervalued, overlooked, and underutilized. By drawing on the strengths of those around you, staff development can be more personalized and less expensive.

Remember that staff development needs are ongoing. One-day workshops can sometimes provide a needed shot in the arm, but real learning occurs when follow-up study and dialogue take place. Book talks or study groups are vehicles for achieving ongoing development and dialogue. They are also easy to facilitate and cost little.

Study groups (Matlin & Short, 1991) have recently become popular to add professionalism to the school climate. Sometimes these groups are led by a principal, a curriculum leader, a teacher, or an outsider as the chairperson. The group selects books or articles to read in common and comes together to discuss them at appointed times, such as once every two weeks after school. Sometimes these groups focus their study on a topic, such as multiage learning or assessment. Key educational books may be the focus, such as *In the Middle* (Atwell, 1987), *Literature Circles* (Daniels, 1994), *Assessment and Evaluation for Student Centered Learning* (Harp, 1994), or even this book! These groups often report back to the faculty as a whole or to the district with recommendations based on their learning. Some districts pay teachers during summer break to participate in such a study group as a task force to lead local changes.

Parent and community growth and understanding should also be ongoing. Some schools have created a parent and community inservice calendar offered throughout the school year for anyone interested in attending the sessions. The inservice topics are usually based on a needs assessment given during previous school years or early in the academic term. The sessions are then based on what people have indicated as needs and might occur after school, during school hours, in the early morning, or in the early evening. Some schools in which we've worked have included sessions on divorce and death, dysfunctional families, positive discipline, and summer reading programs. Others held a family fun night with a book swap or a family math night. At Moody Elementary in Florida, the guidance counselor held successful coffee klatches on a variety of topics at 7;30 a.m. to accommodate working parents.

Some schools have difficulty getting good attendance at any school function except school plays or musical performances. Sometimes parents leave as soon as their child has performed. Fortunately, we have some ideas for dealing with this type of problem. Some of you may feel there's an element of sneakiness in this, and we admit that there is!

We have been at schools that begin with the first two acts or songs of the evening. Suddenly, everyone freezes at an appropriate pausing point, and the principal introduces a group of teachers or parents who do a minilesson on some selected topic. The show continues after this short interlude. This pattern is continued as many times as the staff feels they can successfully get away with it!

Another idea we have come across is to attach food and/or babysitting with an evening of learning. Topics such as discipline and testing tend to draw large numbers of people. Offering a small incentive like a doorprize, or attaching the inservice to a family spaghetti dinner or schoolwide potluck supper, will probably increase the attendance.

Other means of ongoing education for parents might include professional literature for them to check out from your parent library. Books, or excerpts that are carefully selected, and journal articles can be a good source of information for parents. Brochures and articles can also be made available for parents to read, borrow, or purchase. Putting inservices on videotapes and audiotapes permits those who could not attend, or maybe those who do not read well, to grow in their knowledge of multiage education and other pertinent topics.

An additional valuable source of parent information is a monthly newsletter. This could include a research brief, written in an understandable format, as well as any other necessary parent information. News of the parent-teacher organization and student birthdays may be included. Many schools allow such a newsletter to be created by parents or managed by older students in the school with contributions from the principal and the teachers.

Clipboard

The main points of chapter 2 are as follows:

1. Change is a complicated process that requires time, energy, and perseverance.

2. Changing the organizational structure of a school requires planned, second-order change.

3. Before people will commit to change, they must feel a great need or sense of urgency.

4. Change requires commitment and continued support by those immersed in the change process.

5. Many types of people exist in our schools today. We cannot allow those opposed to change to shape our children's destinies.

6. Understanding what beliefs exist among the school community members is the first step toward developing a common vision.

7. Communication, unification, implementation, and ongoing self-renewal are all part of creating a vision by which the school can live.

8. Ongoing staff and parent inservices are a must in creating the understanding and acceptance needed for lasting change.

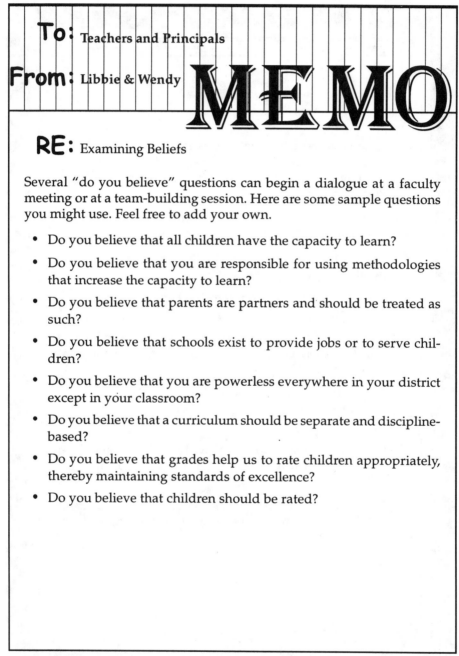

To: Teachers and Principals

From: Libbie & Wendy

MEMO

RE: Examining Beliefs

Several "do you believe" questions can begin a dialogue at a faculty meeting or at a team-building session. Here are some sample questions you might use. Feel free to add your own.

- Do you believe that all children have the capacity to learn?

- Do you believe that you are responsible for using methodologies that increase the capacity to learn?

- Do you believe that parents are partners and should be treated as such?

- Do you believe that schools exist to provide jobs or to serve children?

- Do you believe that you are powerless everywhere in your district except in your classroom?

- Do you believe that a curriculum should be separate and discipline-based?

- Do you believe that grades help us to rate children appropriately, thereby maintaining standards of excellence?

- Do you believe that children should be rated?

Memo 2-1

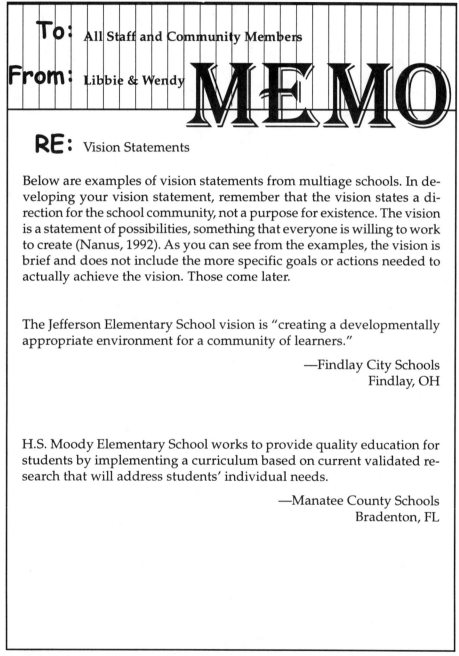

To: All Staff and Community Members

From: Libbie & Wendy

MEMO

RE: Vision Statements

Below are examples of vision statements from multiage schools. In developing your vision statement, remember that the vision states a direction for the school community, not a purpose for existence. The vision is a statement of possibilities, something that everyone is willing to work to create (Nanus, 1992). As you can see from the examples, the vision is brief and does not include the more specific goals or actions needed to actually achieve the vision. Those come later.

The Jefferson Elementary School vision is "creating a developmentally appropriate environment for a community of learners."

—Findlay City Schools
Findlay, OH

H.S. Moody Elementary School works to provide quality education for students by implementing a curriculum based on current validated research that will address students' individual needs.

—Manatee County Schools
Bradenton, FL

Memo 2-2

PART II

Inside the School

● ●

This section includes two chapters that describe the prerequisites for the creation of a multiage school as well as some practical suggestions for beginning a multiage program. Chapter 3 discusses how to structure the school, group children in classrooms, and determine types of multiage settings. Characteristics of multiage teachers are then described. Information on discipline and staff development is followed by considerations for special area teachers. Chapter 4 delineates how to facilitate consensus meetings, ideas for parent involvement, advice from principals, and evaluating the school's progress. Each chapter offers numerous practical ideas and samples for those ready to begin a multiage program.

CHAPTER 3

Designing the Multiage School

Many people comment that multiage classrooms are not new, and they're right. The first American nongraded movement began in the early 1960s with the publication of Goodlad and Anderson's first edition on nongraded schools (1959/1987). Immediately, nongraded education became the panacea for all educational ills. Unfortunately, the philosophy did not last long because implementation in most places was poorly done.

In 1969, Henry Otto, a professor at the University of Texas, published a report on the needs of a nongraded schooling structure. Otto was curious about why nongraded schools were not lasting very long in the United States. He discovered several reasons that nongradedness failed. Otto's work became a guideline for schools that were working toward nongraded structures, and his findings still apply today.

Foundations of a Multiage School

Otto contended that four things must happen for schools to become nongraded in their approaches. First, nongradedness, or multiage classrooms, *cannot be mandated*. Rather, ownership is important for lasting change to be secured. Second, the people with the most effect on schooling are *classroom teachers*; decisions related to curriculum and instruction are best made by those who know the children best—teachers. Third, without appropriate *materials*, such as those needed for hands-on work, innovative grouping is not successful. Fourth, school governance should support these changes through *consensus-style leadership,* in which decisions are shared by everyone involved in the child's education.

Each of Otto's points supports the multiage grouping pattern used within a nongraded schooling structure. We will now elaborate on Otto's suggestions in order to help make multiage education a reality in your school.

Mandating Prohibited

Otto states that a nongraded philosophy cannot be mandated, and we agree. How many times have we seen things fail in our professional and personal lives because they were mandated? Mandated results lack personal commitment to a project as well as the sense of ownership that is needed. Mandating actually *prohibits* the commitment in many cases.

Mandating the philosophy and imposing it on parents is a time bomb. Parents, like staff members, deserve a choice in their child's education. Most parents have been raised in a graded system with textbooks, homework, and grades. To remove their children from the known into the perceived "experimental" classroom environment without much preparation and choice is detrimental to multiage classrooms. Their fear of the unknown will work against the success of multiage grouping.

Providing choice for parents may mean that the school should run both a graded and a nongraded system, each requiring its own structure and guidelines. As more parents learn about multiage, more multiage classes may be needed. Without a choice for parents, it is very likely that the program will be protested and perhaps stopped by the parents through attendance at board meetings, letters to board members, letters to the editor of the local newspaper, and more formal means of protest. Allowing a choice at first will let parents become comfortable with the new grouping patterns and methodologies.

Commitment of Classroom Teachers

Otto suggests that the person closest to the classroom, the teacher, has the greatest impact on the success of the nongraded structure. The teacher must be committed to the grouping pattern and have ownership in the school program for it to be successful.

Teacher leadership is a necessary component of schools. Teachers need to be able to make decisions based upon research and best practices that will serve children in their classrooms. Multiage teachers are typically teacher leaders who determine that they want to teach in a different structure. From our various experiences with multiage teachers, we have generated a list of characteristics exemplified by a quality multiage teacher (see Figure 3-1). You may notice that many of the characteristics are the same ones you would list for any quality leader, boss, teacher, or clergyperson.

The ABCs of Quality Multiage Teachers

A = Able
B = Broad-minded
C = Creative
D = Determined
E = Energetic, Enthusiastic
F = Facilitator
G = Good listener
H = High expectations
I = Interested in kids
J = Just
K = Kid watcher
L = Lifelong learner
M = Mentor
N = Nurturing
O = Outgoing
P = Professional
Q = Quality teacher
R = Risk taker
S = Sculptor (Sower of seeds)
T = Talented
U = Unselfish
V = Vigor
W = Well-informed
X = eXcited about learning and teaching
Y = You
Z = Zestful

Figure 3-1

In many schools, multiage teachers are selected from volunteers. If the school has openings that are advertised as multiage, then the teacher is hired as such. In either case, the teacher buys into the nongraded philosophy and cutting-edge teaching methods.

Teachers need time to plan and organize their multiage classrooms. This time can be generated through extra days, substitute days, or school retreats. Staff development is also included in this planning and organizational time. Attendance at multiage conferences and workshops requires time away from the classroom as well.

Appropriate Materials

If materials relevant to the multiage classroom are not available, Otto and others contend that the classroom will not reach the ultimate level of success. Materials should be assessed for potential multiage classrooms. What do you already have that will be appropriate in a multiage classroom? What might you use in a different way? What is still needed to make the classroom more hands-on and inquiry-based? Are there materials in the school that can be redistributed or shared?

Several materials, such as spelling charts or textbooks in large quantities, are no longer necessary in the multiage classroom. Only a few copies of a variety of grade-level textbooks are needed and are only used as a reference guide for children who cannot yet use encyclopedias or other reference books. The use of technology and the library—both school and public libraries—becomes necessary in the multiage setting. Traditional textbook adoptions must be modified to include software, reference, and hands-on materials. A graded textbook indicates that learning is confined to a specific age or grade, and this is contrary to the structure of the CP philosophy outlined in chapter 1.

Consensus Leadership

Nongraded schooling structures necessitate a different type of leadership, according to Otto. These schools require that those closest to the instruction be part of the decision-making process. Teachers and parents become part of the team that decides what's best for the children. Instructional decisions are made by teacher teams that include the administrator as an equal member; decisions about children's educational goals are jointly made by parents and teachers; and decisions that affect the school as a whole are made by parents, teachers, and administrators. The effort to include all involved parties in a decision is a tedious one; however, the benefits outweigh the time and effort required.

Conclusion

Although Otto's work is based on the nongraded structures of the 1960s, the same four ideas hold true for today's multiage classrooms. The nongraded philosophy is the foundation of the multiage grouping pattern. Without the four ideas in place, success will be more difficult to achieve. What Otto has described is a second-order change—not merely a change in the way we group children but a change in the total structure of how we educate our children.

As we study the mistakes of the past, we can avoid those same problems today. If your school does not have the appropriate materials, a choice about multiage, consensus-style leadership, and teachers that believe in the philosophy, then much work must be done before implementing multiage classrooms. These elements are *essential* as you begin the first steps toward designing the multiage classroom or school.

Practical Decisions

Once the prerequisites are in place in your school, it's time to make practical decisions about the school and classrooms. These include ability grouping, heterogeneous class lists, and who should be a multiage teacher. We then describe schoolwide discipline needs and staff development for teachers and administrators in the multiage school, including special area teachers.

Structuring the School

Grouping to Create Classrooms   Grouping in schools has always been an interesting topic of discussion. Many of us were educated during the era of ability grouping, many of us experienced whole-class grouping, and some of us even experienced the individually guided education of the 1970s. Some of us may have been in a school with the "Joplin plan" for grouping, in which students move during the day to a teacher who is teaching the basal level that is correct for them. For example, if Stephan, a 6-year-old student, is a very fluent reader, he would go to Mrs. Jones, who is teaching the fourth-grade basal for reading time. Jill, a 10-year-old struggling reader, would go to Mr. Ellis, who is teaching the second-grade basal during reading time.

Grouping by ability persists in classrooms today even though research has shown that it is not beneficial to most learners. This section will discuss the unfortunate legacy of ability grouping and the promise of creating heterogeneous learning communities.

A true story from one of our third-grade experiences will illustrate the lasting effects of ability grouping. The classroom was arranged so that 20 students were aligned in a long row with their desks facing and touching each other. This double row of 10 desks was clearly separated from another row of only 6 desks, where 6 boys sat segregated from the rest of the students. The classroom teacher spent a great deal of time giving the 20 students smiles and independent opportunities for work. They even had the privilege of putting up the bulletin boards when the pile of assigned papers was completed. The segregated boys were always quiet, deathly quiet. For some reason, every time the teacher worked with them she became angry and used her "mean" voice. The class didn't know the boys very well because they sat so far away and never even went to recess with the rest of the class.

As the class continued through the school years, those six boys gradually disappeared. They never graduated, and most class members could hardly even remember that they had been there. Who were those invisible children? Where are they today? What did education do for them or to them that dramatically affected the rest of their lives?

About Ability Grouping   Ability grouping, although it has been prevalent, is an ineffective way of grouping children. As researchers (Oakes, 1985; Slavin, 1988) have indicated, ability grouping is directly related to socioeconomic status in the majority of cases. It does not provide for children who need more time, who are late bloomers compared to typical age mates, or those who are different in background or culture.

According to Slavin (1988), ability grouping has been criticized for sorting and unfairly labeling children since 1917. The most common characteristics of ability grouping are educators' judgments of a student's cognitive ability and predictions of a student's future achievement (Wheelock, 1994). Educators are only guessing how students will achieve and how smart they really are. This sorting and classifying of students leads to a different type of teaching and different types of curricula for the "levels" that have been artificially created. It is unconscionable that teacher impressions can determine the fate of a child.

During Libbie's doctoral work, she did a brief study on ability grouping in a nearby public school system. The study consisted of 11 classrooms of first- and second-grade students. Each child was given a literacy attitude survey, and each teacher was given a survey about their attitudes toward teaching reading. Observations were made in each of the classrooms.

The results of this study indicated that teacher attitude, ability-group placement, and socioeconomic status were interdependent. The teachers believed that ability grouping was a necessity and that the low-ability-group children were "slow" or "low functioning." They did not consider that the children might simply be developing at a different rate than their age mates. In addition, the teachers thought that the creative teaching strategies suggested by leading researchers were appropriate for use in the classroom, yet the observational data indicated that none of those cutting-edge strategies were used with the low-ability groups. Implementation was limited to the high-ability groups.

The survey data from the children indicated that the majority of children in the low-ability groups were on free lunch or from a lower socioeconomic class. The children in the low-ability groups received significantly more "skill and drill" practice. The high-ability groups were observed reading and writing, whereas the low-ability students spent much time doing workbook pages. For example, teachers spent much less time reading and discussing with low-ability students. Instead, "round-robin reading" or an inordinate amount of vocabulary skill and drill occurred.

The saddest incident occurred after several first graders had been "skilled and drilled" for approximately 20 minutes on a list of about 55 vocabulary words. They then received directions for five workbook pages which, incidentally, were all different skills. They were sent back to their desks. As Libbie watched the children, their hands went up to ask for directions again, or their heads went down on their desks in defeat.

How can they ever develop?

The compelling issue about this brief study is that children who may be developmentally behind are automatically tagged as being "slow," or "lazy," or even "dull." How can we continue to create such labels for children because of their social status or their limited exposure to school or school-like experiences? Where are the high expectations for *all* learners?

A number of myths about ability grouping nevertheless persist. Some people believe that it is too difficult to reach all the students when they are not placed in "levels." Others believe that gifted students are held back and slower students' needs are not met. Still others believe that the only group that receives what it needs in a heterogeneous class is the average group. All these statements are myths and are not supported by research (Oakes, 1985; Wheelock, 1994; Hunter, 1992). The overall conclusion of the research is that *ability grouping is an ineffective means of grouping students on yearly class lists.*

Let's compare the concept of ability grouping in classrooms to an industrial setting. In a factory, the materials are sorted prior to coming onto the production line. Unqualified pieces of materials are discarded, leaving only the higher quality of materials with which to work. In the industrial production line there is no need to remediate, intervene, or individualize. Products or materials that do not measure up are either recycled or discarded. Does this remind you of the stories we just shared?

Fortunately, education is not a business or an industry. Students are humans who develop in different ways and at different rates and times. This is natural and to be expected. As a result, our responsibility is to see that *each* child has the same opportunity and chance to achieve his or her maximum potential. Ability grouping acts to discard individuals rather than serve them.

Like all classrooms, multiage classrooms require a heterogeneous mixture of children. The teachers recognize that each child has different interests, needs, and abilities, but by individualizing and adapting instruction, these needs are successfully met. The comments of multiage teachers throughout this book reflect this notion.

Differences among children are viewed as assets in multiage learning communities. To be a truly heterogeneous environment, classrooms must be very balanced. Thus, classrooms with unusually high numbers of gifted students or special needs students are not truly multiage; they are actually inclusive classrooms.

Structuring the Classroom

Making the Classroom Heterogeneous   Arranging a multiage class roster may be complicated at first. The multiage team and the school administrators should both be actively involved in setting up the rosters.

Two ways of generating class lists are recommended. The first method is for classrooms in which teachers do not know their incoming student populations. For example, some schools may be newly opened. Other situations may arise due to changes in demographics or district boundary lines. The second method is for known or predictable student populations.

Designing class lists in a newly created or changed multiage school requires some basic knowledge about each of the incoming students. This can be gathered through both formal and informal assessments. For example, at Central Academy in Middletown, Ohio, new class lists were determined through teacher-made tests, parent literacy surveys, informal interviews with parents (principal-conducted), and team meetings to discuss all the findings.

In addition, teachers designed simple assessments for math, reading, and writing. Each prospective student spent half an hour on each of the three areas with a teacher on the assessment team. The math assessment consisted of a primary and an intermediate checklist of applications. For example, students were tested at a table filled with math manipulatives, including clocks, cubes, rods, and two-sided counters. On the primary math checklist, students were asked to show "3 o'clock," for example. The expectation was that the student would use a clock, a personal watch, or the clock in the room to indicate the response. Success was noted on the checklist with a plus sign; a blank space meant that the skill was undeveloped.

The primary assessment consisted of approximately 15 items, whereas approximately 22 were on the intermediate list. Each item had a valued application based on the district's math course of study or teacher experience. Facts sheets with addition and subtraction were used for younger children (ages 5–8) to assess number sense and computation skills. Approximately 12 items were on that sheet. For intermediate-age students (ages 9–12), fact sheets included multiplication and division. Each child was given the opportunity to demonstrate skills as far along as possible in order to provide an accurate individual profile.

The writing assessment was given in a different room with another teacher. Each child worked with the teacher at a table filled with writing supplies. The teacher talked with each child for a few minutes and then began to describe an event to him or her. After the description was complete, the teacher would draw and/or write a sample, depending upon the age and development of the child, who was then asked to respond to a similar prompt in whatever manner possible. For example, students might be asked to draw or write about where they would like to spend their summer vacations. Younger children might draw pictures or dictate stories, whereas older children might produce fluent writing.

Reading was assessed through several means. A literacy survey was taken, with each child responding to a series of questions and choosing an appropriate pictorial response (McKenna & Kear, 1990; Rhodes, 1993). Children were asked to choose a book from a table in the middle of the room. The teacher then followed a standard whole language checklist identifying book-handling abilities (Clay, 1972/1979; Goodman & Altwerger, 1981). For more fluent readers, a commercial informal reading inventory was given to confirm the teacher's perceptions of each child's reading abilities (Burns & Roe, 1993; Goodman, Watson, & Burke, 1987).

The parent survey asked parents about their children's literacy with questions such as "Does your child like to read alone?" and "Does your child understand what has been read?" The staff thought that if they understood the parents' beliefs about the children's development, they could better help each child. Informal interviews with the parents were used to gather information about each child's previous school experiences and parents' expectations and goals.

Upon completion of the authentic assessments, all the multiage teachers met and discussed the results, recording the information on index cards. Sharing the results and impressions was important for determining the instructional needs of the students, who were identified as *emergent, early,* or *fluent* writers and readers (Mooney, 1988; Renwick & Department of Education, 1985). In math, students were identified by their developmental needs. The information received from the parents' interviews and surveys was used to confirm impressions or hunches about each child's literacy and previous schooling experiences. After determining the developmental levels of the children, the staff would "check" their decisions with the children's past records if these were available.

In conducting these evaluations, authentic assessments rather than standardized-norm reference tests were used, for the latter are not designed to yield substantive information about individuals on which curricular decisions can be based (Goodman, Bird, & Goodman, 1992; Harp, 1994; Hart, 1994; Kamii, 1990).

After completing the team meetings, the principal took the index cards describing each child's attributes and perceived needs and sorted them into equal numbers of 6-, 7-, and 8-year-olds. Each pile, or class list, included equal numbers of "fluent" 6-year-old girls, "fluent" 6-year-old boys, and so on. The development of class lists continued until each classroom was heterogeneously balanced by gender, ethnicity, age, interests, achievement, and abilities. The preliminary class lists were shared with the teachers for additional feedback before becoming permanent.

In a situation where the prospective students have attended the school prior to moving into the multiage classroom, extensive assessments are not needed. Teachers can identify the characteristics of each child, and this information can be used to generate a heterogeneous class list. For example, Mrs. Jones will keep about half her class, but the others will move into the next age-level grouping. Mrs. Jones will need to identify the characteristics of the children who remain with her so that the incoming students can be added to form a heterogeneous class list. She should also identify the characteristics of the children who leave her in order to begin to generate next year's suggested class lists, which will be heterogeneous as well.

The principal then takes the rosters that the multiage teams constructed and adds them to the next age-level lists of remaining students in order to complete the heterogeneous class rosters (see Appendixes E and F). This procedure allows teachers from the "early primary" to create half a class list for their colleagues in the level above them. The benefits of this type of planning include the regrouping of students who do not get along well or who have developed differently. Who can better determine the best class make-up than the teachers who have just had the students for two years? The principal, however, determines which teacher receives which team-generated list to be added to his or her returning students.

Different Kinds of Multiage Settings   Multiage classrooms can be either open or self-contained physical spaces. When management will not permit walls to be altered or removed, it may be necessary to remain in a self-contained physical space. In our experiences, either physical arrangement will work.

Open-space classrooms are often the setting in which teams of teachers work with a large number of students. In the self-contained classroom, one teacher usually has a class of 20–25 students. Both types of multiage classrooms require room arrangements with multiple work areas to allow for flexibility in planning.

We have found that putting quiet work areas in one section of the room— or, in a team-taught situation, in half the double room—and the centers and technology in another section works best. Students know that the quiet zone is where the tables or desks are located and the interactive zone is where the other materials are located (see Figure 3-2).

Arranging Age Groupings   Several combinations of ages are appropriate for multiage classrooms. Many experts suggest various groupings. However, any decision about grouping of ages should be based on your students' needs.

Multiage Classroom Structure

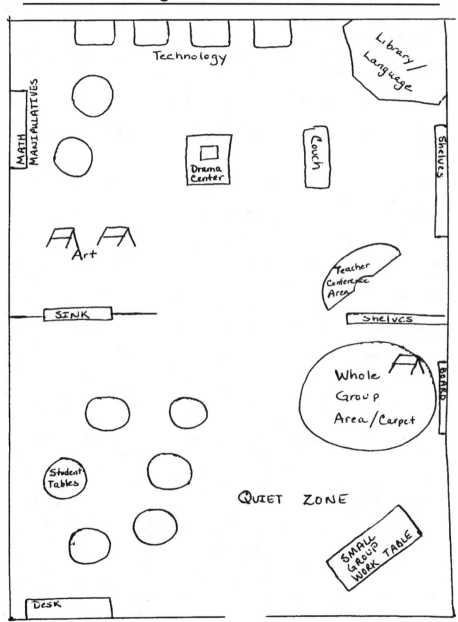

Figure 3-2

For example, Goodlad and Anderson (1987) describe 6-, 7-, and 8-year-olds together (in graded terms, first and second graders); 8-, 9-, and 10-year-olds together (third and fourth graders); and 10-, 11-, and 12-year-olds together (fifth and sixth graders). Kasten and Clarke (1993) did research in a highly successful classroom that began as a kindergarten and eventually became a multiage classroom of 5-, 6-, 7-, 8-, and 9-year-olds (grades K–3). Many schools create groups in a K–1, 2–3, and 4–5 grade pattern, whereas many others group in 1–2, 2–3, 3–4, 4–5, and 5–6 grade patterns. Still others, after experiencing composite (two ages) multiage groups, create triads of grades K–2, 1–3, and 4–6. The decision is up to you and the members of your school community.

Some areas have half-day kindergarten, which makes it somewhat difficult to include K–1 in your plan. It poses an interesting challenge, and schools that have decided to include half-day kindergarten students in their multiage primary have handled it in one of two ways: Some have the kindergarten students arrive later in the day to join their slightly older classmates; others have some kindergarten-age students arrive in the multiage classroom in the morning and some in the afternoon. In both cases, the day is planned first and foremost around the needs of the all-day, older students. Visiting kindergarten members are included in the activities of the existing class members, especially in the beginning of the year. Later, some separate groupings and activities are planned for new entrants to meet their specialized needs.

Some school buildings include only primary, such as K–3. If this is the case in your school, it may be decided that grade 3 cannot participate in the first years of becoming multiage, or perhaps kindergarten is not included at first. These decisions need to be carefully decided based upon student needs, not only teacher willingness to teach a specific age level.

In Libbie's current school district, there are K–4 buildings and a 5–6 building. They have made the decision to group grades 1–2, 3–4, and 5–6 (composite multiage) because of the natural breakdown of the school buildings. Kindergartens, though developmentally appropriate, have not been included yet because of busing problems. In Harrisburg, Pennsylvania, a school started with an all-day kindergarten program that within two years had expanded into a multiage grouping of K–2. Outside Philadelphia, a school system began with grades 1–2 in a multiage group and moved by two age levels each year through middle school. Still other schools have allowed teacher requests to determine some of the groupings, so they are not consistent. Moody Elementary in Bradenton, Florida, has some K–1 multiage classes, one 1–2 multiage class, several 2–3 multiage groups, and several intermediates consisting of 4–5. Many options are available, and they are workable as long as they are carefully considered before beginning.

One important yet often forgotten issue is what to call the multiage classroom groupings. Although we describe them by grade levels here, we try to avoid grade-level terms at all costs inside the classroom and around the school. By only referring to grade levels as they are required on mandated state or provincial reports (if the reports have not yet been updated to include multiage classrooms), an ungraded community can be formed. Many schools call their multiage classrooms *early primary, early intermediate, late primary,* and *intermediate*. Others call the units *families* or *pods*. *Primary house* or *intermediate house* is used in some locations. Multiage teachers often allow their students to vote on class names, such as Explorers or Moonwalkers. Some multiage classes we've visited have used names such as Spectrum (continuum of the colors of the rainbow), MAG (multiage group), and some have even given the classroom an address, such as Lolli Lane or Kasten Place. It is very necessary to avoid terms that have been used in the past to indicate success or placement, such as Pod A and Pod F or Unit 1 and Unit 2. Perceptions of these terms tend to relate to what has been experienced, so Pod A and Unit 1 may automatically be thought of as the "best" groupings or the first-grade level. Avoiding these types of terms is the best way to prevent misperceptions about the multiage classes.

Our advice is to begin with composite multiage classes (two "grade levels" together). Numerous schools that began with three groupings found that the transition was more difficult for teachers and that parents were unsupportive. We believe that beginning with two ages together enables a smooth transition. Later, as teachers and parents are comfortable with the implementation, a third level (or more) can be added. It's better to start small and be successful.

Perhaps your team will decide that two ages are appropriate for students and never move into a third grouping. Composite multiage classes are generally highly successful and are quite acceptable if they serve your students and community. Many successful multiage classrooms house two age levels and never move to a third age level.

Continuous Progress for Students   Schooling structures that permit DAP include a flexible vertical grouping pattern. CP, as we have discussed in chapter 1, allows children to move to the next age level when they are ready. There is no specific requirement of number of days spent at a specific "level"; there is only a requirement that the child has demonstrated a need in the social, emotional, cognitive, physical, and aesthetic developmental areas. For example, curricular benchmarks or achievements specified for the age level have been demonstrated; social needs have indicated that the child needs the peer association of a different grouping; and emotional needs have indicated that the child is ready for more challenges than are possible in the current age grouping. These indicators point to the need for the child to move into the next age-level grouping.

CP requires vertical grouping to be in place. As children move up through the age levels, the normal grade-level barriers and time constraints are lifted. Children move as they need to move without being held back because of space, class size, rotation of new students into classes, or other administrative or teacher-created barriers to the children reaching their maximum potential. CP and the "how to" should be discussed before opening the multiage classrooms. Without CP, we continue in the same fashion as a graded classroom by limiting the child's opportunity for the most effective environment.

Why is vertical grouping flexibility so important? Ian was a member of a 6-, 7-, and 8-year-old group. As he entered the class in September, he was 8 years old and very happy to be in the classroom. As Ian became an "older" 8-year-old in the classroom, he began to voice his irritation at being with those "babies." He complained of boredom and became a discipline problem. It was already 7 months into the school year, and Ian could survive for 2 more months. But as the situation became more intolerable for him, he became very disruptive in the classroom. What could make a child who was a "shining star" until then turn into this sort of student? No major changes had occurred at home, and no major changes had occurred at school. Ian simply needed the challenge of more sophisticated learners. His time line was different than most of his age mates. Ian needed to be moved to the next grouping of multiage classes, and so he was.

Don, another case, was a "special needs" child. He was not pulled out for any additional instruction and participated as a class member in the 6-, 7-, and 8-year-old group. At the conclusion of the school year, Don, who should have been moving into the next multiage level, remained in the same classroom. His parents and the multiage teaching team determined that Don needed a little more time with his current teacher. Don came back in the new year to a familiar classroom with half a class he knew from the previous year, so he felt secure and comfortable with his teacher and friends. By the end of the semester, Don was ready to move into the next level of multiage classes, which he did very successfully. There again he saw old friends from the previous year, so his comfort level was increased.

Another case in point was Peter, an African American student in a Florida second-grade room. Peter had been retained in a previous grade and was a year older and quite a bit more mature than the other class members. He became an inappropriate center of attention with disruptive behavior. The real issue was boredom. Peter's developmental growth spurt had made his membership in second grade no longer appropriate.

In this school, which has both multiage and traditional classes, Peter was moved into a multiage 2–3 grouping at the midyear point. In the new setting, he was academically challenged and fit in much better socially. His disruptive behavior greatly diminished as he discovered that the antics that had amused other second graders were not similarly received in a class where half the students were "third graders" (the term used on paper). In the new environment, Peter had an academic growth spurt and began to perform more like the older students. After being in this classroom for only half a year, Peter was sent on to an intermediate placement, where he began to thrive.

A vertical grouping pattern permits this kind of movement whenever necessary to meet the student's ever-changing needs. Without vertical grouping and CP, Ian, Don, and Peter would not have been as successful in their school endeavors. Perhaps they would have become disruptive, turned off to learning, defeated, disenfranchised, or even angry. CP permits students to develop and grow in their own time rather than the school's time.

Using a CP Team   Several issues arise when CP is practiced in schools. Contractual issues related to class size become a major stumbling block if teachers have not agreed to accept students on the CP cycle. Of course, we are not advocating that the accepting teacher's class load become extreme or unmanageable. The flexibility to accept one or two new children and send others on at various times in the year is necessary, however. It is advisable to periodically sit down with the entire multiage team, including the principal, to discuss potential movement of students. About 10% of your students will probably be discussed in a year. Some ideas for the discussion include the following:

- The student's name is brought to the group.

- Pertinent, concise information and samples of work are shared.

- The child is described socially, emotionally, physically, aesthetically, and cognitively.

- The principal asks others who work with the child to do the same.

- Input from the music, art, and physical education specialists, the librarian, the secretary, and so on is important for the discussion.

- Everyone thinks about the information and asks any clarifying questions.

- A decision is made on whether someone from the next level of multiage should observe the child. If so, arrangements are made.

- The observer reports back in 1 week to the team.

- A decision is then made by all on potential movement or a continued watch.

- If potential movement is suggested, the parents are brought in to discuss the idea.
- At the conclusion of the meeting with the parents, the parties decide if movement is appropriate.
- The child is consulted and movement is arranged.

A child is not moved if anyone is uncertain about the need for it. It is a travesty to move children to another age level only to end up moving them back. If in doubt, don't move the child, or move the child for a portion of the day as a trial.

Flexible In-Class Grouping   Another type of grouping that must exist in the classroom is flexible in-class grouping. This implies that no group remains together for an extended period of time. Teachers who practice a whole language philosophy are accustomed to this type of flexibility. Children come to small groups for needs, interests, learning styles, enrichment, and reteaching. These small groups remain together only until the objective is accomplished. If a student achieves the objective ahead of the rest of the small group, that student leaves the group. It is very possible that a child may participate in more than one small group within a week. If the group stays together for more than 2 weeks (other than emergent readers working together), the potential for it to become a fixed group is strong, and it could become an ability grouping. More on grouping uses and practices is provided in chapter 7.

About Multiage Teachers

Earlier we described the characteristics of a multiage teacher. This section deals with a continuum of beliefs about teaching, curriculum, and learning and the teacher's placement on that continuum. The multiage teacher believes that "less is more." In other words, less teacher control equals more student empowerment and choice, and less curriculum coverage equals more in-depth learning. Multiage teachers believe that student choice is paramount in keeping students motivated and interested. Student choice does not imply chaos or an "anything goes" attitude. On the contrary, choices are made with guidance, and parameters are set to ensure quality academic learning.

Child-centeredness is a guiding principle in the multiage classroom. Decisions about curriculum, organization, activities, and assessment all revolve around the question, "Whom does this decision serve first?" Is the classroom organized around the teacher's choices and interests, or is it truly flexible enough to allow the children to have a choice about activities and learning experiences? Children gain responsibility and independence by being permitted to take some safe risks and make some decisions about their learning.

Child-centered classrooms provide the opportunity for students to discover, take risks, and develop at their own rate.

Multiage teachers believe that learning requires a variety of experiences and mediums. They know that the brain develops differently in each person; therefore, all children learn in their own way and in their own time (Armstrong, 1987, 1994; Hart, 1983; Healy, 1987; Jensen, 1996; Sylvester, 1995). Multiage classrooms respect and celebrate those differences. Children are not squeezed into a curriculum or textbook that doesn't fit; instead, the curriculum and materials are designed to meet the child's needs.

"What first attracted me to multiage classrooms was my level of frustration with single-graded classrooms. By that I mean grade levels like first, second and third grade. What I found was that we created a mold for children and expected all of them to fit that mold. We know that's not how children are."

—Diane Kittelberger
Massillon, OH

Box 3-1

Teachers in multiage classrooms serve as guides, providing miniskills lessons as appropriate, and as facilitators of the learning process. Facilitation comes in the form of gathering materials and providing the necessary time, space, and guidance for the students to find and develop the information that is needed for in-depth understanding.

Multiage teachers recognize that materials must include use of the Internet, public and school libraries, reference materials, materials from students' homes, and periodicals. The use of textbooks as the sole resource is no longer appropriate. As information continues to grow at a rapid rate, textbooks are not likely to contain the most current knowledge. Similarly, the curriculum is based on concepts, not the literal or factual knowledge found in textbooks.

Multiage teachers believe that continual assessment guides instructional needs for the class and for the individual. Group tests or worksheets, such as those given after a class finishes reading a chapter in a textbook, are not appropriate in the multiage class because they assume that all students are the same. This type of assessment also assumes that all students have studied the same information in the same book. Assessment serves as a tool to determine what will be taught next; it is not just an end to the learning unit or topic, as in a graded classroom.

Multiage teachers, like all good teachers, are lifelong learners. Much time is spent on reading, reflecting, and dialoguing with others about classroom practices. As serious professionals, multiage teachers also attend university courses, conferences, and workshops to enhance their own understanding and growth.

We recognize that effective teachers in graded classrooms also exhibit many of the child-centered characteristics listed for multiage teachers. However, graded schooling structures limit opportunities for students because of adopted grade-level curricula and materials. Even when thematic units are used in graded classrooms, it becomes very necessary to cover the curricular objectives of that grade level, thereby limiting the availability of CP along the curriculum continuum. When we taught in our graded classrooms, we were required to enrich our children horizontally, as opposed to using CP or vertical movement, because the teachers of the next grade level wanted to avoid infringement on their objectives and materials. In a multiage setting, the students remain with one teacher for two or more years, so the infringement issue is lessened.

Team Teaching   Many multiage classrooms are team taught, with two or more teachers in a room with two or more classes. Team teaching usually takes place in an open-space classroom or in a classroom that has expandable doors between two rooms. Without the physical arrangement of a double classroom, teaming becomes more difficult. Teaming, according to Anderson and Pavan (1993), "calls for groups of teachers to work closely together in all dimensions of teaching, and to share responsibility for aggregations of children who would otherwise, under conventional circumstances, be subaggregated into so-called self-contained classrooms" (p. 93).

Teachers on a team plan and organize the lessons together. In the early days of teaming, many felt that this meant "tag team" teaching or "turn" teaching. That is, one teacher would teach social studies while the other teacher prepared worksheets for teaching science later in the day. In other words, one teacher taught 50 students in a type of classroom departmentalization. As Slavin (1988) has indicated, departmentalization is *not* the best choice for student grouping, so this type of teaming did not improve learning as anticipated. Tag teaching is neither a good team model nor a good context for multiage education, in our estimation.

Teaming requires both teachers to be actively engaged in the classroom experiences. For example, while one teacher is giving a minilesson, the other teacher is recording observational data to be used later in the assessment of instructional needs. While one teacher is working with a small group, the other teacher may be doing individual conferences. Both teachers are actively involved throughout the day.

Since both teachers are actively involved with every aspect of children's growth and development, both teachers are also involved in the assessment process. Each teacher spends time gathering anecdotal information as well as doing formal assessments during conferencing or small group times. Both teachers are responsible for reporting student progress to parents. Conferences are attended by both teachers, and progress reports are jointly generated.

"Once it was decided that we would be a team in a multiage classroom, we began talking and talking! Neither of us had ever seen the other teach, but we were told that our student expectations and work ethic were similar. We met often during the summer to share information about our teaching. We needed to decide which routines and activities from previous years were ones that we had to use and which ones we could live without. After talking about "my way" and "your way," we came up with "our way" for day-to-day procedures."

—SueBeth Arnold and Barbara Kidwell
Findlay, OH

Box 3-2

Partial Teaming   In schools that structurally cannot support open classrooms or open walls, partial teaming can be very effective. Partial teaming requires multiage age-level teams to jointly plan units and lessons. Libbie's former school used partial teaming. Every Wednesday after school, teams of age-level teachers would meet and decide how the next week's lessons would look. Ideas for minilessons, experiments, center activities, technology, and literature were shared by team members. The rotation cycle for shared materials was determined, as was the list of assignments, such as who would shop for the cooking center materials or other special supplies. This partial teaming enabled the students to have the expertise of the team even though they spent the majority of their time with one teacher. Collegiality was also fostered among team members.

Specialization Opportunities   Another form of partial teaming can occur in the multiage setting. When children are involved in a thematic or concept unit, specialization can be developed. Teachers of the 6-, 7-, and 8-year-old group can decide during a unit on cycles that one of the teachers will provide a concentrated time for learning about seasonal cycles, another teacher may provide the opportunity for the water cycle, and another may provide the life cycle. Each teacher is responsible for meeting the study objectives of the day; however, the opportunity for a student to become an "expert" is given during a block of time, perhaps in the afternoon when no one is in music, art, or physical education class. Students choose a topic of study based upon their interests, and they move to that classroom for a designated number of days to develop their expertise. Each child creates a product that indicates the level of understanding he or she has developed. These products are presented to the "homeroom" multiage classroom upon completion of the "expert" time. The benefit of this type of partial teaming is that one teacher provides an in-depth understanding of a topic of interest to children within a unit. Children also benefit from being with children and teachers from the other multiage units.

> "We say that there are 26 teachers in the class and 26 learners. Twenty-five are children and one is an adult."
>
> —Nancy Norman
> Palmer, AK

Box 3-3

Self-Contained Multiage   Although some people have called this "self-contaminated" classrooms, we believe that with cooperative planning, the old adage can be changed. To avoid just closing the door and teaching, the teacher works closely with others in the multiage units but keeps the children all day. Integration and assessment continue to be seamless parts of the instructional day. Self-contained classrooms can become wonderful learning communities.

Role of Specialists in the Multiage   *Special teachers*, for our purposes, include anyone who is not a member of the classroom team. Music, art, and physical education teachers are examples. However, speech and language pathologists, reading and math lab teachers, educational assistants, special education teachers, and even parent volunteers are also included. The roles of these various positions may seem different, but in a multiage setting they are very similar.

Special teachers from around the country have numerous questions about multiage and their subject area. It is understandable that many will need to change their lesson plans and possibly their teaching strategies. However, anyone who teaches children has the duty to do the very best that they can for students. Specialists in a multiage setting become members of the multiage team. This membership includes planning the school, as described earlier, as well as planning the units that will be used to teach students.

In making school changes, these special-area teachers are often omitted from staff development and discussions, creating a problem of ownership and even acceptance. One school that we worked with held yearly retreats to evaluate the past year, plan for the next year, and envision 5 years down the road. All special teachers were expected to be involved in this retreat. While in-depth planning occurred among age-level team members, specialists planned their involvement in the units with these teachers, and at other times during the retreat they planned only with the "specials" team.

As we consider specialists in the multiage classroom, three major themes seem to surface: (a) the importance of these teachers in the school environment, (b) the integration of their areas of expertise into the multiage setting, and (c) the teaching of their own curricular requirements. Each of the themes is important in having an excellent multiage program.

Before any discussion of multiage begins, all special teachers must be invited to the discussion as well as to the resulting study groups, inservices, or other staff development sessions. Nothing is worse than learning through rumors that you will have to accommodate two "grade levels" of learners at the same time. Everyone, as we've noted, needs preliminary information about multiage classroom practices. Specialists need to have an opportunity to voice their doubts, concerns, and joy as part of the planning. Including everyone who teaches the children in the process of determining how multiage will occur opens the door for more creativity as well as ownership.

Integration of the arts or physical education curriculum into planned units connects more information for children. Classroom teachers and specialists can benefit from brainstorming together, even with time constraints. In this way, needs can be met for both curricula. A free exchange of ideas can lead to a more positive attitude about multiage classrooms.

One of us was a music teacher for a portion of our career. Nothing caused more rebellion than when the fifth-grade teacher arrived at the door and said that a unit on Mexico was going to start. The expectation was that the music she listed would be taught immediately! Because the unit lasted only 2 weeks, there were only two music classes during that unit. Special teachers do not mind being part of integrated units if they are allowed to be part of the planning and to do part of the choosing, or if they are given sufficient advance notice to help fill a special need.

Something often forgotten by those of us involved in the planning of units is that special teachers are also responsible for teaching their own curricula. Requesting that all classes be devoted to the unit will not permit the special teacher enough time to develop his or her course of study. A joint agreement about amount and time is needed to ensure that the special curriculum has a place in the multiage class. Although some of the specialist's curriculum can be integrated with the classroom content, time may need to be set aside to accomplish other required objectives. Here mutual respect between classroom teachers and specialists is the key. Each needs to communicate their needs and concerns so that arrangements suitable for all can be made.

How can this joint partnership between special teachers and classroom teachers occur?

- Begin the dialogue about multiage together.

- Take special teacher concerns seriously.

- Provide visitation opportunities for special teachers to multiage classes.

- Provide time for follow-up discussion of what has been seen.

- Be inclusive with all planning.

- Allow special teachers to have a major voice in the integration of the curriculum.

- Understand that everyone has a curriculum for which he or she is responsible.

Lesson Planning for Special Teachers   A complaint heard from most special teachers is the double planning necessary for multiage classrooms. This problem exists mainly because many special teachers have lost sight of the developmental needs of their students. Not until recently have the arts and physical education been basalized and graded. In any place other than school, music, art, and physical fitness are multiage experiences. Yet we have permitted textbook companies to determine what song a 5-year-old can sing or play and what type of artwork that child is permitted to experience. How many physical education teachers have 6-year-olds who arrive with exactly the same developmental abilities? No one has a class of identical 6-year-olds, even in a first-grade setting. Children come to us at individual developmental levels, and we are responsible for teaching them at that level. Likewise, in planning a lesson for a multiage 1–2 or a first- or second-grade classroom, the activities should be appropriate for a variety of abilities and levels. One lesson plan with a variety of practice ideas is all that is needed.

For example, a physical education teacher has planned a lengthy unit on basketball. It is unheard of and educationally unsound for the teacher to throw out the ball and say, "Play." Quality physical education teachers recognize that first, lessons and practice on ball-handling skills need to occur. The teacher models various ball-handling skills and then allows children to practice these skills, first in isolation and then at a station where a game with the new skill is incorporated with other previously learned skills. As more skills are taught, the games become more sophisticated. After a long period of this type of activity, the teacher begins to put the basketball game together. First the games may comprise running, dribbling, and passing relays; then running, dribbling, shooting from the foul line, and bounce passing to the next person on the relay team. The teacher builds the skills and abilities until the majority of children can easily participate in a short basketball game. The lessons described above are easily implemented in either a graded classroom or a multiage one.

The teacher must recognize the steps that are needed in any lesson to meet the various needs of all the children. Each lesson includes a focus taken from the curriculum. After that, the lesson proceeds to include the practice of previously taught skills or a guided practice of the new skill. This practice takes place through a variety of multilevel activities. The practice time is also a prime opportunity for the teacher to integrate the classroom curriculum.

Music teachers are required to teach children about various rhythms. Suppose a current lesson is the introduction of the eighth note as an important rhythm. The teacher welcomes the students to music and facilitates a brief discussion of the "Composer of the Month," playing a short excerpt of his or her music. Kodaly syllables are used to warm up voices as well as for ear training. Rhythm cards with quarter, whole, and half notes are clapped or patschened (thigh pats). The teacher then gives a minilesson on the eighth note. Various examples are given, and the written symbol is introduced into the rhythm-card exercise. Children practice by clapping or patschening the rhythm, either in isolation or through the use of poetry or rhyme. Songs are then sung and accompanied, or a dance is taught. The activities include the new rhythm. Children with previous musical training can accompany the class on Orff instruments, playing a melody or even improvising using eighth notes. Children with less understanding can accompany simply by keeping a steady beat. This multilevel approach to the practice of activities develops the children's abilities.

Music, art, and physical education teachers can stretch their curricula out in the same manner as classroom teachers do. The question becomes, "What should an 8-year-old leave my class knowing?" The answers become the benchmarks or performance objectives for the multiage class. Assessment of these benchmarks becomes the reporting mechanism to parents in these subject areas.

Other Specialists   Speech and language pathologists, special education teachers, occupational therapists, and reading and math lab personnel can work inside the multiage classroom. Scheduling for the best use of everyone's time should be prearranged and be flexible when student needs dictate. Speech teachers can arrange their schedules to be available during a language workshop time or center time. Special education teachers, if not permanently assigned to a multiage team, can schedule themselves in multiage classrooms during the part of the day where extra assistance is needed. Of course, the math and reading lab teachers should try to schedule their visits during the time when their "subject" is the focus.

Building Collegiality   Multiage grouping is difficult when one does it alone. Life becomes more pleasant and actually easier when people work together to achieve the same goals. Teachers benefit from being collegial. Building this type of community in the school is not an easy task, but it is well worth it.

Even in schools that have not become multiage, there always seems to be a small number of teachers who choose not to be collegial. Have you ever worked in a school where one or two people went off on their own and created their own "islands"? This happens in many schools where changes are occurring, whether the changes are multiage groupings or something else. In one school that we visited, two teachers refused to participate in the school retreats, the schoolwide concept units, and the use of the technology that was rapidly surrounding their classrooms. Instead, they created their own publicity through the use of "glitz and glitter" activities. Newspapers enjoy printing articles about cats or rabbits in the classroom or students who supposedly have made a quilt on their own. Unfortunately, recognition of such classrooms promotes isolation and competition.

In another school, where everyone was working together on schoolwide projects or units, all the teachers shared ideas and materials with each other. They found it so much easier to work together across the entire school. The children also benefit from such a collegial environment. All the resources in the building, rather than just one teacher's ideas and materials, were used to support the learning.

Building a collegial group within the school requires everyone's concerted efforts. In a building we visited, the teachers' workroom included a happy-face poster and an unhappy face. When asked about the two symbols, the teachers indicated that an age-level team or an individual who feels left out of important decisions, discussions, or plans indicates that by posting the unhappy face. This then becomes an item of discussion at the next faculty meeting. Many times, in the fast pace of our lives, we may have a discussion with one group and forget that another group or member of the group was not present. This can be easily remedied as we consciously work on community.

Discipline

Consider the idea that discipline affects both the students and the teacher. Leading researchers (Curwin & Mendler, 1988; Kohn, 1996; Nelson, 1987) contend that, after violence in society and excessive television viewing as factors requiring discipline, the problems that exist in classrooms are directly related to teacher behavior and curriculum. Approximately 80% of all students in any class want to learn and do not misbehave. Another 15% tend to misbehave "frequently," and about 5% misbehave "continuously" (Curwin & Mendler, 1988). Problems that cause 95% of the class to become behavior problems include lack of choice, lack of clarity about expectations, and boredom. In other words, teachers have control over some of the causes of discipline problems in their classrooms, and in understanding this relationship they can begin to solve the problems.

Lack of Choice   In many classrooms, discipline serves as a means to have power over children. Libbie's oldest son experienced this type of power struggle as a fifth-grade student. The two teachers, who regularly engaged in sarcasm, determined that students who did not cross a *t* or dot an *i* deserved a -1 from the total score each time the offense occurred. These two teachers also determined that students should have at least 2 hours of redundant, boring nightly homework. More examples of their petty practices could be shared, but you get the idea. During this fifth-grade year, Libbie spent many evenings doing her son's homework. He felt angry, frustrated, and turned off to learning. Having come from a wonderful multiage setting, this teacher power-struggle environment was quite a shock to him.

Concern over details and acting on personal pet peeves are not part of a quality education and frequently lead to student discipline problems. The students sense a lack of respect from the teachers and consequently lose respect for their teachers and the educational system. This does not create a learning community.

Lack of choice, whether in issues large or small, results in students feeling no ownership in the classroom. They are powerless to make decisions that directly affect them. For adults as well as students, decisions that are forced upon a person are met with either compliance or rebellion. The 80% who want to learn and are "good" students have learned the schooling game: compliance. Those who rebel have either chosen not to comply or are unable to comply.

Clarity of Expectations   Students need to be aware of expected behaviors and have models of acceptable behaviors presented to them. Teachers who model kindness and respect earn the same from their students. Likewise, teachers who model sarcasm and unfairness will receive the same. By asking students what their expectations are and adding your own, you communicate that the classroom belongs to everyone.

Students often do not know what expectations are. For example, five students go to the pencil sharpener during writing workshop time, and the teacher indicates in a very unhappy voice that this is inappropriate. Were students told this beforehand? If not, how can we expect them to follow the "rules"? Expectations such as "respect others" need to be clearly defined, discussed, and modeled for the class. What does *respect* mean to a 6-year-old?

Boredom   Often, students who do not usually act out will suddenly begin to misbehave (with no apparent change in the home situation). This is because they are bored. Teachers need to analyze the curriculum and the level of work assigned to the individual. "Teacher talk" or even cooperative learning groups become boring to children when used continuously. Teachers need to vary strategies to maintain student interest and motivation.

The curriculum itself is often a cause of boredom. One of us recently had a lengthy discussion with an inner-city teacher who was deeply concerned about the lack of student control in her primary classroom. When asked about student choices within the curriculum, the teacher indicated that the state required specific objectives to be taught. The discussion continued with the fact that students need to be taught at their levels, not molded into a curriculum that does not fit them. The discussion ended with the teacher committing to trying some choice topics for the students within the framework of the curriculum. The context of the curriculum will be explored in later chapters.

> "There are many things that make a multiage classroom easier to teach. Students are never bored in my room. Learning makes sense when it fits into a theme instead of isolated exercises. This eliminates many discipline problems. Other behavior problems are reduced because students aren't all going through the same stages."
>
> —Jackie Robbie
> Colorado Springs, CO

Box 3-4

Multiage classrooms require discipline plans that are consistent with philosophical beliefs about children and learning. Discipline should be *an integrated part* of a total learning environment. Rules that apply only to the classroom and not to life outside it do not usually occur in a multiage school. Discipline centers on developing skills for lifelong use, such as honesty, respect, and trust. Obeying the rule of raising your hand to speak becomes less important when you've learned the larger lesson that listening is an important skill in life!

Discipline is also *individualized* in a multiage school, and blanket punishments are avoided. Consequences are usually determined by the child, the parents, and the teacher or administrator. In Libbie's former multiage school, she rarely saw children in the office for disciplinary action. When it did occur, the questions she posed to them were almost harder to answer than dealing with the punishment. These children (who fell into the 95% category described earlier) were asked to name the school rules, which included *truth, trust, personal best, no put-downs,* and *active listening.* Upon completing the list, the students were required to identify which rules they had broken and then determine their own "punishment." Most of the time, the students suggested far worse consequences than were warranted, so Libbie would discuss the relationship between the violation and the nature of the consequence with them.

Effective discipline requires that students develop *responsibility* for their behavior. In the multiage classroom this is a natural process. Students are permitted to be part of the decision making through "family meetings" or discussions, including the creation of rules for the classroom. The multiage environment provides the opportunity for children to learn that the skills that are needed for home, school, houses of worship, and other community institutions are the same. There are no separate rules just for school. Figure 3-3 describes several beliefs about discipline in any classroom.

In one multiage school where we've worked, the teachers opted to change from an "assertive" model of discipline to a discipline program they called "Skills for Life." These skills were taken from a book called *Tribes* (Gibbs,

---

Beliefs About Discipline

- Discipline should be individualized.

- Group punishment is never acceptable.

- Students need to be treated with dignity and respect.

- Students need to clearly understand the expectations and the offenses.

- Parents need to be actively involved before the problem becomes too large.

- Consequences should fit the misbehavior and not be malicious or vindictive.

- Discipline rules and regulations need to be the same throughout the school, in every classroom and every area of the school.

- Discipline needs to be an integrated part of the learning process.

- Discipline is based on real-life lessons for democratic living.

Figure 3-3

1995), which delineates Native American community norms of truth, trust, personal best, no put-downs, and active listening. Learning the skills was then followed by 10 weeks of learning about "megaskills" (Rich, 1992), which include motivation, effort, responsibility, perseverance, common sense, problem solving, initiative, confidence, caring, and teamwork.

Students coming into the school had all been under an "assertive" plan for several years, and the teachers themselves were very comfortable with the "assertive" practices, although they did not feel that these were the best possible procedures to use. Students entering at an older elementary age had the most difficult time adjusting to a responsibility-based program where the consequences depended upon *self*. Because they were used to the other system, the older students were often the ones that the principal saw and that parents were summoned to intervene with immediately.

Chet, an African American student, arrived in this building as a third-grade-age child. Chet and his mother believed that he never did anything wrong. His mother believed that everyone else got Chet into trouble. One day, after Chet and another boy disrupted the classroom for the umpteenth time, they were sent to the principal's office. The principal removed the students from class for the rest of the afternoon, occupying them with reading materials from the classroom.

The next day both sets of parents visited the principal together. They had copies of the student code of discipline and made threats about attorneys. Fortunately, the principal was not frazzled by the irate parents. Instead, responsibility-based discipline and the option of emergency removal from school were discussed. After quite a while, both sets of parents left, committed to helping their children learn how to manage their behaviors responsibly instead of accusing others. The boys' behavior did not improve immediately, but the diligent effort of the teachers and the principal to keep the parents and the boys recognizing their roles did pay off within the next 2 years.

Switching from a teacher-centered discipline program to one that puts the responsibility on the students is not easy. Midway through the first year of trying such a program, two veteran teachers approached their principal and requested to return to a more "assertive" program. The principal worked with them on the problems in their classrooms. By the end of the school year, both teachers realized that the change did indeed require time for the students to learn and accept it, as well as time for the teachers themselves to adjust to it.

Substitute teachers need to be aware of the discipline program in the building. In one building we visited, the principal related the story of a substitute teacher in the music classroom. The principal stood in the hallway during the afternoon to watch the children move from special class to homeroom and vice versa. As he was watching the children leave the music room, several children quickly moved toward him to register a complaint about the substitute music teacher. The children stated that they did not want the substitute to come back because she said "shut up" to the class, and that was not appropriate in their school. The principal realized that the children were appalled by this treatment. The discipline plan had therefore had some effect on them. (The substitute was told about the comments, and when her reply was anger, she wasn't invited back!) Figure 3-4 describes some steps to implement a responsibility-based discipline plan in the multiage school.

Staff Development

Successful change requires quality staff development. The majority of multiage teachers who have great success have participated in professional development for years prior to becoming a multiage teacher. Staff development implies that time is required to achieve the outcomes, unlike inservice, which is typically a one-shot opportunity to "get the message." National Staff Development Council standards describe the type of staff development that should occur in the school or district. These are as follows:

- Staff development involves and benefits everyone who influences students' learning.

- Both individuals and organizations have the inherent responsibility to define and achieve their own excellence.

- School improvement results from staff development.

- Effective staff development is based on research and theory and proved in practice.

- The value of staff development should be measured by its impact on the staff and the students they serve. (Caldwell, 1989)

In the last decade, staff development has become an opportunity for teachers and administrators to learn about themselves as practitioners while also learning about their students. From this staff development movement, the theme of "teacher as learner, leader, and colleague" has surfaced. We believe that this is also applicable for the principal. The following types of staff development opportunities are therefore critical for schools that are implementing multiage classes. These include staff development for teachers and administrators as learners, as leaders, and as colleagues, as well as for individual and district-based needs.

Teachers and Administrators as Learners   Opportunities for staff development must center on the adult learner. Adults construct meaning as children do. We adults just happen to have many more experiences than children, so

---

Implementing Responsibility-Based Discipline

- Introduce the staff to the philosophy through visitations to schools that use it; study the philosophy, discuss it with those who use it, and bring in consultants.

- Identify the major barriers to this type of program. Brainstorm solutions to alleviate the barriers.

- Create an action plan for implementation. Remember that older students will take longer to adjust. Younger students don't know other types of discipline plans.

- Teach the skills for life to your students. Central Academy (Middletown, Ohio) uses a videotape the first 5 days of school to teach students the skills for life, one skill per day. The first year, the principal and administrative assistant read a story, told an anecdote, or talked about each of the skills and what they meant to the entire school. At the conclusion of the daily lesson, the teachers switched off the video and talked to students about that skill and their classroom. After the 5 days of videotape, teachers used the next 10 weeks to teach the predesigned megaskills lessons.

- Teach parents about the new program. Provide them with ongoing help to implement the skills at home. Newsletters with a "Discipline Dialogue" or "Management Moment" can give parents helpful hints.

- Teach custodians, bus drivers, substitute teachers, cafeteria workers, and volunteers about the plan. Alert them to the fact that other forms of discipline are not recognized in the building.

- Follow through with the plan. When students begin to forget or become disruptive again, review the plan. Stop, reteach, and reimplement.

- Post the skills for life in every area of the school on the same-color paper. If you choose to use the megaskills, which are registered under copyright law, permission to post them is required. However, they should be posted if you adopt the program.

Figure 3-4

our meaning construction is different. Oja (1980) suggests that four focal points will help teachers and administrators. The first is *practical application followed by reflection*. As staff members hear and learn new strategies or techniques, they need time to apply these in the classroom or school. Following the application, time to reflect is necessary. Was this applied the way it was meant to be applied? Did my students respond? Colleagues can help each other through this reflection period.

In a district in which one of us worked, the teachers were staff-developed and staff-developed, yet no real changes in classroom practices were occurring. The problem was that the new learning was never applied or expected to be applied. Without that application, the learning did not really take hold, so changes did not occur.

Teachers and Administrators as Leaders   Oja (1980) describes the *need for more complex role taking* in the adult learning stages. Teachers or principals as leaders provide this opportunity. We have already noted the importance of everyone being part of decision making. The responsibility that comes from decision making increases the complexity of the roles that we play. This role taking requires that leaders be able to put themselves in another's role in order to come to an understanding and a consensus. It also requires an increase in interpersonal skills and communication abilities. Through this type of development, educators become better equipped in the classroom as observers, facilitators, and leaders.

Teachers and Administrators as Colleagues   The final two focus points that Oja makes about adult learning center on a *supportive environment* and *peer supervision and advising*. Staff development that focuses on the staff working together in a collegial manner is imperative if the school goals and vision are to be achieved. Each of us is stronger because of all of us.

"The three of us [who were to become multiage teachers] had no other prior training of any kind in multiage. We had each other. We made the time to meet together. We had a healthy interest in sharing ideas, asking questions, reading the literature, and solving our own and each other's problems. We also had a very supportive principal who encouraged risk taking and who did not expect perfection from us."

—Nancy Norman
Palmer, AK

Box 3-5

Some suggestions for types of staff development will be given for personal growth as well as for growth concerning the achievement of school goals. For individual staff development, we recommend a keen understanding and the implementation of DAP. DAP staff development includes understanding child development, how it applies to school today, and what practices are not compatible with a developmentally appropriate classroom. Guidelines for DAP are listed in Appendix A.

Schools that have converted entire school programs to DAP have used several types of staff development to achieve this. One district in Pennsylvania used outside consultants to conduct summer academies on DAP, which were repeated the next year at an advanced level as well as at the beginning level. After three summer academies, teachers became in-district trainers, and their "model" classrooms were used for site visitations.

Another district used a study group to begin converting its practices to DAP. These study groups were open to anyone who chose to attend and led by a curriculum specialist from the district's central office. They occurred weekly and were based upon the National Association of Education for Young Children (NAEYC) book on DAP (Bredekamp, 1987). Each week one section of the guidelines would be discussed, based on old practices and what would need to be changed. Teachers returned to their classrooms to try some of the ideas generated by their colleagues. Although this was an internal form of staff development, it was still highly effective.

A second type of staff development in moving toward multiage is the understanding and use of a whole language philosophy. Whole language implies meeting individual needs in reading and writing, meaning-centered practices, and learning from the whole to its parts. Teachers often have a difficult time understanding how to facilitate this in the classroom. Management of whole language practices in reading and writing requires organization and confidence. The principles of whole language are outlined in the glossary and in Appendix B.

Many schools we have worked with began this process as an elective choice for teachers. Staff development included teachers teaching other teachers as well as literacy experts from local universities providing the theoretical framework. Several districts offered teachers the opportunity to declare where they were on a 3- to 5-year path toward whole language philosophy. For example, some teachers still chose to use the basal units for a period of time and then stopped to teach a short author-study unit with a bibliography of the author's books from which students chose their reading materials. Another teacher may have been ready to totally integrate the language arts with topical units of study, and yet another was ready for a totally integrated inquiry classroom. The districts usually supported these teachers with funds diverted from those typically used for workbooks, in order to embellish classroom collections of big books and trade books.

Use of hands-on, minds-on mathematics and science materials is also an excellent staff development series for teachers in multiage classrooms. Many materials already found in classrooms can be used as manipulatives for customizing the needs of students. For example, most classrooms have access to beans (for two-sided counters), rods, tangrams, and so on. These become materials that the individual, rather than the whole class, can use in working toward abstract thinking. Choice and management of manipulatives to enhance the scientific and mathematical explorations of the classroom as a whole are also topics for staff development. Teachers need to understand the various uses of the manipulatives for large-group, small-group, and individual work. The best source for these types of sessions is usually teachers who have actually implemented manipulatives. Another quality source for manipulative use is the education department of most universities or colleges.

One school district we visited used a university professor, who helped develop the National Council of Teachers of Mathematics (NCTM) standards (see Appendix G), and a trained teacher to conduct an extended series of math staff development opportunities. Teachers received manipulatives for their classrooms through federal grant money for math and science as a result of attending the series. Each session included a research-based discussion of the standards and their practical application using manipulatives for concrete learning and eventually for abstract thinking.

Another district participated with a local university in a massive retraining of teachers for science inquiry. Extensive staff development occurred over a 2-year period, with teachers expected to begin teaching other teachers at the conclusion of their own development. This series included science and literature, science with toys, science as inquiry, and science as an integrated part of life.

Technology in the classroom is critical for the individual teacher's staff development. Using technology as more than a skill-and-drill or busy-work activity requires knowledge about the various types of software available to students as well as the use of the Internet. Teachers who are unaccustomed to technology in classrooms must have awareness and beginner sessions on using computers. More advanced staff development can occur after their comfort levels have increased.

In the Nordonia Hills Schools in Ohio, the district offers a Technology School for teachers. This series of 78 hours of technology training includes two strands—a beginner level and an advanced level. Teachers who attend the entire series receive a computer workstation for their classrooms and for their private practice during the series. Sessions in the series include basic application programs, use of the Internet, use of technology as a tool to support the inquiry classroom, multimedia presentation programs, use of various ancillary products such as quick-take cameras and video editing equipment, and troubleshooting. This highly successful program meets the needs of the individual teacher as well as the goals of the school district.

The key to successful individual staff development is to permit teachers to self-evaluate and identify what their learning needs are for the coming year. Each customized plan of staff development offers choice to teachers and administrators. After the staff development series concludes, don't forget to apply what's been learned and take the time to reflect on both practice and student response.

District or school-based staff development tends to focus on achievement of the district or school goals. One example might be a building-identified goal of becoming a consensus team. The staff development series offered to (and often required of) the entire staff would center on creating collegial teams. Often this type of staff development is left until last and, consequently, never gets done. This type of staff development is probably more important in the context of converting schools to multiage than is the customized individual work. Collegiality makes us all stronger.

Recommended staff development of this nature includes team building, consensus building, conflict resolution, and assessing progress. First, team building by outside consultants is usually more successful than through use of the principal or a teacher. Each member of the staff must be able to participate freely in the series without worrying about planning and facilitating the sessions. Team building is not just "warm fuzzy" work; it needs to focus on dialogue and discussion in an open, honest manner. Some work with making "artificial" decisions, such as whether to stay in or leave the Arctic tundra when your plane crashes, will help to prepare you for the real decisions that face the team. However, teams also need to have the opportunity to try to solve real issues during the staff development sessions.

Consensus training is needed so that staffs can move away from a win–lose (majority rules) or lose-lose (top-down dictated) manner of making decisions. Consensus, while not difficult to understand, is time consuming and requires a commitment to full participation. Consensus trainers typically work with staffs to develop an awareness of personality and work styles found in the group. Knowledge of the various styles found in the group helps everyone to recognize and respect individual differences.

Conflict resolution is probably the most powerful staff development tool for building consensus. Recognizing that each person has a conflict style, and how that may play out in a team situation, is all part of the process. If several people continually agree with a vocal minority on the team merely to avoid conflict, imagine how little "new thought" a team will have. Conflict styles allow team members to grow and develop, which helps the team as a whole to grow and develop.

Assessing the progress of both the team and the movement toward school or district goals requires some staff development. Most of us are not in the business of disaggregating scores or analyzing survey data, yet we need to

The difference in multiage, of course, is that it takes the lid off learning.

—Frank Sibberson
Dublin, OH

Box 3-6

be able to determine, both qualitatively and quantitatively, whether the work being done is effective. Most major research universities can assist in this type of group staff development.

Staff development is the most important factor in creating a successful multiage classroom. With both individualized and schoolwide opportunities, multiage classrooms will be successfully developed and implemented. As teachers learn and practice new skills of consensus, team building, and decision making with their colleagues, two payoffs are possible. First of all, schools should run more smoothly, with better interaction between teams. But just as important is the notion that newly trained teachers will bring these new skills into their classrooms. Students need the same skills that the teachers have learned to support the development of classrooms that are true communities of learners.

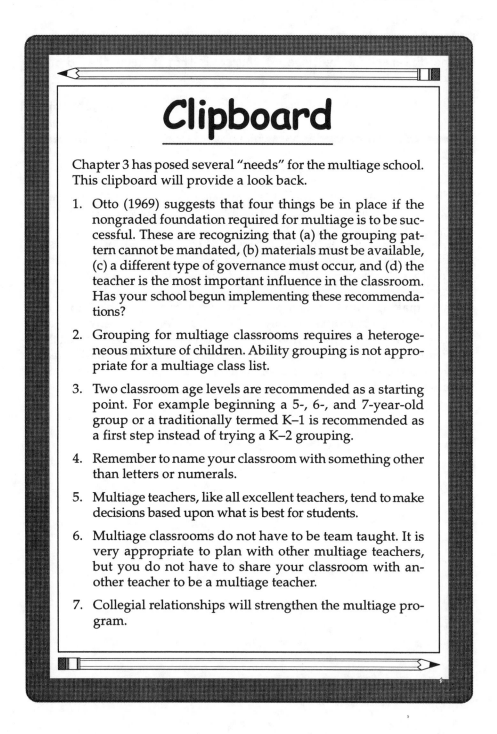

Clipboard

Chapter 3 has posed several "needs" for the multiage school. This clipboard will provide a look back.

1. Otto (1969) suggests that four things be in place if the nongraded foundation required for multiage is to be successful. These are recognizing that (a) the grouping pattern cannot be mandated, (b) materials must be available, (c) a different type of governance must occur, and (d) the teacher is the most important influence in the classroom. Has your school begun implementing these recommendations?

2. Grouping for multiage classrooms requires a heterogeneous mixture of children. Ability grouping is not appropriate for a multiage class list.

3. Two classroom age levels are recommended as a starting point. For example beginning a 5-, 6-, and 7-year-old group or a traditionally termed K–1 is recommended as a first step instead of trying a K–2 grouping.

4. Remember to name your classroom with something other than letters or numerals.

5. Multiage teachers, like all excellent teachers, tend to make decisions based upon what is best for students.

6. Multiage classrooms do not have to be team taught. It is very appropriate to plan with other multiage teachers, but you do not have to share your classroom with another teacher to be a multiage teacher.

7. Collegial relationships will strengthen the multiage program.

To: Teachers & Principals

From: Libbie & Wendy

MEMO

RE: Grouping Children

When you group your children, begin with an index card for every child. Write all information that would be important for making a heterogeneous class list.

Name _____ Age (at end of school year) _____

Parents in home _____ Gender _____ Free/Reduced lunch _____

Emergent/Early/Fluent   Math _____

Race _____ Special needs _____

Discipline needs _____   Friends _____

Friends to avoid   _____   Interests _____

This type of card can help you sort children into very mixed classes, thus avoiding overloading any one class in the building with any one type of student.

Memo 3-1

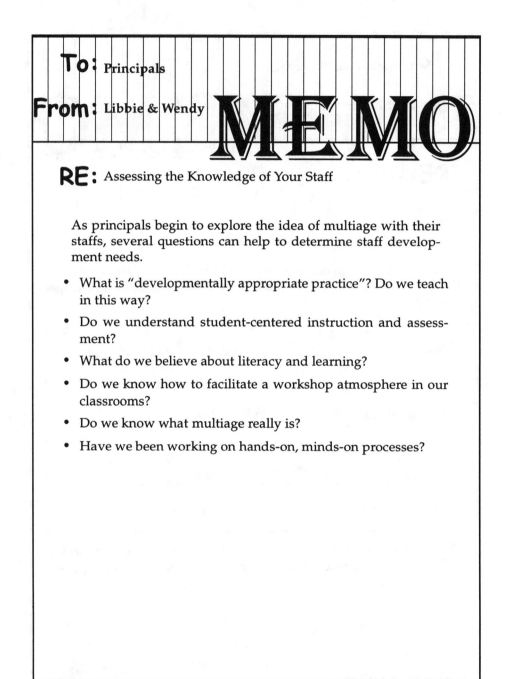

To: Principals

From: Libbie & Wendy

MEMO

RE: Assessing the Knowledge of Your Staff

As principals begin to explore the idea of multiage with their staffs, several questions can help to determine staff development needs.

- What is "developmentally appropriate practice"? Do we teach in this way?

- Do we understand student-centered instruction and assessment?

- What do we believe about literacy and learning?

- Do we know how to facilitate a workshop atmosphere in our classrooms?

- Do we know what multiage really is?

- Have we been working on hands-on, minds-on processes?

Memo 3-2

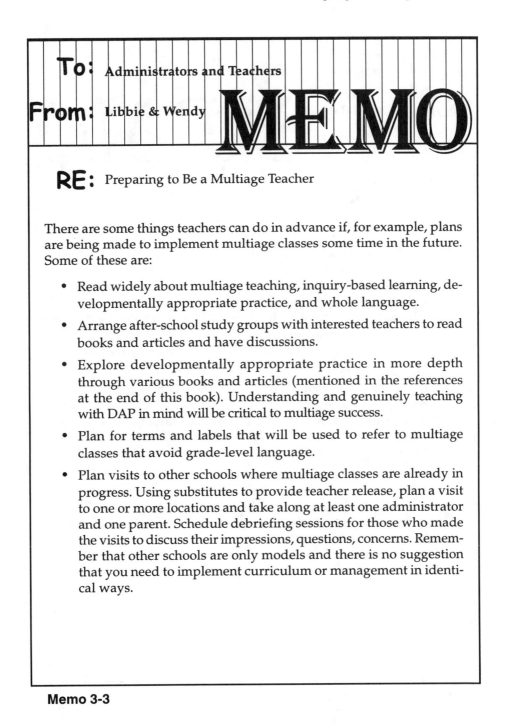

To: Administrators and Teachers

From: Libbie & Wendy

MEMO

RE: Preparing to Be a Multiage Teacher

There are some things teachers can do in advance if, for example, plans are being made to implement multiage classes some time in the future. Some of these are:

- Read widely about multiage teaching, inquiry-based learning, developmentally appropriate practice, and whole language.

- Arrange after-school study groups with interested teachers to read books and articles and have discussions.

- Explore developmentally appropriate practice in more depth through various books and articles (mentioned in the references at the end of this book). Understanding and genuinely teaching with DAP in mind will be critical to multiage success.

- Plan for terms and labels that will be used to refer to multiage classes that avoid grade-level language.

- Plan visits to other schools where multiage classes are already in progress. Using substitutes to provide teacher release, plan a visit to one or more locations and take along at least one administrator and one parent. Schedule debriefing sessions for those who made the visits to discuss their impressions, questions, concerns. Remember that other schools are only models and there is no suggestion that you need to implement curriculum or management in identical ways.

Memo 3-3

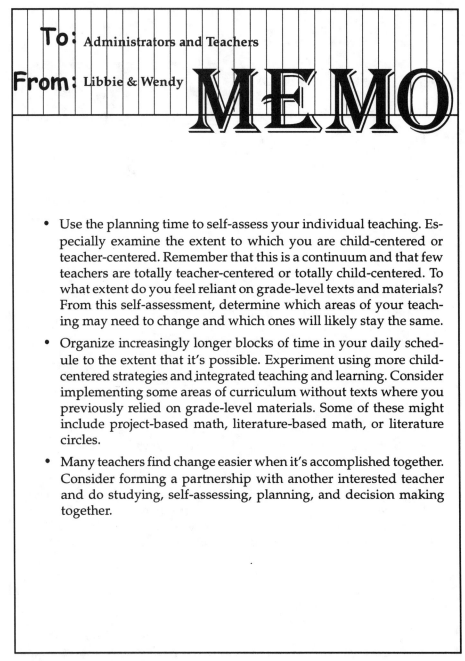

To: Administrators and Teachers

From: Libbie & Wendy

MEMO

- Use the planning time to self-assess your individual teaching. Especially examine the extent to which you are child-centered or teacher-centered. Remember that this is a continuum and that few teachers are totally teacher-centered or totally child-centered. To what extent do you feel reliant on grade-level texts and materials? From this self-assessment, determine which areas of your teaching may need to change and which ones will likely stay the same.

- Organize increasingly longer blocks of time in your daily schedule to the extent that it's possible. Experiment using more child-centered strategies and integrated teaching and learning. Consider implementing some areas of curriculum without texts where you previously relied on grade-level materials. Some of these might include project-based math, literature-based math, or literature circles.

- Many teachers find change easier when it's accomplished together. Consider forming a partnership with another interested teacher and do studying, self-assessing, planning, and decision making together.

Memo 3-3, continued

Schoolwide Considerations

●●

This chapter deals with many issues that are directly related to the entire school organization. Consensus-style meetings, parent involvement, helpful hints for administrators, and evaluation of the school's progress are all important and appropriate topics for the multiage school.

Consensus Teams

As described earlier, consensus is the decision-making style of choice in multiage schools. Although it is understood that all decisions cannot be made by consensus, decisions that relate directly to instruction and learning can be. Before practicing consensus, staff development on team building, consensus, and conflict resolution should have occurred, as discussed in chapter 3. Commitment from all staff members should have been gained for active participation and the time necessary to reach consensus. Figure 4-1 shows a possible membership plan for the consensus team.

The size of the consensus team depends on the size of the school. Most recommend that a team consist of 15–20 members if the school is large. This group must be representative of all members of the staff, including custodians, secretaries, and media specialists if they choose to be part of the team. If the school is small, everyone may choose to participate.

The keys to successful consensus teams include communication, honesty, organization, leadership, and ownership. *Communication* during a consensus meeting requires that everyone listen to the speaker. When side

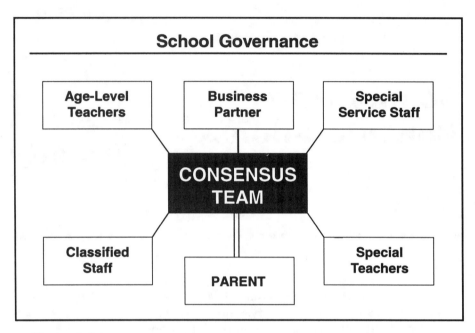

Figure 4-1

conversations occur or body language is negative, communication is jeopardized. Each speaker is expected to be concise and respectful, the listeners are expected to be respectful and actively listening. After meetings are concluded, notes or minutes are prepared and distributed to all staff members. These notes become part of the archives of the building as well.

Honesty during consensus meetings is often difficult to achieve. Many teachers are afraid to speak up or afraid of hurting others' feelings. These teachers leave meetings and continue to do things as they have in the past without hurting anyone or having caused conflict. Consensus teams require a commitment that each person will actively and honestly voice his or her ideas, concerns, suggestions, and disagreements. Before consensus is reached, the leader of the meeting should attend to each person who has not spoken and ask if he or she accepts the decision being discussed or has a different idea. Being required to speak in front of the group is part of the commitment to participate in the decision-making process. A basic rule is: Don't leave a consensus meeting without requesting that everyone speak up.

In a school in Wyoming where one of us did a series of staff development sessions on consensus decision making, the following occurred. As decisions were made utilizing the usual consensus guidelines, staff members would either agree publicly or sit quietly. It appeared that consensus had been reached. However, later two people who either did not speak or did not "get their way," went from room to room trying to dissuade individuals from agreeing with the meeting's decision. Such subversion leads to a failed consensus process by undermining collegiality and trust. The subverters had to be told by those they visited that they should have spoken in front of the group or forever held their peace.

Organization of the meetings is the third major key to success. How long will the meetings last? Will items other than those on the agenda be accepted? Who makes the agenda? When and where will meetings be held? Each of these questions, as well as others related to the overall organization of the meeting, can be answered at an organizational team meeting.

In some schools the agenda is jointly developed by submitting items to the leader or the office. In other schools the agenda is developed by the leader, a role that may rotate among staff members, for a particular meeting. However the agenda is developed, we advise that you do not permit other items to be added at the meeting. Many times the focus of the meeting is lost because someone comes in with an item that is of concern only to that individual. These types of concerns should be addressed with the principal and not take up valuable consensus time.

At Central Academy in Middletown, Ohio, the consensus team met weekly. During the first year, several meetings occurred where one or two teachers had to leave early or did not attend at all. The team discussed this at the end of the year and determined that if consensus was really important to them and their school, attendance should be required. This self-governance led to more productive meetings and to a sense of commitment to the process by all staff members.

Leadership on the consensus team should not be solely the responsibility of the principal. Initially, as the team is learning to efficiently operate, the principal may run some of the meetings. However, teachers and other staff members on the team should eventually take this responsibility. Some schools nominate and elect a leader, whereas others rotate the leadership according to a sign-up sheet. This type of procedure is also used to select the note taker, who will record decisions for the school archive.

One positive effect often observed in multiage classrooms is the fact that children function as both leaders and followers within a school week. Rotating leadership on the consensus team can have the same effect for teachers and other staff members. Although management of a group of adults is different from that of a group of children, running a consensus team enables one to develop the latter skill. Managing an agenda and keeping everyone "on task" is quite a learning experience for most staff members. Another responsibility of the leader is to question whether the decision being discussed is child-centered or adult-centered. The type of thinking required to facilitate the discussion helps the leader to grow in communication skills and knowledge about child-centeredness.

As we have worked with principals around the country, the majority of them agree that consensus is the way to run a school. The problem is that they are then stuck with carrying out all the decisions made. In a consensus situation, it is also the responsibility of everyone to divide the actions and follow-through to completion. *Ownership* is thus essential on a consensus team. You cannot own the process yet not own the responsibility for the actions. Before leaving consensus meetings, choices must be made about who will carry out the decisions, what the time frame is for completion, and what the reporting-back procedures will be.

Consensus is a powerful tool for decision making. Figure 4-2 describes some of the recommendations we would make to those beginning or trying to revise their decision-making procedures.

Guidelines for Consensus Meetings

- Who will take minutes, type them, and distribute them?

- Who will lead meetings and how will they be led?

- What is the time frame for and frequency of meetings?

- What are the rules for meetings (e.g., "no side conversations," "active listening")?

- What are the monitoring procedures for group interactions (e.g., "Is the decision child-centered?" "Are we on-task?")?

- Who will follow through with the actions decided?

Figure 4-2

Parent Involvement

If educators view children simply as students, they are likely to see the family as separate from the school. That is, the family is expected to do its job and leave the education of children to the schools. If educators view students as children, they are likely to see both the family and the community as partners with the school in children's education and development. (Epstein, 1995, p. 701)

Schools that are recognized as outstanding share many common elements. One of the most prominent elements is parent involvement. Much has been written supporting the use of parents in schools (Barth, 1990; Baskwill, 1989; Glatthorn, 1994; Joyce, Wolf, & Calhoun, 1993; Schmoker, 1996). Several themes about parent involvement emerge in the literature. They include reaching out to parents, being accountable to parents, using parents in decision making, and educating parents. This section will discuss each of these areas and offer practical suggestions for involving parents.

Reaching Out to Parents

The cry continues from schools, "Our parents don't care. They won't come to school. How are we supposed to get volunteers when we can't depend on them to show up?" Why won't parents come into our schools and classrooms and help out? Perhaps they don't care about their children; perhaps they don't have time; or perhaps they feel unwelcome.

Although many parents do have a difficult time juggling careers and child rearing, few fit the category of not caring about their children. Parents, just like children, need expectations to be set for them. Even the busiest parent, if expected, will find time to attend a parent-teacher conference if it will truly benefit the child. Parents do care and want to be involved in some way with their children's education, yet on an almost daily basis they are discouraged from doing so by the often unconscious, unintentional actions of school personnel.

What happens too often in schools is that the communication tends to be one-sided and many times condescending. How often do we *really* listen to parents and try to work out their concerns? Baskwill (1989) states:

> We have the power to impose—or simply allow—an unbalanced relationship that puts too much guilt on one party, too much authority and responsibility on the other, so that no real communication, no real sharing of ideas and information can occur. The problem is how to prevent that kind of imbalance, how to ensure shared understanding and joint goals. (p. 5)

Parents must feel welcome and develop a sense of belonging if the old paradigm is to be broken. Examining school behaviors and rules is a first step. Inside the school, are parents welcomed in a friendly and courteous manner? Or are they overlooked as staff members continue conversations or the secretary works at the computer? Is input about their children's education sought and used? Do parents participate in more than bake sales? Figure 4-3 indicates the level of parent participation that schools should expect and

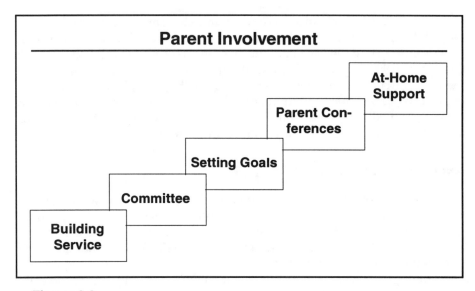

Figure 4-3

be willing to positively support. How each level of participation is structured needs to be determined by both staff members and parents.

Suggestions for reaching out to parents include the creation of school councils on which parents and students serve with teachers and administrators. The charge of such a council could be to determine accountability reporting to oversee the movement toward school goals, or to review and restructure the curriculum. School councils can be frightening for some teachers and principals because of the possibility of losing control. The key to a quality school council is to use it for real purposes and to set the parameters of the council's power before initiating the council. Clear, definitive expectations and job descriptions of the council will alleviate problems later.

Another opportunity for involving parents is the creation of school committees that truly have a role in children's lives. For example, parents could, with the help of staff members, determine what type of assemblies best fit the requirements of the curriculum or the themes for the school year. In one school, parents served on a committee that met with teachers to discuss possible field trips and assemblies for the year. Once the decisions were jointly made, the parents then scheduled the assemblies and arranged for the field trips, with final approval remaining with the principal. These parents were active participants in deciding their children's experiences.

Another committee in this same school coordinated all the special projects in the building, such as the book fair, holiday gift shop, portfolio making, and community service project. Each of the events was discussed with the staff before and after the decisions were jointly made. The parent committee then took charge and facilitated the completion of each project. Imagine not having to worry about these major projects!

Even parents who work outside the home can be involved in volunteerism. Many times teachers need work completed that can be done at home after the children are in bed. Parents can help with some of these tasks as their time permits. For example, many publishing centers in schools use cardboard covered with wallpaper samples, or folded booklet formats. Parents can assist the school with these types of projects in their homes. Many parents can take a day from work and chaperone a curriculum-based field trip. These parents probably have other ideas about how to assist. Don't be afraid to ask them for help.

Parents in many of the multiage schools we visit are surveyed about their special talents, interests, and volunteerism desires. Results from these surveys can help school personnel to determine if there are special committees, such as the ones cited above, that can be formed to achieve some of the school's goals. A sample parent survey can be found in Appendix H.

Ideas for involving parents in their child's education are also important. Teachers have begun to realize that project work is often parent work and that homework is merely a practicing of errors. What, then, can parents do to help their children at home? The most important thing that any parent can do for a child of any age is to read to him or her and discuss what is read.

Reading and discussing materials at home facilitates a continuation of language learning. Many teachers, including most multiage teachers, will send a book bag or backpack home with children throughout the week. In one school, after the child's individual conference with the teacher, a large plastic bag containing the child's reading materials and journal was sent home. The parents had been taught that when the book bag arrived, they were to look at the color of the bookmark to determine if they should read the book to the child (red), if the child could read the book with help (yellow), or if the child should read the book to the parents (green). Parents also responded to their child's weekly writing in the journal. Both items were sent back to school the next day. For those parents that cannot be depended on to return materials the next day, have alternative materials for the child to use until the other materials are returned. Most parents are dependable if they know the expectation, so be sure to communicate the procedures.

Other ways to involve the parents include sharing ideas about appropriate software. Many parents today have access to technology and want to help their children learn to use it. Software fairs for parents to view software and actually order from the company are helpful and can be facilitated by the school. Parents can then use the appropriate software at home to help their children conduct research and learn how to use technology as a tool.

Home math is also workable for parents. Advising parents about giving children an allowance to manage on a weekly or monthly basis will increase children's sense of economics. Taking children to the grocery store with a fictitious amount of money to spend allows them to use calculator skills and to shop comparatively. Children can also learn math skills in the kitchen through reading recipes and weighing and measuring the ingredients. Ideas are limitless for math reinforcement at home.

Accountability to Parents

School personnel are responsible to the community they serve, and parents are a major part of that community. Accountability to parents, especially when changing the way that things are done in schools, is critical. Reporting what the changes are, as well as seeking input from parents about the changes, is necessary to avoid sabotage.

Multiage grouping creates several questions in parents' minds: how the curriculum will be covered, how skills will be taught, the appropriateness of grouping young children with older children, and discipline (Gayfer, 1991; Kasten & Clarke, 1993; Lolli, 1994). In an effort to answer these questions and be accountable to parents for changes, several ideas are offered.

Covering curriculum as well as the teaching of skills can be addressed in the form of communiqués to parents. Quarterly newsletters describing up-coming units of study and possible at-home activities can be created and sent to parents before the start of the unit. Additionally, weekly bulletins describing possible minilessons and special projects for the week can alleviate unnecessary concerns about whether or not "real teaching" is occurring. The parent-school newsletter can also serve as a vehicle for updating parents about curriculum trends and how they apply in the multiage school. Samples of these can be found in Appendixes I and J.

Individual accountability for each parent's child can be achieved through setting individual goal plans, which is discussed later in this section. Quarterly reporting on student achievement of these goals can be accomplished with parent conferencing or student-led conferences. Narrative report cards can also provide an accounting of student growth and achievement of goals.

Another means of being accountable to parents was mentioned in chapter 2. Yearly surveys provide feedback to the school about its progress and child-centeredness. These survey results must be analyzed, and some resolution sought for the complaints or concerns that appear frequently. Once the resolutions are determined, schools should inform parents of the changes that will occur as a result of their concerns or complaints. In this manner, the school is accountable to parents and committed to making the school a truly joint facility (see Appendixes D and K).

Parents and Decision Making

Parent roles on school councils and special committees have been discussed. Parents can also be part of the instructional decision-making process. They can help to determine appropriate curricular objectives as well as the individual needs of their children. This is not to say that all control is given to the parent. However, parents have valuable knowledge of what their children need, and teachers can benefit from hearing those ideas.

One very frustrated parent and friend of ours described how she had tried to alert the teacher that students in the class had completed an in-depth study of ocean animals during the previous school year. The parent suggested to the teacher that perhaps jungle animals, farm animals, or any other kind of animals might better maintain the students' interest. The teacher failed to listen to the parent's suggestion and continued instead to make the students read the science chapter on ocean animals. Needless to say, for several weeks the children complained about how boring the work was and how silly the book sounded because they had created multimedia presentations the year before.

In the majority of multiage schools we are familiar with, CP is practiced. Because of this, each student needs a customized goal plan for each school quarter. Parents can help to negotiate these goals for their children. As you become more comfortable with setting individual goals, the children can begin to set their goals with you. These goals and the assessment of them sometimes result in students moving to new placements during the year.

Setting goals occurs before each quarter begins, with parents expected to meet and plan along with the teachers. This of course requires extra time. Many schools use grant money to hire substitute teachers so that conferences can be held during the school day, whereas others pay teachers a small stipend for their evening or weekend time. Jackie Robbie of Colorado Springs holds parent nights one evening a month. Students give presentations to parents on their progress and then set new goals (see chapter 9, the section on Learner Responsibility in Assessment).

Goal setting can be met with three approaches. Parents may arrive with their goals already set (on a sheet that was sent with the conference notice). Other parents will arrive with no goal sheet and a hopeful expression on their faces. These parents will usually say that they trust teacher judgment, so teachers can make recommendations to them. The final type of parents will state that their children are ready to attend the university, so do your best to create goals that indicate that!

Regardless of the type of parents, teachers must take time to teach them about developmental needs. Such conferences will typically last for at least half an hour, so a minilesson about growth and development can be given subtly. Comparing last quarter's completed goals with the goals that seem appropriate for the upcoming quarter often helps parents to realize their child's needs.

For those parents who do not understand developmental needs and continue to insist on inappropriate goals, it will be important to simply state your position and mark the goal with an *R*, signifying parental request. If the goal is not met by the child during the next quarter, the parent may then see that it was inappropriate. If the child does reach the goal, everyone celebrates. Goals that remain on the goal sheet but are unmet for more than two quarters are probably inappropriate goals for the child. The three to five goals that are indicated for the child should be attainable during one quarter, not unreachable until much growth has occurred.

When Libbie's son, Benjamin, was an early primary-age student, he requested to take the mandated district math-facts tests. In the district, second graders were given the tests, not first graders. Benjamin had seen several of the other children in his classroom taking these tests, and he decided that he also wanted to take them. Both Libbie and the teacher were doubtful, but they agreed to let him try. Benjamin passed each timed test that he took for the remainder of the year! Without the input from the student, both the parent and the teacher would have missed a CP opportunity for him.

One danger in goal setting for teachers is marking or identifying too many goals per child per quarter. Goals are the individualized work of the child, achieved during small-group or individual conference times. Too many goals are not realistic, and they are impossible for the teacher to manage. Three to five goals in major areas, such as language arts and math tools, are sufficient and manageable.

Parents should be expected to attend goal-setting and reporting conferences even if they have no ideas to contribute. Education about their child and developmental theory is an important outcome of these conferences. Even when parents do not attend conferences and teachers have rescheduled numerous times, it is important not to give up. Principals can write a letter or make a call indicating that one more time will be arranged or that a home visit by someone can be made. Most parents do not want a home visit (they may have to clean the house or serve cookies!), so they will make the effort to get to school. Following through with this expectation will keep your parents actively involved in their children's progress.

Parents should also be asked how they would like progress to be reported. Diane Kittelberger and Lyn Dreurey, multiage teachers in Barberton, Ohio, held a parent meeting at which parents were shown the traditional graded report card, a developmentally appropriate checklist, and a narrative. With each example, the pros and cons were discussed. Overwhelmingly the parents determined that they wanted to be reported to through narratives. Most parents, when given the opportunity to discuss and visualize progress reports, will choose something other than grades. At first this difference is very uncomfortable for many of them. However, allowing them some choice lessens the dissension. Remember, letter grades are inconsistent with the philosophy of nongraded, multiage classrooms!

Parent Education

Educating parents is an ongoing process in a school that is implementing change. Parents, like staff members, need opportunities to learn about the changes, reflect on them, and respond to them. Several ideas for parent inservices were described in chapter 2, so this section will deal with a few other ideas for keeping parents learning.

Research briefs about specific areas of change are important before changes are implemented. For example, a school that was planning on switching to multiage grouping at the beginning of the next school year began sending briefs home halfway through the current year. These one-page flyers talked about DAP, whole language philosophy, CP, and, eventually, multiage grouping. Each flyer described in common terms what the research literature indicated about the practice or philosophy. Teachers then wrote their thoughts about how they applied it in their classrooms or how they felt they would need to apply it the following year. This school found that the parents trusted the teachers' comments much more than the research literature. Switching the grouping pattern then faced relatively few objections when the final phase of the plan was announced.

"We used informational meetings and evening preview meetings with district multiage teachers and the Assistant Superintendent for Curriculum and Instruction. We offered to supply articles to read and invitations to visit and participate in multiage interactions."

—Myna Matlin, multiage principal
Tucson, AZ

Box 4-1

Parent study groups can be facilitated in much the same way as teacher study groups. Parents or a staff member can facilitate the study. Articles or videotapes may be used for these study groups. Time for discussion and reflection is needed for parents to accept and understand the changes in the schooling structure. Remember, most parents were educated in a graded system. That makes changing more difficult.

"Meetings were held with the parents of incoming kindergarten students to explain the [multiage] program. We established a team of administrators that included the superintendent, supervisor of elementary education, building principal, and myself, as committee chairperson, to present the information and answer questions. We also developed handouts for the parents. Principals met one-on-one with parents who had additional questions and concerns."

—Stephanie Acri,
principal & staff development coordinator
Harrisburg, PA

Box 4-2

Other ideas for updating parents include the use of brochures, pamphlets, booklets, and even visits (see Appendix L). Each of the written materials can describe the components of the multiage school and classroom. The booklets can further explain expectations or benchmarks for children as well as parent volunteer opportunities. One school took all the principal's monthly columns from the school newsletter and put them into a booklet that was distributed to all parents, visitors, and grandparents. Because the articles highlighted aspects of the multiage school, parents received a concise, easy-to-read booklet about their children's school. Visits to their children's classrooms or to other multiage schools are also a means of increasing parent awareness of the multiage classroom. A word of caution about visits: Be sure procedures and expectations are clearly identified. You do not want Mrs. Quimby showing up to "visit" her child's classroom every day of the week, nor do you want her sitting beside her child, interfering with the instructional process. Specific days and visitation rules must be clearly established for everyone to follow.

"Several parents went along on the school visits in Ohio and Michigan. Meetings were held to describe our pilot program and to explain the benefits that we hoped to gain."

—David Rossman, principal
Findlay, OH

Box 4-3

Parent involvement, when facilitated to serve children, can be a blessing. Parent involvement that doesn't help children in classrooms is not a blessing. Parents who have nothing more to do than micromanage the school can create havoc in a volunteer program. Parents who cannot keep a confidence about a child's ability can create havoc in the community. Sometimes the principal must step in and say "no" to volunteers who believe they are serving the school. An example occurred during the second year of a successful volunteer program in a multiage school we visited. A very enthusiastic, stay-at-home parent designed a plan to increase parent participation in the multiage classrooms. Parents would sign up for any day and then just show up at the teachers' doors. The principal, after recovering from cardiac arrest, proceeded to explain that instruction would constantly be interrupted because the teacher would be required to stop and instruct the parent on what to do and possibly how to do it. Needless to say, the parent who designed the plan was not at all happy with the principal. However, the children were not being served first with the parent's idea.

Helpful hints about volunteers include setting up a *sign-in procedure*. Parents or other volunteers can report to the office to sign in before going to teachers' rooms. *Badges* or *nametags* should be available to identify the person as a legitimate visitor to the school. *Volunteer training* should occur prior to anyone working in a classroom. This training can be facilitated by parents and teachers. Issues such as confidentiality and the "how to" of the volunteer projects are discussed. Many schools teach parent volunteers how to listen to children read, facilitate emergent journal writing, audiotape readers for their portfolios, use classroom technology, and work in the learning centers. Each of these tasks is based on DAP, so a volunteer should not be heard telling a child to "sound it out, sound it out" when listening to him or her read. Instead, appropriate child-centered strategies are taught to the volunteers.

At the conclusion of the year, schools often honor their parents and other volunteers in various ways. Many schools have a luncheon or breakfast where the total number of volunteers and hours of volunteer time (including the at-home time spent by working parents) is announced and celebrated. As with other award situations in multiage classrooms, no one is singled out as being the "greatest" or "most committed." Each person, no matter how small the contribution, is recognized as an involved parent or volunteer.

Volunteerism helps to create a sense of the school as a community. One parent in a multiage school did not have the same level of economic resources as most of the other parents. Karen lived close to the school, so she walked her children to school daily and always stopped in the office to ask if anything needed to be done. Karen volunteered in two of her children's classrooms on a daily basis and often helped with other projects around the school. Whenever she saw a book or an item that she thought the school could use, she either purchased it or traded for it. At the close of one year, when the volunteers were to be recognized, Karen walked her children to school and tried to hurry out of the building. The principal approached her and asked why she wasn't staying for the recognition ceremony. Karen responded that she only had jeans to wear and would not be properly dressed. The principal insisted that everyone was a member of the school family and that she should be recognized. Fortunately, Karen trusted the principal and attended the ceremony and actually felt comfortable with the other guests. This type of acceptance of parents is vital to the creation of the school community.

This section has described ways that parents can be involved at the building level on committees, with goal setting, at conferences, and in decision-making. Parent involvement at home has also been discussed. Parent involvement or disenfranchisement can make or break the multiage program. The benefits, in our opinion, far outweigh the risks and the hard work required to keep parents coming to the school.

Helpful Hints for Administrators From Administrators

This section is based solely on advice from one principal to another about converting to a multiage school. While many of the suggestions have been discussed earlier in the book, several overarching themes surface from these experienced administrators. They include suggestions for facilitating the change, dealing with sabotage, working with those who don't buy in, and general advice. The format for this section is quite different from the previous sections, as extensive quotes are used.

Facilitating the Change

Each of the principals who responded to our survey questions indicated that long-range planning had occurred in some form or another. This long-range planning led to the research and development phase of creating a multiage classroom. The following statements are comments from several of the principals.

> The implementation plan reflected a 3-year phase-in, with the first year being full-day kindergarten; the second year, multiage was used with the kindergarten and first-grade students; and the third year, multiage was expanded to include kindergarten, first-, and second-grade students. We believed that this 3-year phase-in would allow teachers and parents to adjust to the program. (Stephanie Acri, Pennsylvania)

> As the principal, I facilitated a staff needs assessment, set goals to address identified needs, and planned strategies for

reaching those goals. I secured resources and made arrangements for staff development. I arranged parent meetings and shared responsibility with several teachers for the presentations at those meetings. I also served as the liaison with the central office administration. (David Rossman, Ohio)

I first introduced the concept [multiage] in conversation and shared articles with teachers. I talked with key parents and PTA leaders. Teacher visitations and release time for teachers to attend multiage conferences with parents were provided. I listened to problems and concerns, smiled, and often said, "I understand." I am also willing to problem solve with teachers and parents. (Myna Matlin, Arizona)

I initiated discussions with teachers, parent groups, district representatives, and school board members. We built the concept over a 2-year period with the groups mentioned above. We developed a plan that included restructuring resources, planning sessions, staff development, ordering, and grant writing. Teachers were given time out of class to visit other schools. I encouraged and supported teachers. I even built the change into teacher goal-setting conferences and the development of the school goals for the last 3 years. I worked with parents. I worked carefully on staffing and assignment of students to classrooms. I developed and sometimes taught college classes for the staff. (Virginia Juettner, Alaska)

Dealing With Sabotage

As described in earlier chapters, sabotage sometimes occurs when changes are initiated. Each of these principals has dealt with sabotage in one manner or another. Principals offer this advice to those who must deal with sabotage through their change processes.

We openly discussed in faculty meetings that it's okay to have different philosophies but that it's not okay to be damaging to other's beliefs. Furthermore, I let the staff know that I didn't expect to go to the grocery store, or anywhere else in town where I may have contact with parents and community members, and hear that Ms. So-and-So said that multiage is no good or doesn't work.

We agreed to disagree in some areas of our philosophies, and we agreed that we would be supportive of one another regardless. Fortunately, we didn't have a great deal of this! (Judy Joachim, Florida)

> There have been a few negative comments by other teach-
> ers, and the multiage teachers and I have taken the high road
> trying to ignore these. Our biggest problems have come from
> parents who have attempted to sabotage the multiage classes.
> We keep meeting with any parent, providing information,
> and inviting them in to visit. We are attempting to educate
> the wider parent community, especially the positive leaders
> so that they will help us pass on the positive news. We have
> also invited and had the mayor, superintendent, and other
> district officials visit to "give their blessings." (Myna Matlin,
> Arizona)

> I could write a book on this issue. From the very beginning
> we had a small group of parents, mainly from one geographi-
> cal area, who were extremely vocal against the multiage pro-
> gram. They did not like the use of whole language philosophy,
> mixing children of different ages, the integrated curriculum,
> the report card, staying with a teacher for more than one year,
> and on and on. They spoke at every board meeting for two
> years. (Stephanie Acri, Pennsylvania)

Not all principals we interviewed reported attempts at sabotage, but the
problem does occur in many cases with this as well as other kinds of school
changes. Thus, being prepared will be helpful.

Dealing With Reluctant Participants

Several principals have indicated that multiage grouping in their schools is a
choice for both parents and teachers. Again, we support the opportunity for
choice because it leads to commitment and buy-in.

> With some parents I asked them to trust me and hang in there.
> This has worked well with proactive teacher follow-up and
> regular contact with these parents. If a parent flatly demands
> to have their child moved, I do so. This is not a battle worth
> fighting. All multiage teachers have made the request for
> changing to multiage. I won't force a teacher to take a
> multiage classroom. (Virginia Juettner, Alaska)

> We are still giving parents an option of placement in a
> multiage classroom or in a self-contained first or second
> grade. We secured a commitment from all teachers at the
> outset that they would not stand in the way of changes that
> the staff deemed to be beneficial to students. They agreed
> that if they were unwilling to implement those changes, they

would seek a transfer to another building. (David Rossman, Ohio)

Helping people to not feel threatened by new ideas was our main concern. We tried to let them know that we respected their talents and current knowledge and were willing to offer every kind of support possible that would empower them to be risk-takers. Hopefully, the message was, "We respect the work you're doing with your learners, but let's all take a look together at new possibilities—we're all in this together." (M. Ruth Davenport, Oregon)

General Advice

The last portion of this section on principals consists of general advice about multiage classrooms or schools. While all of us have many areas of expertise, it is extremely helpful to be able to pick up ideas from others who are willing to share.

- Know why you are doing this and how it fits with all other components of the school program.
- Find ways to provide your staff with time for planning and ongoing meetings for collaboration. Plan to work 3–5 years on this.
- Allow teachers to choose to teach multiage.
- Involve your parents. Get them on board from the beginning. They will be your best support.
- Always listen to your students. They will be your best teachers. Just as you don't want to "do" multiage to your teachers, we don't want teachers doing multiage to their students. Allow a learning community to be created.
- Be prepared to "wander in the wilderness" for a while.
- Be prepared to give information again and again.
- Support the teachers and parents through the change process.
- Take care of yourself, and keep smiling.
- Use a consultant with multiage expertise to provide staff development and parent education.
- Start slowly, and have a plan.
- Go for it! You've made a smart decision, and your children will be the winners!

Evaluating Progress

The final section of this chapter highlights some ways for multiage schools to evaluate their progress in reaching their goals. Surveys were discussed in chapter 2, with some samples found in the appendixes. This section deals with other types of assessment that can be used to evaluate the school's progress.

Quantitative Test Results

Although standardized achievement and ability tests for young children are developmentally inappropriate, several states or districts require them to be given. Multiage classrooms are rarely exempt from this type of testing. We do not advocate these tests but we understand that they may be mandated.

Children in multiage classrooms should be given the test that is most appropriate to their developmental levels. This may mean that an 8-year-old may be taking a test that was originally designed for a 6-year-old. Teachers and parents must understand that the test is given at the developmental level rather than the age level. In districts where this is unacceptable, children will probably be required to take the "grade level" test. In these unfortunate instances, it is important that the parents understand that developmentally the child may be working at a different place than the test results will indicate. As we have indicated throughout this book, this is the old factory model of schooling clashing with the developmental one. Age and grade tests are the quality control of the assembly line.

Once these quantitative results are in, staff members need to analyze the data identifying curriculum strengths and possible weaknesses as well as individual results, and then they should put these results in proper perspective, as one limited source of information. The staff is responsible for using whatever results are workable to better the program or increase student learning. Often, results are published and compared with nonmultiage classrooms, as inappropriate as this may be. Over time, we are certain the results will be positive, and long-term research supports this. No one in a multiage classroom is at a disadvantage because of the structure (see chapter 1).

Another form of testing used to measure school achievement is proficiency or competency-based testing. This type of format claims to determine whether the curriculum is being taught and learned. Most of these tests are relatively new and require problem-solving abilities rather than rote memorization of facts or figures. Extended answers, short-answer essays, and multiple-choice answers are typically used on these tests. Many of them can be helpful to multiage teachers as a means to assess the curriculum as well as student problem-solving capabilities. Since most proficiency tests are new, assessment and periodic revisions may be needed as educators become more experienced with these instruments.

Qualitative Assessments

Information about schooling success should be moved from the realm of tests and test results. According to Schmoker (1996), we need to focus on short-term goals and long-term goals, realizing that more usable information will be gained. Schmoker also states that we need to analyze not only standardized tests and academic achievement but also local assessments, ongoing process-improvement data, and progress toward short-term goals. We therefore offer the following ideas to add to your school portfolio.

School climate can be successfully measured through student interviewing. Multiage programs tend to be highly rated by students. Gathering this type of information is as important as quantitative results, and it speaks to parents who care deeply about their children's experiences. Plan on spending time talking to students about their previous school experiences and their current experiences. Documenting these comments, interviews, or surveys will provide additional information to the test results. Using published attitude scales or self-esteem measures can also be helpful. Such instruments are available from school counselors and school psychologists.

Two other pieces of data that speak to positive results are tracking school *attendance* and *discipline records*. Some administrators have noted, anecdotally, that truancy has subsided and that discipline referrals have decreased with multiage classes. Although little research is available to date on these two areas, we feel there is great potential for schools that wish to document these trends.

Retreats

Multiage staff members benefit from an annual retreat in the spring. During this retreat, three things can occur: reflection on the past year, short-range planning for the next year, and long-range planning and reflection on the school's vision and goals. Retreats should be well planned and held off school grounds.

Many schools develop the retreat agenda during the school year. For example, several teachers may attend a conference on math journaling and become greatly excited about this. The subject might then be added to the agenda for the upcoming retreat to avoid introducing one more new thing during the current school year. Other agenda items might include discussion of group functioning during consensus meetings, how to take the next step in the multiage journey, and even how to revise the school assessment plan.

Time for social activities as well as work time is important at a retreat. Several schools plan a nice evening meal to complement a hard day's work. Other social activities can include a midmorning break for group activities such as swimming or golfing. The key is to balance work and play and avoid teacher burnout.

Most retreats occur over a 2-night period, usually beginning after school on a Friday and culminating on Saturday night or Sunday midday. Of course, the retreat schedule depends on the staff. For participants to gain the most benefit from the retreat, the agenda should be followed, with resolutions recorded for later implementation.

Some schools may have difficulty facilitating retreats because of association contracts or collective bargaining agreements. Perhaps teachers would feel so committed to the decision-making process that they would attend without worrying about the contract, but in some places this is not possible. One suggestion is to keep attendance voluntary if contract issues arise. Judy Joachim, a multiage principal in Florida, allowed teachers to leave immediately after the students were dismissed for several days (instead of staying through until contracts or collective bargaining agreements dictate) in order to make up the time spent in planning.

Goal Reporting

Schools need to spend time reflecting on their progress toward the goals that were set earlier and creating additional goals as needed. Reflections can be recorded in a narrative format under each goal statement. Artifacts or evidence of progress can be included with the reflections. Muldoon Elementary in Anchorage, Alaska, identifies a "report card" for the school, which is used to measure progress on the goals set for the school year. Each goal is identified, an expectation is printed, and action plans for achieving the goal are listed. As each action is completed, a check-off and evidence or artifacts supporting the goal are placed in a cumulative report (see Appendix M).

Summary

This chapter has explored the topics of consensus teams, parent involvement, best advice from principals, and evaluation of the school's progress. Each of the topics is important in the development of the multiage school. Otto (1969) described the structure needed for nongraded philosophy to be successful, and consensus teams provide the vehicle for that structure. Parent involvement can enhance or detract from the school climate. It is better to involve the parents and gain their support than to ultimately lose the multiage groupings because of nonsupport. Administrators have a major job in facilitating the multiage change process. They must be willing to fight the saboteurs, involve parents, and evaluate the school's progress with an open mind. The creation of the multiage school is not easy, but from experience we can tell you that it is well worth it!

Clipboard

Chapter 4 describes several schoolwide considerations.

1. School governance can take the form of a consensus team, following the guidelines of communication, honesty, leadership, organization, and ownership.

2. Involving parents in the multiage building is a must. Parents can be involved in decision making and other school-based activities, such as volunteerism.

3. An open-door policy along with sincerity will help parents realize that their presence is wanted in the multiage school.

4. Ongoing quality information should be shared with parents. Too much misinformation can lead to doubts and efforts to ban the multiage classrooms.

5. Advice from principals includes not mandating the program, informing parents, and developing the staff.

6. In evaluating school progress, both quantitative and qualitative measures are needed.

7. Creation of a building portfolio to share artifacts and evidence of progress toward achieving goals can be very worthwhile.

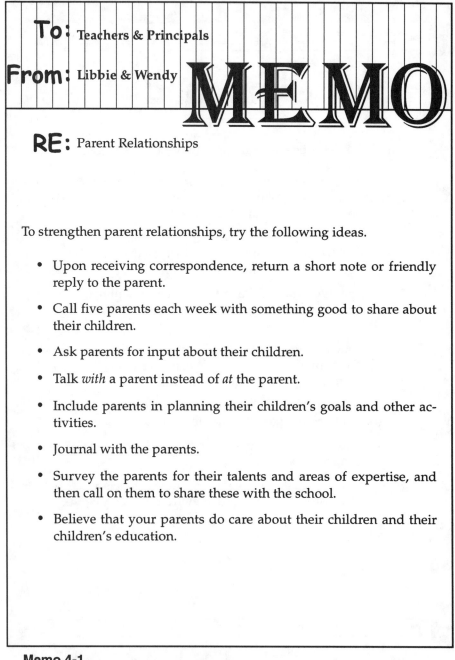

To: Teachers & Principals

From: Libbie & Wendy

MEMO

RE: Parent Relationships

To strengthen parent relationships, try the following ideas.

- Upon receiving correspondence, return a short note or friendly reply to the parent.

- Call five parents each week with something good to share about their children.

- Ask parents for input about their children.

- Talk *with* a parent instead of *at* the parent.

- Include parents in planning their children's goals and other activities.

- Journal with the parents.

- Survey the parents for their talents and areas of expertise, and then call on them to share these with the school.

- Believe that your parents do care about their children and their children's education.

Memo 4-1

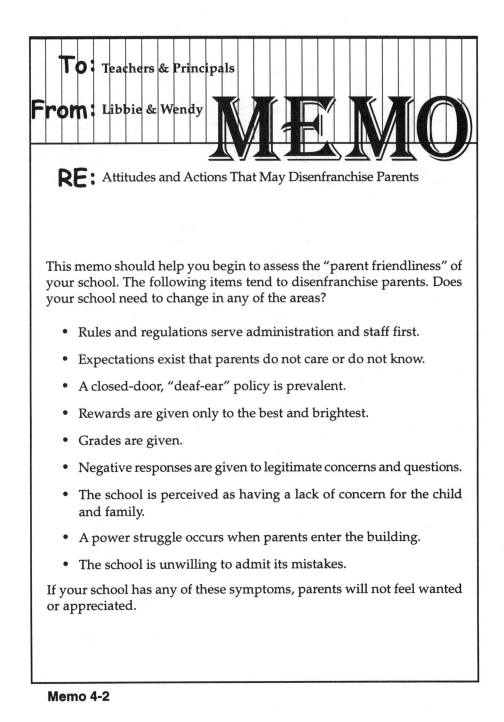

To: Teachers & Principals

From: Libbie & Wendy

MEMO

RE: Attitudes and Actions That May Disenfranchise Parents

This memo should help you begin to assess the "parent friendliness" of your school. The following items tend to disenfranchise parents. Does your school need to change in any of the areas?

- Rules and regulations serve administration and staff first.

- Expectations exist that parents do not care or do not know.

- A closed-door, "deaf-ear" policy is prevalent.

- Rewards are given only to the best and brightest.

- Grades are given.

- Negative responses are given to legitimate concerns and questions.

- The school is perceived as having a lack of concern for the child and family.

- A power struggle occurs when parents enter the building.

- The school is unwilling to admit its mistakes.

If your school has any of these symptoms, parents will not feel wanted or appreciated.

Memo 4-2

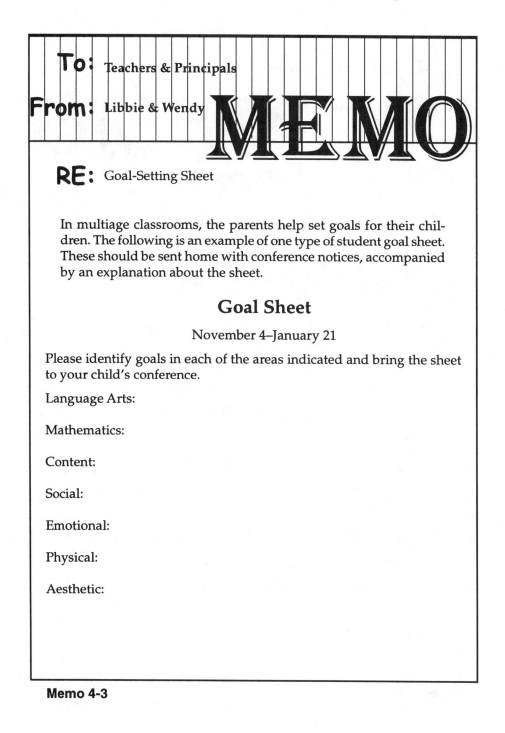

To: Teachers & Principals

From: Libbie & Wendy

MEMO

RE: Goal-Setting Sheet

In multiage classrooms, the parents help set goals for their children. The following is an example of one type of student goal sheet. These should be sent home with conference notices, accompanied by an explanation about the sheet.

Goal Sheet

November 4–January 21

Please identify goals in each of the areas indicated and bring the sheet to your child's conference.

Language Arts:

Mathematics:

Content:

Social:

Emotional:

Physical:

Aesthetic:

Memo 4-3

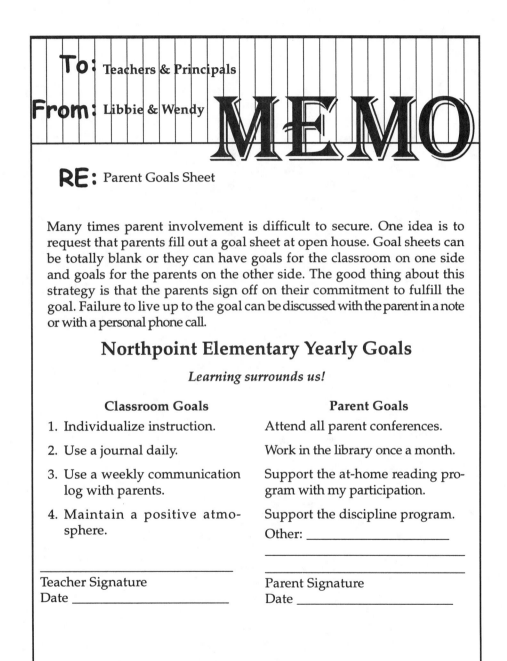

To: Teachers & Principals

From: Libbie & Wendy

MEMO

RE: Parent Goals Sheet

Many times parent involvement is difficult to secure. One idea is to request that parents fill out a goal sheet at open house. Goal sheets can be totally blank or they can have goals for the classroom on one side and goals for the parents on the other side. The good thing about this strategy is that the parents sign off on their commitment to fulfill the goal. Failure to live up to the goal can be discussed with the parent in a note or with a personal phone call.

Northpoint Elementary Yearly Goals

Learning surrounds us!

Classroom Goals	Parent Goals
1. Individualize instruction.	Attend all parent conferences.
2. Use a journal daily.	Work in the library once a month.
3. Use a weekly communication log with parents.	Support the at-home reading program with my participation.
4. Maintain a positive atmosphere.	Support the discipline program.
	Other: _____
	_____

_____
Teacher Signature
Date _____

_____
Parent Signature
Date _____

Memo 4-4

PART III

Inside the Classroom

● ●

> I believe that the individual who is to be educated is a social
> individual, and that society is an organic union of individu-
> als. If we eliminate the social factor from the child we are left
> only with an abstraction; if we eliminate the individual fac-
> tor from society, we are left only with an inert and lifeless
> mass. Education, therefore, must begin with a psychological
> insight into the child's capacities, interests, and habits. It must
> be controlled at every point by reference to these same con-
> siderations. These powers, interests, and habits must be con-
> tinually interpreted—we must know what they mean. They
> must be translated into terms of their social equivalents—
> into terms of what they are capable of in the way of social
> service.
>
> —John Dewey, *My Pedagogic Creed* (1897, p. 6)

Part III, the largest section of this book, includes several chapters that address the specifics of teaching and curriculum in an elementary multiage setting. Included are chapters on curriculum in general, designing curriculum,
implementing curriculum, logical or mathematical thinking, and assessment.

One caveat, however, is that this section will not offer recipes or easy
answers. Each teacher must find his or her own way to teach, using individual strengths and making any of our suggestions his or her own. No book,
or set of materials, releases teachers from the responsibility to make the best
decisions for their community of learners. Teachers are professionals.

CHAPTER 5

Setting the Stage: Curriculum and Instruction in a Context

As the quote by Dewey suggests, curriculum doesn't happen in a vacuum. Curriculum is embedded in the context of a classroom that includes an instructional leader, a class of youngsters, a physical space, and miscellaneous materials. A great deal takes place as these components interact.

What Is *Curriculum*?

When people in your district use the word *curriculum*, exactly what do they mean? Often there's a tacit assumption that everyone has the same definition, but this usually isn't the case, in our experiences working with schools. For example, some people mean *content* when they say *curriculum*. To them, it's the stuff in the books, or the numerous pages locally written into some curriculum guide or course of study. Other schools use *curriculum* as in "We have just purchased a new social studies curriculum." In this case, they really mean *materials* and the tables of contents of those materials. Still others lump *curriculum* and *instruction* together as two sides of the same coin—one being what you teach, and the other being the methodology by which you teach it.

Entire books are written on the subject of curriculum, and some of them never actually define the term. McCutcheon (1995) defines *curriculum* as "what students have the opportunity to learn in schools" (p. xv). Noting, however, that this definition inherently contains topics that are stated explicitly to be learned as well as topics that are more implicit, McCutcheon recognizes that the definition of curriculum is muddy. We agree.

We will take McCutcheon's definition quite literally and note that students have an opportunity to learn many things in schools that go far beyond their traditional content. Some of these may include learning about themselves as learners; learning about themselves as individual human beings, including their hopes, capabilities, and levels of confidence; and learning who they are in relation to the rest of the world. Consequently, *absolutely everything that takes place in classrooms and in school becomes part of the curriculum.*

What takes place in school goes far beyond the tables of contents in textbooks. Curriculum, then, includes the environment, the relationships and interactions in that environment, and the content and methodology used in the environment. One implication of this definition is that we don't plan and direct everything that students will learn in the "curriculum." They will learn lessons of many kinds that weren't in anyone's planbook. Another implication of this definition is that maybe we should care about the rest of those lessons. After all, students may forget facts. Years from now they won't remember the names of state capitals, the important dates of history, or the parts of a flower. They *will* remember how they were treated in school, how they felt about themselves during school hours, how to be a learner, and how those lasting impressions translated into their eventual adult life.

Curriculum isn't something you buy from a catalog. You might purchase some materials from a catalog that support your curriculum. Those purchases aren't cures or the keys to change, and they will not by themselves solve any problems in a school or district. In Part I we talked about long-term goals and about schools having and publicizing a mission statement and vision. Any discussions and deliberations about curriculum should take those visions and goals into account.

What Is *Instruction?*

Instruction is "an effort to assist or to shape growth" (Bruner, 1966, p. 1). Hopefully, instruction is a catalyst for learning. Another long debated and much studied aspect of education, instruction includes all the deliberate and nondeliberate actions that influence student learning. These actions go beyond "covering the curriculum." They encompass all the methodologies, materials, and experiences that take place in classrooms. In other words, instruction is a subset of curriculum.

Once upon a time, instruction was equated with lecturing or telling. Instruction was also the sole domain of the teacher. Now most of us would consider that lecturing is only one way in which instruction might take place, and hopefully only a small part of it. During earlier times, little was known about learning, and so instruction consisted primarily of the traditional method of teachers telling and students listening, sometimes enhanced with visual aids or demonstrations.

Today learning theory has come a long way. The passive model of instruction may be appropriate at times but is no longer thought of as being the most effective method. In fact, the entire traditional scene—the teacher at the front doing all the talking, the students individually doing all the listening, and uniform assessments determining success and standards—these are all notions right out of the industrial model, as we suggested in chapter 1. It's all part of the assembly line.

Since the industrial model and the assembly line is what we are trying to reform with multiage classrooms, we will focus on curriculum and instruction that are not teacher-centered or textbook-based. Teacher-centered ways of doing things, as we discussed in Part II, are not well suited to a multiage environment because the class has not been constructed to be homogeneous. The discussions in the rest of this section will capitalize on the diversity of the multiage environment.

What Is the Context?

No matter what the curriculum, no matter what the instruction, both are imbedded in a *context*, or environment within the school. Can you imagine, for example, a teacher whose skills at instruction are excellent and whose content or curriculum includes good and interesting material but who hates the students she teaches? Of course, many of us would argue that such an individual is not a good teacher, because attitudes are just as important as learning.

In fact, we argue that the context is an integral part of the learning that takes place. We believe that certain basic principles apply to every classroom at every age level, whether those classrooms are multiage or not. First of all is the principle of *student respect*. Teachers should respect students and treat them with the same dignity given to adults. There will be times when students' behaviors are unacceptable, but the human beings inside those behaviors need guidance and respect. While to some this may seem obvious and should not need to be said here, we can assure you from our extensive travels that respect does not exist in every classroom.

There is never justification for inflicting upon students words or actions that belittle them. Nothing is gained, and much is lost. Their behavior might be reprimanded, scolded, or even punished severely, but the human being must not be lost in the transaction. Respect is deserved by all students from all backgrounds, no matter who their parents are or from where they come.

Another principle that applies to all classrooms is *acceptance*. As we mentioned in chapter 1, learning happens better when learners feel accepted, respected, and not afraid. In other words, every single learner has an equal right to be there, to be nurtured, and to be supported toward the most growth possible, no matter what the person's background or economic situation. Accepting all our learners means that we *assume* they all can learn, we *assume* they are all teachable, and we *assume* they will all succeed. It also means that we *assume* they all want to learn. If it doesn't appear that they all want to learn, then it's also our job to find and light the fire within them. If school learning is totally foreign to them and seems to bear little resemblance to real life, then we should question the school learning and not the students.

The classroom context includes the attitudes, climate, and culture that is modeled, promoted, and supported, first by the instructional leader (teacher) and eventually by members of the classroom. When this occurs, the group isn't just a classroom, it has become a community. Creating community does not happen all by itself but, like all worthwhile endeavors, takes effort. It must be nurtured. It's difficult, and it takes time. In the previous section we stated that school faculties should learn to become communities. Here we will share some tips on creating community in the classroom.

Figures 5-1 and 5-2 present contrasting views of curriculum. Figure 5-1 illustrates an industrial-model view of curriculum and instruction similar to the one with which many of us grew up. One teacher did all the teaching, which mostly meant telling information in a format we have come to refer to as a *transmission* style of teaching. Learners gathered or absorbed identical information and were required to process it for later evaluation, generally in the form of a test.

Figure 5-2 presents a more elaborate model of curriculum and instruction in a holistic, constructivist, or whole language paradigm. Curriculum is more broadly defined as educational experiences; learner factors, such as background experience, are taken into account. All are embedded in a context that includes the classroom climate, culture, and attitudes. Outcomes may be less predictable and aren't uniform, but they serve individuals and their needs.

Figure 5-1 depicts the funnel-like quality of curriculum in an industrial model. Content, delivered through the teacher and the materials, is fed into students systematically. The expectation is that individuals process the information fed into them in a more or less uniform manner. Evaluation is generally formal, such as a single paper-pencil test that may take a variety of forms (essay, multiple choice, true-false), but is rarely if ever adjusted to meet individual needs, such as different learner strengths, intelligences, or development. This "sink or swim" attitude is designed to discard outliers (those who fail) just like imperfect merchandise on the assembly line. Not everyone is expected to succeed.

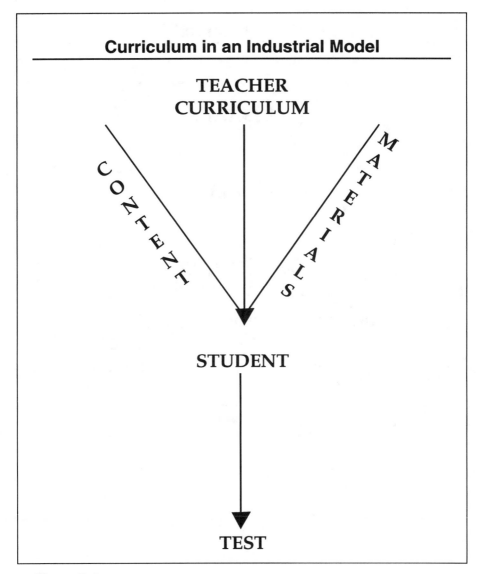

Curriculum in an Industrial Model

TEACHER
CURRICULUM

CONTENT

MATERIALS

STUDENT

TEST

Figure 5-1

Figure 5-2 depicts curriculum in a constructivist model. Planned with a vision of success in mind and having goals consistent with the vision, daily school experiences are more varied as content, instruction, and the individual considerations of learners constantly interact. These parts are all embedded

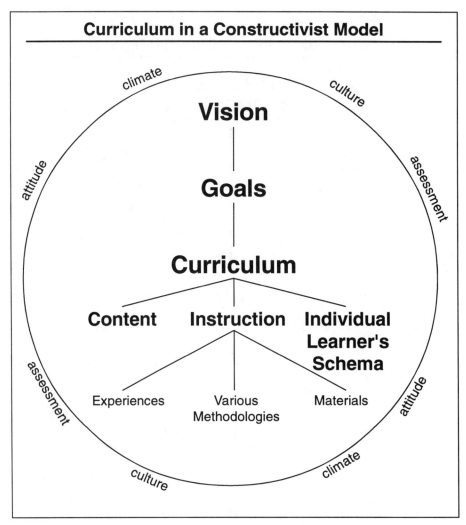

Figure 5-2

in a context that includes positive attitudes and expectations, a climate of individual acceptance, a culture that values diversity in learners in many ways, and assessment that is part of teaching rather than a separate entity following instruction.

Which do you think is a better model in which to raise human beings for a democratic way of life?

Creating Community in the Classroom

Teachers have long known that the difference between a good classroom and an outstanding one greatly depends on the climate and atmosphere. *Climate* is a tone or ambiance that the teacher, as classroom instructional leader, sets and nurtures through attitudes, models, policies, management, and general discipline. This aspect of classroom life is intangible. Another way of looking at this, according to Jalongo (1991), is that good teachers teach their students as they would want their own children to be taught.

One of the aspects of classroom climate that a teacher may create is a sense of community. A community is a place where people rely and depend on each other; they work both alone and together, often sharing in the responsibilities of everyday life. We strongly believe that classrooms need to have this sense of community and that this contributes to an effective learning environment.

"We are constantly working toward building and strengthening a sense of community in the classroom. Class meetings, class discussions, learning buddies, responsibilities in classroom maintenance, cooperative group work, and creating classroom guidelines together and discussing consequences are just some of the ways that we build community."

—Marybeth Phelps and Gloria Morrison
Danielson, CT

Box 5-1

Certain teachers we have met over the years have a gift for creating a beautiful community. Other teachers think they need tips and guidance in this area. Having given some thought to the commonalities of the classrooms we have observed that have a good sense of community, we outline some helpful suggestions here.

A community is highly similar to a well-functioning family. Although different families have a variety of ways of organizing themselves, there are still jobs to be done, and it somehow has to be decided who will do what. Whether it is based on a specialization of roles (the same person always does the laundry), or a rotation of roles (everyone takes turn clearing the dishes from the table), everyone plays a role in an environment that functions as a community. The payoff is that the members of that community feel a sense of belonging and ownership because their contributions are vital parts of the operation.

Basic Beliefs About Children

One aspect of community that we have found with the teachers we have studied is their basic underlying positive beliefs about children. This is true whether or not the classroom is multiage. These teachers have a firm belief that children are good people, that everyone has gifts, and that everyone will learn and grow. No child is judged to be unteachable. Although this statement may sound too obvious to some readers and too simplistic to others, we believe that positive attitudes toward children and learning are a prerequisite for entering the teaching profession. That requirement includes a commitment on the part of teachers to best serve all the children they teach, no matter what their backgrounds or their abilities.

Both of us are former classroom teachers, and we will not suggest that it's an easy job. Quite the opposite—it's about as emotionally demanding a job as there is in life. Many children arrive at school with serious personal and family problems that cannot be ignored in the process of teaching. These influence our ability to help students learn, and we frequently need the intervention of social workers, health care professionals, or counselors. A malnourished child may not be able to stay awake to learn during the school day. An abused child may not be able to pay attention to class lessons. A child with a dying parent may need class time to grieve. The list is endless.

Children with difficult situations are worthwhile human beings with certain gifts and capabilities that the teacher and other students can help to identify. It may be unfortunate that teachers sometimes have to become advocates for the children they teach, but today, more often than not, it's part of the job.

"We present several plays each year. This builds more class unity, gives students confidence, and makes students rely on each other."

—Jackie Robbie
Colorado Springs, CO

Box 5-2

Building Class "Resident Experts"

The relationship between self-esteem and learning has long been recognized (Canfield & Wells, 1976). Students who feel valued, accepted, and worthwhile are in a more advantageous position to take risks with learning. As we mentioned in Part I, many readers can relate to a time at work or in school where they felt either valued or unappreciated, and this affected their situation.

We are using the term *experts* here very loosely and for lack of a better one. The notion stands that finding, acknowledging, and nurturing student expertise helps class individuals to thrive and feel like a member of the community. Within any class, someone might be your resident dinosaur expert. The child whose parents participate in dog shows may be your canine behavior expert. Someone who has grown up in a computer household may be your most able computer technical assistant. The child of the migrant farmworker family is your resident expert on agriculture.

As you mine your classroom for individual gifts and talents, it will be important to note that some gifts consist of process more than content knowledge. One or two children may be the most diplomatic and can help solve minor disputes, especially with some training. Others may be excellent hosts to give tours when parents and others visit your classroom. Often, pairing an experienced expert with a less experienced one will mentor someone into an important role, providing for continuity as class members change and grow beyond your classroom.

Another important thing to keep in mind is that some children may not arrive with an obvious expertise and may need more nurturing. Recognition of their strengths may result when they are assigned to become responsible for something. For example, almost every classroom has a child who is well organized and meticulous about personal property, assignments, and so on. That student might be the candidate to set up a system to keep track of the classroom library or to take over attendance and lunch counts.

Classroom Traditions

Traditions and rituals help a group to feel like a community with meaning. Most organizations have rituals and traditions. Girl Scouts/Guides have special songs, closing ceremonies, and services for when someone leaves or joins. Boy Scouts/Guides have special handshakes, laws, and symbols. Piano classes have recitals or concerts. Classrooms need their traditions as well.

Peterson (1992) mentions how some classrooms always light a candle when it is reading-aloud time. Others celebrate student accomplishments with parties or special events like assemblies. Peterson contends that traditions help to fill a human need for meaning within a group and provide a sense of reassurance. Jodi Kinner and Beth Bonner of Iowa City practice some "adoption" rituals when a new student arrives. Some teachers have traditions they practice from year to year, and sometimes schools have time-honored traditions that a teacher may inherit, such as a particular field trip, social event, outdoor education trip, or end-of-the-year festival. Libbie's former multiage school planned a culminating activity at the end of every schoolwide theme. For example, after 9 weeks of a thematic study on plants, the school planned and planted a joint garden. After 9 weeks of intensive study of animals, everyone went to the zoo. Whatever the traditions, whether they are student- or teacher-initiated, they can add to a sense of community.

A composite class that one of us visited in Australia started each part of the day by coming together in a circle on the floor. This time was used to share personal stories, review the daily docket, give reassurance where needed, and provide necessary instructions. The calm and gentle nature of these brief meetings set the tone for the morning, afternoon, or after returning from an event.

Coming together was also a tradition in the multiage classroom where Wendy and a colleague studied multiage learning for 4 years. In this primary classroom, the community came together on the only carpeted area of the room at the day's beginning and end. The closing circle provided an opportunity to find out if the students had had a good day or not. Each class member would respond with "thumbs up" or "thumbs down" in judging their day. This enabled the teacher to notice which students might have had bad days (if she had missed it earlier) and provide reassurance or have a chat with these individuals. Another multiage teacher, Kittye Copeland from Missouri, began and ended every day with a classroom meeting. These student-led sessions accomplished many purposes, including reviewing needs, instructions, sharing, solving community problems, announcements, and anything else that may have arisen.

Another class we visited began and ended every day with a song. Certain songs were thought of as special class songs, but others were for fun or related to classroom content. Music is part of many traditions in different kinds of groups and has a powerful influence on the mood of those present. Still another class began and ended each day with a poem.

Student Responsibilities

Sometimes, under the guise of being nurturing, parents and teachers do too much for those for whom they care. Children want and need responsibilities that are age-appropriate. Duties that contribute to the common good build self-esteem and a sense of belonging. One good thesis is that everything that *can* be done by children in the classroom *should* be. If you, as teacher, think you'll spend time after school putting up a bulletin board, assembling a new center, downloading files from the computer, or doing other teaching-related duties, then you might consider whether these tasks can be done by a student or perhaps a small group. Student responsibility has learning value attached to it (whereas you, as a teacher, probably already know how to do it). So why miss a learning opportunity for a youngster?

One multiage primary classroom we visited had students taking on many of the chores done in some schools by maintenance staff. Students filled soap dispensers in the class lavatory and replaced toilet paper and paper towels. They replenished classroom paper supplies in places where paper was meant to be accessible. They washed chalkboards and desktops and emptied the trash into hallway containers. These activities were not necessarily done only at the end of the day. This teacher taught these students that if the dispenser ran out of towels, she didn't even want to hear about it. Students were either to replace the towels themselves or find a friend to help them do it.

Once students see the classroom as a place that belongs to them, these types of responsibilities become quite natural and even expected. Sometimes these issues need special explanations to parents who are not accustomed to classrooms that are run like communities. For example, one affluent parent whose son had just willingly and voluntarily washed the class desks after a messy project visited the school and informed the teacher indignantly that her son "doesn't *do* maintenance." The teacher had to explain the value of taking turns to help out in a classroom, which is unrelated to career expectations or aspirations.

Responsibilities go far beyond the mundane maintenance of the classroom, of course. Hopefully, students are learning to take responsibility for themselves as learners—a most important lifelong skill. Opportunities for independent, self-selected study and student participation in the assessment process are two ways to develop responsible learners. In adult life, learners are in charge of their own schedules and tasks and need to organize themselves to get things done. These skills are nurtured during elementary school years in order to form lifelong habits that will serve learners, no matter what their personal aspirations.

Taking Risks: Kids Weren't Meant to Be Perfect

A leading educator of this century, Roach Van Allen, has frequently stated that "learning is risk taking." In other words, learning is a risky business because when you learn new things, you are in a position of either being successful or unsuccessful in front of your teacher and peers. If you are successful, you feel good. If you are unsuccessful, your confidence and self-esteem may take a "hit."

Taking risks is a problem for children who are already so fragile that they cannot afford a "hit," or loss. One might say that their emotional bank account is too small for any spending or withdrawal. The child with "limited funds" will withdraw or misbehave rather than risk being unsuccessful. These potential risks might occur with very difficult work, with new experiences at which the child thinks he or she is not very good, or in an environment where people care too much about perfection and correctness. Many teachers have met children who have given up on learning (at least in school) and have observed the resulting antisocial behavior. Such a situation is very difficult to change.

Take a moment to reflect on your own successes as well as your own mistakes, whether in schooling experiences or in other arenas of life. Which experiences were the most powerful teachers? Obviously we learn from both successes and mistakes, but often mistakes are the better lessons. In fact, many great inventions in the world were the result of mistakes, such as the invention of cellophane.

In classrooms, teachers can promote and demonstrate healthy attitudes toward errors. Pointing out one's own mistakes and showing their learning value can be a unique and important model for students. Many of us may have grown up thinking that our teachers were perfect, knew everything, or never spelled words wrong. Although some people may think it's helpful to be put on a pedestal, such a position does not benefit those we teach. Such a position is not real, not a healthy aspiration, and it does not promote lifelong learning.

Another part of risk taking in the classroom is the recognition that learning certain new things is either harder or easier for some people at any given time and that this is a perfectly normal scenario. Learning is gradual. Imagine yourself learning something very new—karate, playing the piano, tap dancing—and being asked to display your new skill for evaluation after only a few lessons! Yet how often do we "cover the material" once and assume that it has been taught and that our students should have learned it?

The multiage classroom has some inherent advantages in developing this positive learning climate. Class diversity makes it natural and expected that the learning pace will differ among classmates. This diversity provides fertile ground for students to help each other. It has always been acceptable to ask an older or more experienced person for help. In age-segregated classrooms, children who always have to ask for help are in a position that has a stigma attached to it. Asking for help is sometimes good, whereas needing it constantly changes one's status within the group. In the multiage environment, helping comes naturally. It might begin with older students helping younger ones, but it easily slips into anyone helping anyone. This phenomenon is reported consistently by veteran multiage teachers.

Modeling takes place regularly and often quite incidentally between classmates. Also, as teachers train students to have supportive attitudes toward each other, this climate will likely continue from year to year because a portion of the class remains constant each year. Modeling, helping, and recognizing individual differences among learners will help to make classrooms places where risks are safe and okay. More risks translate to more leaps in learning.

Teasing

One thing that works against children creating a community of learners is teasing. Teasing may be quite prevalent among youngsters, but it grows from a lack of solid self-esteem among community members. Finding ways to abate teasing can help to strengthen the community environment.

The first strategy to abate teasing behavior is to consider carefully the self-esteem of individuals and work to help strengthen that esteem. Many students lack the knowledge of their own gifts and abilities. Identifying and supporting learner strengths, not just academically but in other parts of school life, can help individuals to feel positive about their membership in the community. Having responsibilities in the group, as mentioned earlier, makes community or organizational success something of a personal investment. Many resources are available to teachers through books (Canfield & Wells, 1976; and others), guidance counselors, or community organizations (religious youth groups, scouting, etc.). Overlooking this issue of self-esteem in learners can undermine the best efforts to create a family of learners.

The second strategy to abate teasing behavior is to directly teach children *about* teasing. One multiage classroom where one of us spent enormous amounts of time successfully discussed teasing with primary-age students. Helping children to understand what teasing is, its causes, and its effects on people led to its gradual decline. Eventually, attempts to tease others were met with disapproval by class members who recognized and labeled the undesirable behavior.

A key to the disapproval was the children's understanding that the behavior was rooted in poor self-image and was deliberately hurtful. All students admitted that they disliked being teased and that their motivation for teasing others was selfishness. Students learned alternative strategies for dealing with sadness or fear and for settling interpersonal disputes. Selected class members were trained to act as mediators and proceed through a series of questions and exercises at a classroom table, sometimes dubbed the "peace table." This mediation served other disputes besides teasing.

The end result of all these efforts was that incidents of teasing eventually became rare. Generally, when one did occur, it was initiated by a newer member of the community who was less familiar with classroom rights and responsibilities. These attempts were met with both disapproval and reprimand by more experienced community members, who informed the violator that "we don't *do* that here." After a great deal of effort on the teacher's part, kindness became a mainstay of the culture in this ethnically diverse classroom in which all students qualified for free or reduced lunch. Parents later reported that these new strategies spilled over to the home (there were 16 sets of siblings in this classroom), where sisters and brothers treated each other better.

Attitudes and Actions That Divide the Community

For many, the most frustrating part of being a multiage teacher is the structures and traditions that continually work against the community of the classroom. One district, for example, had such a long-standing tradition with field trips that they could not readily bend to have individual multiage classes go on field trips together. The first year, members of one class attended different field trips with their respective "grade levels" instead of with their class.

This situation was unacceptable to both the students and the teachers. The value of a field trip is partially tied up in the common experiences from which the community can jointly draw, in future lessons as well as in personal memories. Some negotiating with district personnel was eventually rewarded with multiage classrooms being permitted to choose the field trips they would attend. Similar issues came up with the school lunch program, where the lunchroom personnel found it difficult to reorganize their record keeping by some method other than grade level. Still other grade-level programs, such as "drug awareness" or "family-life education," were designed by nonschool personnel who had little or no knowledge of school reforms. Some of these outside programs and the people who taught them found it difficult to be flexible, and they did not want children of mixed grades to attend.

"The perception has been that we are actually two classes, two grade levels, and not one class! This has begun to improve after much fuss from us. For example, 'Uh-oh. Here comes the multiage group into the assembly. Should they sit with the first grade or the second grade?' Ugh. As the program met with success and the children were actually learning, the staff began to view the program in a more accepting light."

—Marybeth Phelps and Gloria Morrison
Danielson, CT

Box 5-3

In another school, where an outside program was offered on dental health, toothbrushes and other materials were to be provided to all first graders. Multiage teachers had to advocate that *all* children in the multiage primary classrooms needed information about dental health and should receive sample toothbrushes. After some persuasion, the facilitators provided toothbrushes to all primary-age students in multiage classes so that class members could learn about good dental care together.

Each of these situations presents challenges and obstacles that, though annoying, are not impossible to overcome. As with any change, individuals need education of their own to understand school changes concerning their own areas of expertise. After personal contact and time to adapt, most professionals have found ways to work with diverse classrooms. The same issues often arise with special-area teachers, such as those for art, music, and physical education. (For more information on special-area teachers, see Part II.)

> "The idea of making learning in the classroom fit the students instead of making students fit the learning made us believers in individualized instruction and the multiage configuration."
>
> —Barbara Kidwell and SueBeth Arnold
> Findlay, OH

Box 5-4

Summary

If there's one thing we hope readers remember from this chapter, it is that discussions of curriculum and instruction alone are not sufficient without also examining the context or environment in which they are taking place. Students spend 6 or more hours a day in school, which is a significant number of their waking hours. While these students are in our charge, we are responsible for not only the traditional academic concerns but the humane ones as well. People learn and function better when they are in an environment where they are accepted and feel a sense of ownership. Teachers and schools can influence those environments to maximize the learning potential—for all kinds of learning—that can take place.

Once our children grow up and find jobs or careers, they will still need to learn and will be able to learn many new things. Skills like math and writing can be remediated, improved, or built upon for the specific needs of their jobs. But how do we remediate their abilities to get along with others? In school, we must not ignore the parts of their education that are vital in their youth: being kind and productive human beings. Children don't come to school with only their minds and leave their spirits at home. In school, we have the whole child, and we should do our best to educate that whole child.

Clipboard

The following are questions to ponder from chapter 5.

1. When you say *curriculum*, what exactly do you mean? How do others in your school think of this word?

2. What are some classroom traditions that you practice? That your school practices? Are there some you'd like to initiate?

3. Do you honestly think that the students in your class can readily take risks? Are there ways to enhance risk taking?

4. Can you think of a time in your life when you learned a great deal from a mistake? Are mistakes valued in your class? Perhaps the value of mistakes would be a good discussion topic in your room (start with yourself as a model.)

5. Do you believe that all your children have special gifts? Perhaps making a list would help you to remember what skills need identifying and reinforcing.

6. Were you teased as a child? Perhaps sharing with students could lead to a discussion about teasing and its effects.

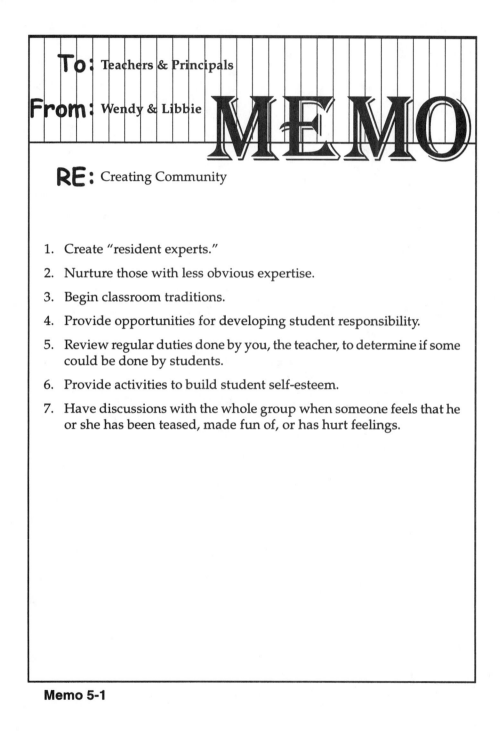

To: Teachers & Principals

From: Wendy & Libbie

MEMO

RE: Creating Community

1. Create "resident experts."

2. Nurture those with less obvious expertise.

3. Begin classroom traditions.

4. Provide opportunities for developing student responsibility.

5. Review regular duties done by you, the teacher, to determine if some could be done by students.

6. Provide activities to build student self-esteem.

7. Have discussions with the whole group when someone feels that he or she has been teased, made fun of, or has hurt feelings.

Memo 5-1

CHAPTER 6

Designing the Multiage Curriculum

● ●

Early in this chapter it should become obvious that all our recommendations about curriculum in multiage classrooms will work in other child-centered, meaning-centered classrooms as well. In fact, as we have discussed in Part II, our advice for teachers preparing to become multiage involves self-assessment of teaching styles and movement toward child-centered practices (see Memo 3-3).

Simply put, if you are treating students as individuals and moving away from the industrial paradigm of "everyone gets the same" and the traditional transmission model of teaching (where one person does nearly all the talking and teaching), then you are meeting the needs of any diverse setting, which can include multiage, groups with varied abilities, and classes with inclusion students. The bottom line is that *more child-centered teaching with DAP meets individual needs and conforms schooling to the needs of children rather than trying to conform children to the structures or convenience of schools.*

This chapter will address designing curriculum: the considerations that enter into planning, including expectations of teachers from a variety of sources; multiple intelligences and multiple ways of knowing to meet the needs of a diverse group of students; guidelines from learned societies; and working within the parameters of graded courses of study and other external expectations.

Considerations:
What Do We Teach in the Multiage Class?

We have already defined curriculum and instruction as highly interrelated, and we have also gone on record with the strong belief that multiage teachers should begin to move toward more child-centered curricula. However, decisions still need to be made about what to teach.

Decisions about content come from a variety of sources and rarely from just one. These sources include district expectations, community considerations, school-based decisions, learned societies, students, and teachers. One constituency should not make these decisions without regard for the others. However, when it comes to nuts-and-bolts decisions that affect the everyday life of the classroom, decisions should be made by those closest to the children—teachers—taking all the factors into account.

District Expectations

Many larger school structures—whether they are by district, county, state, province, or some other variation—offer guides and courses of study in an attempt to organize and coordinate the scope of topics to be taught. Although these guides can be very useful in deciding what should be taught, a quality guide is deliberately written in broad and general terms so that teachers can carry out the ideas in a variety of ways. Guides are just that—*guides*. They do not replace responsible professional decision making, and they cannot be held accountable for the quality of teaching.

Many well-written guides are organized by strands or larger topics, such as *People and the Earth; Cultures of Peoples; Structures of Governments; Matter and Energy;* or *Living Things.* Often, broad topics such as these cross age levels, with gradually more complex concepts arising at successive levels. Although such guides are also typically organized by grade levels, guides are not *mandates;* therefore, flexibility is inherent in the structure. Teachers are often led to believe that these guides are meant to be for more than the purpose of guiding. Where this is the case, midlevel administrators who are the instructional leaders in the school should clarify flexibility and how to make use of it.

After all, if *guides* were *mandates*, then that would be precisely like the assembly line: All first graders get *this*, and all second graders get *that*. No good educator really believes that children should be treated the same as cars on an assembly line. If they do, we would suggest some adjustments in personnel. If, in preparing for multiage classrooms, teachers and administrators discover that district guidelines and courses of study are outdated, unacceptable, or otherwise in need of revision, then plans can be made to articulate curricular expectations among the faculty at the school level, such as meetings of teachers of similar-age children to outline logical ways of proceeding.

Community Considerations

Often, local issues, culture, geography, and other community concerns are incorporated into curricular decisions. For example, areas with issues of economic pressures and environmental safety might study the issue as part of science and social studies education. Traditionally, students have some focused study of local and state (or provincial) history and geography. Sometimes parents and community leaders feel strongly about including issues they value, such as substance-abuse education, family-life education, understanding child abuse, or other issues in the news. Parent and community input should be taken into account when making decisions. This is not to be confused with community or parent groups micromanaging schools, which is educationally inappropriate. Although outside input is highly valued, educational expertise lies within the school walls. School personnel are held accountable for decisions, educated to make those decisions, and should be making informed and responsible choices. Of course, all this presumes a well-educated professional staff that keeps up with current trends in theory, practice, and school law through staff development, continued education, professional journals, and the recommendations of learned societies.

Learned Societies

Every discipline has a society that governs accreditation to ensure quality programs consistent with current theory and practice. Because teaching is a profession, new knowledge is constantly being added to the professional repertoire. Today, in addition to research done at colleges and universities, teachers have become researchers as well, all in an effort to provide best practices for students. The continuing use of timeworn practices, regardless of research and updated guidelines of learned societies in reading, mathematics, science, social studies, and early childhood development, is simply educational malpractice. Malpractice is not acceptable with physicians, nor is it acceptable in schools. Every educator is charged with the responsibilities of lifelong learning and keeping up with current trends.

Each learned society publishes guidelines that synthesize the best practices to date for education. Based on mountains of research, such guidelines can serve as vehicles to assess and possibly update local courses of study or curriculum guidelines, and they can also be used for school-based program evaluation. These include guidelines for DAP, language arts and reading, mathematics, social studies, science, and a synthesis of best practices. All these are summarized in Appendixes G and N through Q.

Students

Currently, one of us in engaged in a monumental research study with colleagues in northeast Ohio looking at students' opinions of the various assignments given in school. Students from early childhood through college level are being interviewed about what educational experiences they feel they learned the most from over the years. Conversely, they are also being asked what assignments or experiences yielded little if any learning value.

Preliminary results from all age groups point to student choice in learning as a key element in making learning memorable and meaningful. *Choice* emerges from every interview, from little children to grown-up students. When students have input into what they study or the manner in which they study it, they believe they learn more. As one college-age student said, citing an independent study project in a high school class, "I learned that I could learn!" This student's realization that she could control her learning, and that learning doesn't come just from teachers and school, was a lesson for life.

We are not advocating that students do anything they want anytime they want. Quite the contrary, for even *choosing* is a skill that is learned over time and with effort. Some students will know less about themselves and their interests than others. Many of us can cite an incident where an interest, perhaps a lifelong one, came into being because of a teacher or other adult who introduced us to something new and wonderful. One of us has a sibling who is an electrical engineer today, and although his interest and aptitude for electronics was inborn, it was his sixth-grade teacher who set the ball rolling when she gave him a simple crystal radio in a soap dish. Sometimes we learn about something we like or are good at because of significant others.

We are advocating that each unit of education at every level take into account the role of student choice and input. Where and when can students study what interests them? How do we provide for further study when students have been "turned on" by something the teacher has introduced? Where do we provide opportunities to create, dream, and have wonderful ideas? Finding ways to allow and promote student choice (as well as helping them to make choices) is an important part of developing lifelong learners.

Having choices and room to grow, create, and innovate is an important aspect of education. One of us once had a job tutoring a Japanese child whose father was in the United States on a 2-year assignment studying cancer at a major research facility. This man, his wife, and their three sons were struggling to get along with little fluency in English and were trying to encourage their children to make optimum use of the opportunity of living in a foreign country.

This man, as a scientist, made some assumptions upon registering his sons in American public schools. He believed that his children would be more advanced than their American age mates. A year later, he was humbled as he compared his children's education in the United States to that in Japan. His conclusion was that although his sons knew more terms and formulas, especially in mathematics, they lacked the understanding to apply them and create. Their prescribed, traditional rote learning had not included choice, creativity, or application of concepts.

His concluding comment was noteworthy as he elaborated on the positive changes he observed in his sons' new abilities. "We [the Japanese people] are so good at taking other people's ideas and making them better, smaller, and less expensive," he said thoughtfully. "But did you notice that we never *invent* anything new?" Clearly, he equated the lack of invention he perceived in his own culture with the nature of its educational system.

His compliment to American education aside, students need to *learn* choices and have opportunities to be in charge of their own learning—so that they can "learn that they can learn," as our interviewee said. This point has hit home for both of us, as we have been "host families" to graduate students from the former Soviet Union at Kent State University. In getting to know these individuals and helping them through the necessary culture shock that almost anyone experiences while living in a foreign country, we have noticed that one of the overwhelming issues for these students is the number of opportunities to make choices. Coming from a political structure where there was little or no room for choices or decisions of any kind, these students are overwhelmed (and express this articulately) by being forced to make so many choices on a regular basis—shopping for personal clothing and school supplies; selecting from restaurant menus, banks, bank account types, and university class schedules; and myriad others. This can be frightening even for *adults* who are inexperienced at such things.

In designing curriculum, one element to consider is the students. Remembering that good curriculum allows some room for student choice, creativity, and personal independent investigations will make for a successful program. This element of a quality curriculum cannot be ignored if we are to create lifelong learners.

Teachers

Teachers are closest to children and are charged with the ultimate responsibility for what happens within classroom walls. Using all the factors we have outlined, teachers are faced with decisions about exactly what will happen in the classroom. No matter what model of education is subscribed to, teachers are still the primary instructional leaders in a classroom. Their management and nurturing of their learning environment creates (or kills) enthusiasm for learning; stimulates (or stifles) a sense of wonder and awe of the world; and sows (or buries) the seeds for lifelong learning, whatever the subject matter. Teachers are ultimately responsible for learning.

Teachers are further accountable for the best learning for each student in their charge. Wendy once wrote a motto for a fellow teacher to hang on her wall. The teacher was a talented, creative individual, but she worried more about what subsequent teachers would think of her students than was sensible or logical. We have included the motto here; feel free to use it.

Wisdom for Constructivist Teachers

It is my job, as a teacher, to get to know my students—academically, socially, and culturally—and, starting where they are, to take them as far as I can in the time we have together, taking into consideration both learning and developmental factors. It is *not* my job to prepare my students for the mythical expectations of a future classroom or an assembly-line model of schooling. Children cannot be made to fit into preconceived structures of schooling; rather, schooling needs to adapt to suit the realities of growing and developing children.

Figure 6-1

Multiple Intelligences and Multiple Ways of Knowing in the Multiage Classroom

Good teachers and other educators have long known that children's talents and gifts come in many forms. Typically, learners whose strengths lie in language arts (reading, writing, listening, and speaking) and mathematics are the most successful in schooling. Yet other gifts, even ones we label ingenious, exist but are often ignored. The arts, for example, have been less central in schools.

Gardner (1993) and others have articulated the sentiments long felt by teachers that different kinds of intelligences exist. Gardner's pluralistic view of intelligence recognizes many "different and discrete facets of cognition, acknowledging that people have different cognitive strengths and contrasting cognitive styles" (p. 6). Gardner's categories of intelligences continue to evolve; they currently include musical intelligence, bodily/kinesthetic intelligence, logical/mathematical intelligence, linguistic intelligence, spatial intelligence, interpersonal intelligence, intrapersonal intelligence, and, a recent addition, intelligence termed "the naturalist" (dealing with flora and fauna and patterns in nature and species). Since information on multiple intelligences is readily available from Gardner's books, workshops, and even instruments that assess these strengths in students (e.g., M.I.D.A.S.; Shearer, 1996), we will not elaborate on the theory here but only discuss how it applies to multiage classrooms.

Multiple has become a popular word as educators deliberately stray from the industrial paradigm. Others have written about *multiple ways of knowing* in classrooms (Clyde, 1994; Leland & Harste, 1994), which complement multiple intelligences. The practice of multiple ways of knowing recognizes that, since learners vary in their intelligences, they also vary in how they come to understand concepts and information, the value they attribute to different knowledge and information, and the ways in which those understandings manifest themselves. For example, Leland and Harste (1994) advocate that time and space need to be given to multiple sign systems instead of relying on language and math, the dominant forms of knowing in schools, as prerequisites of other knowledge. Other sign systems, such as art, music, and movement are forms of knowing that are better suited to many of the students we teach. Even students' understanding of what they read can sometimes be expressed better in other sign systems (see chapter 7 for some specifics on strategies).

As educators, we make the best use of multiple intelligences and multiple ways of knowing when these concepts are integrated throughout classroom experiences in the curriculum. Various modes and models are utilized regularly to present, practice, experience, manipulate, apply, and assess concepts. As with the other ideas that have been presented about multiage classrooms, all the *m* words (multiage, multiple intelligences, and multiple ways of knowing) help to personalize education, meet individual needs, and teach in a variety of ways to make authentic connections between the world of school and the real-life world. All these notions seek to tie student needs and their learning to the long-term goals for schooling, as we discussed in Part I.

In our discussion of curriculum in the multiage setting, these terms will surface from time to time as connecting threads, as our focus shifts from meeting the needs of school structures to meeting the needs of learners. Figure 6-2 summarizes the considerations for curriculum planning to satisfy a variety of constituents.

Materials in the Multiage Classroom

We are often asked if a multiage environment *costs* more than a grade-level classroom. The answer is decidedly "no," but redistribution of materials and funds for materials may be necessary.

For example, depending on where you live and teach, books and equipment may be treated as the individual property of a particular teacher or program, or, conversely, materials may be shared among classes. As men-

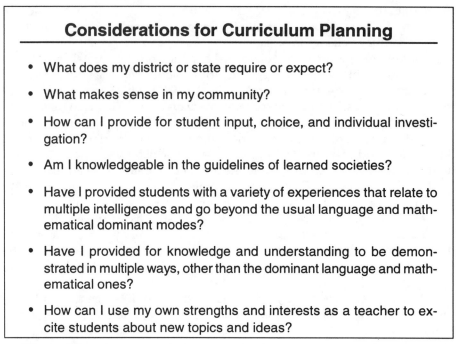

Considerations for Curriculum Planning

- What does my district or state require or expect?

- What makes sense in my community?

- How can I provide for student input, choice, and individual investigation?

- Am I knowledgeable in the guidelines of learned societies?

- Have I provided students with a variety of experiences that relate to multiple intelligences and go beyond the usual language and mathematical dominant modes?

- Have I provided for knowledge and understanding to be demonstrated in multiple ways, other than the dominant language and mathematical ones?

- How can I use my own strengths and interests as a teacher to excite students about new topics and ideas?

Figure 6-2

tioned in Part II, an assessment of what's available may have to be conducted to determine an inventory, noting strengths and needs. Here we list the categories that are necessary to supply the multiage class.

Reading Materials

All classrooms, but especially multiage ones, need a wide variety of available reading materials to suit the needs of the learners and the program. Depending on the area, this need is filled in different ways. As mentioned earlier, some schools share materials schoolwide. This optimizes the use of materials, including books, for the least amount of money. Rather than each multiage classroom having group sets of popular picture books and novels, for example, the school media center might house all book sets for classroom checkout, or each group of multiage teachers may have a central storage unit used for check-out.

Some schools have successfully diverted funds intended for textbook replacement in cases where teachers or teams of teachers have opted not to use new textbooks. In some cases this was a relatively easy process, and in other cases it was a political battle that had to be won for all the classes that wished to spend their money in different ways. Sometimes local policy or law dates back to pre–media center and pre-Internet days, when the purchase of new texts was quite a privilege. Today, individual teachers and schools need more choices in how monies for materials are spent.

Diverted textbook monies have been used, for example, to enhance the school library collection. The sum of money used for one year of one textbook replacement can nicely embellish the school library collection. Another way to fund the school or classroom library is through publishers' book clubs. When students purchase inexpensive books, teachers are awarded credits to spend on available titles. These credits add up quickly and can help even new teachers build significant collections for classroom use.

Other schools have sought external funding for enhancing book collections. Parent-teacher organizations, community service organizations, and business partners are all possible sources to tap for reading materials. Each school and teacher will best know the local resources that may provide needed funds and direct donations. Another popular strategy is the schoolwide book fair. Many bookstores participate in book fairs, where students and parents can shop at regular retail rates that provide payoffs to the school that it can use to purchase new titles.

All in all, several different considerations are necessary for the individual classroom:

- A good media center or library, available either in the classroom, the school, or the local community, with materials that vary in interest, genre, and level of difficulty.

- Sets of four to eight multiple copies of picture books (fiction and nonfiction), novels, and poetry books for small-group study. These will serve both specific content-area study and literature circles.

- Electronic sources such as the Internet and the World Wide Web.

- "Big books" for classes of 5- to 10-year-olds can serve larger groups, both for teaching reading (see chapter 7) and content-area study. Many classes construct their own "big books" as part of class activities, which are then saved and used again when needed.

- Student-produced books and materials supplement even the best collections, because child-authored, school-published fiction, nonfiction, and poetry serve as models and incentives for other students. Students *love* reading the work of other students. (Kasten, 1991)

- Lots of paper (lined and unlined) for different kinds for writing, charts, graphs, art, and book and report covers.

Consumables

Many classrooms have traditionally used consumable published materials of various types, such as workbooks and student journals. Published consumables are expensive and should be carefully evaluated according to the cost effectiveness of the items. Some publishers, for example, offer attractive student journaling booklets, but their prices should be compared with the cost of purchasing spiral notebooks in quantity, which may contain more paper per booklet and may be more versatile.

Some schools have reevaluated traditional workbooks and decided that the same skills or practice could be accomplished better or more cheaply by other means. Saving even a few hundred dollars by comparison shopping might allow you to buy several small-group novel sets or a dozen new titles for the library.

Other popular consumables include the wide variety of black-line masters for reproduction. Again, each item should be considered for value. Are all pages of the reproducible book worthwhile? Generally, in our own experiences, reproducibles geared to content-area study, such as social studies or science, are rarely good enough to warrant the expense. However, other reproducibles, such as puzzles, games, science observation log sheets, or assessment items for portfolios, might be useful. Each item should be carefully evaluated to maximize classroom thriftiness.

Mathematics Materials

Math will be discussed more in its own chapter, but there are certainly several categories of materials that each classroom will probably want to have available. Manipulatives are the basic tools for helping students to understand the conceptual part of logical and mathematical thinking. Not all classrooms need their own personal manipulatives, but there will certainly need to be ample sets in a location accessible to all teachers. Other materials might include children's literature dealing with math concepts (Whitin & Wilde, 1992, 1995), instruments for weighing and measuring, substances to weigh and measure (e.g., sand, water), blocks, instruments for telling time, and art paper (for making origami forms and other shapes). Some of these items might be commercially produced, and others might be of the more homespun variety. For example, a very large button jar goes a long way in sorting, classifying, learning set theory, identifying properties of sets, counting, learning fractions, multiplying, and more.

Materials for Content Study

The materials used in science and social studies are not always entirely separate. For example, good maps and charts may be used in both. The well-developed library, especially of nonfiction and historical fiction, will support the many topics that may be studied in these subjects, whether they are studied separately or as part of a theme study or an inquiry-based model of some sort. Other tools can be shared by classes, such as microscopes, aquariums, cutting and digging tools, boxes to view or display bugs, chemicals, rocks, shells, electrical components, magnets, models, measuring and weighing instruments (the same ones, perhaps, used in math), posters, diagrams, telescopes, and magnifying glasses.

In content-area study, the Internet now plays a huge role. With the expansion of information, textbooks are no longer viable for the most up-to-date information. Surfing the Web for sites sponsored by NASA, museums, national parks, foundations, governments, government agencies, and research facilities yields much more current information than that found in general texts. These electronic sources will supplement the nonfiction book collection available in the classroom, school, or community.

With more teachers teaching thematically in lieu of textbook-based lessons, some schools or districts have invented ways to alleviate some of the burden of preparation that theme teaching requires. In Anchorage, Alaska, the district office offers preassembled materials on a variety of topics that are popular classroom themes. Books (including different genres), nonprint media (films or videos), artifacts (rock collections, shell collection), and more have been collected in a plastic tub, box, or other suitable container. A team of teachers spent time writing theme-teaching ideas to accompany each box, which might span topics like the rainforest, oceans, the tundra, Egypt, and the food chain. The availability of these boxes is advertised like any other media in a catalog, so teachers can request to use the materials for a certain period of time.

Many inventive ways of making the most of monies for materials can be explored in any school or district, as long as cooperation exists among staff members. Some effort early on will save time later so that assembled materials will be well utilized, circulating from class to class instead of spending much of the school year in a closet or on a shelf.

Traditional Reference Books

Many of us grew up using encyclopedias. Though a wonderful resource in the past, these multivolumed tomes have changed. Once these books were the only sources beyond textbooks in schools without libraries or media centers; today encyclopedias have changed and gone electronic. Using encyclopedias in electronic form enables schools to have more different sources available. This is true for other reference books as well, like dictionaries, thesauruses, books of quotations, and biographical dictionaries. Encyclopedias in electronic form serve as a good introduction and an overview of the topic. The overview can help students select an area for focus and point them to sources that provide in-depth information on it.

Technology Tools

As we progress quickly into the computer age, schools are scrambling to make technology available to all students. We have tried to weave the issue of technology through everything we address, as technology becomes an increasing part of everyday life inside and outside the classroom. Incorporating technology into the multiage classroom is important, not just because it is multiage but because it is a classroom of the future. Computers are here to stay, and students in all sorts of classes need to be prepared for the world into which they will grow.

Like the age-old issue of the value of television (Is it good or bad?), computers and the accompanying technology they represent are neither good nor bad but can be used in more productive or less productive ways. Using a computer to do what a pencil and paper can do just as easily isn't particularly innovative or economical. Drilling students in electronic workbook-type drills is a waste of money. Computers should be considered for their more innovative applications.

Word processing is one way that computers can easily be incorporated into instruction and curriculum. *Writer's workshops* (see chapter 7) already call for students to write substantive texts no matter what their age. As anyone who has word processed quickly learns, computers facilitate writing more; revising more readily, with the ability to move entire blocks of text; and editing and proofreading more easily, with spelling and grammar checks. While few classrooms have enough computers for students to use them frequently while writing, most have the resources to enable students to sometimes write directly on-screen.

Research of any kind in the classroom can be enhanced with technology. Whether it's finding information that was previously sought in book-form encyclopedias, contacting experts directly through e-mail, or downloading current photos and information from the Web, the possibilities are exciting. One classroom Libbie visited was studying space. Using the Web site sponsored by NASA, these students were able to access and download current photographs of Mars taken by the Hubble telescope, in addition to text, to add to their reports.

Other classrooms are constructing reports using presentation software. Designing their reports by screens and a story board, students include written text, clip art, sound clips, and charts and graphs that illuminate their findings. Popular software is learned and readily used by students (sometimes when their teachers are still struggling with it). In some places, these multimedia reports have replaced the ones that many of us knew as children.

Computers can be teaching tools as well. With the help of Liquid Crystal Display (LCD) panels or multimedia presenters, innovative teachers are teaching about content topics using similar software or video disc technologies. These formats can demonstrate charts, graphs, photos, and many other possibilities that cannot be done on an overhead projector. Students use the same formats to show what they have learned in independent or group work.

As we enter a new millennium, these technologies are changing almost daily and are therefore too numerous to mention. Clearly, technology is not only an important part of education today but an exciting frontier for teachers and students.

Figure 6-3 summarizes the kinds of materials that should be considered for multiage teaching as well as materials that will not be helpful.

Designing Your Curriculum

Taking into account all the factors we have presented, there are several way to approach designing your curriculum, either as an individual or as a multiage team. Your choice of methods will depend to a large degree on the amount of empowerment that teachers have in a particular district to make their professional decisions. These will be presented, beginning with the one that we consider the most desirable. However, every teaching situation varies. Although many teachers may see their teaching style in the models we have observed, just as many will have to pick and choose the components that will work in a given environment. Remember, there are no recipes. Each teacher must take from our advice what he or she can and adapt it to suit individual needs.

An Inquiry Model

If we were to go back to the classroom, this is how we both would choose to teach. An inquiry model requires a highly confident and skilled teacher. No topics or themes are preplanned before students arrive. Students, along with the teacher, propose and negotiate a context in which all subjects will be integrated. Also referred to as *generative curriculum*, this process is described by Jill Ostrow (1995), who used it in her Oregon multiage primary classroom.

Ostrow and her students decided on the context in which learning would take place. In the case presented, the context was the study of *tropical islands*. Math and science were explored, practiced, and applied as students planned, measured, and built their island atmosphere with materials such as paper

Materials for the Multiage Classroom

What you *don't* need:

1. Textbooks in every subject for every child
2. Workbooks in every subject for every child
3. Books of generic ditto sheets or black-line masters that are not related to other curricula

What you *do* need:

1. Lots of reading materials, on a variety of reading levels and representing a variety of genres, that support both the reading program and content-area study. Sources for these books may include classroom libraries, school media centers, or public libraries.
2. Math manipulatives and materials for the various levels of concepts that will come up, both for focused math teaching and thematic or inquiry study. Many of these can be shared among classrooms: thermometers, play money, clocks, weighing devices, measuring sticks, adhesive tapes, cups, spoons, objects for creating sets, studying "place value" in math, calculators, and so on.
3. A way in which materials can be jointly used by more than one classroom, by centralizing some materials in the school media center or other curriculum materials storage location.
4. Four to eight copies of various books, including picture books, chapter books, and nonfiction, that will be used by small groups throughout the year.
5. Resources in many forms, including traditional reference books, CD-Rom references, and on-line resources.
6. Different kinds of paper and art supplies for writing, drawing, book making, charts, graphs, posters, murals, dioramas, and so on.
7. Notebooks that are bought or made for journaling, note taking, and personal inquiry organization.

Figure 6-3

mache on chicken wire, refrigerator boxes, cardboard rolls from carpet stores, and other common materials treated with flame-retardant sprays (to create palm trees, island dwellings, and other items). Students formed committees to proceed with various duties and responsibilities.

As Ostrow posed pertinent questions to each committee, realistic and interdisciplinary problem solving began. For example, every community, even a tropical island, produces garbage. Their island's "Outrageous Garbage Company," as one group named itself, faced the following questions: Where does the garbage get taken? What time of day will you need to take the garbage out? Who will take it out? How will our custodian know that we took the garbage out? What else in the room needs cleaning? How much of the custodian's time will be saved by our cleaning?

Through skilled questioning, students were faced with dilemmas that they had to solve together. In the course of their solutions, reading, writing, listening, speaking, negotiation, mathematical, and logical concepts all came into play, in addition to issues of science (waste management), social studies (members' roles and monitoring them), health (proper disposal of wastes), and so on.

For any teacher, this type of teaching poses management and assessment challenges. Teachers who choose an inquiry model need a firm grasp of the developmental progression of skills in language arts and mathematics. Some sort of record keeping is maintained to document student growth as well as the nature and scope of student learning. Teacher resources can help with this process when, for example, published profiles neatly lay out a framework from which to assess student growth (Griffin, Smith, & Burrill, 1995). Often, students participate in the management process in a variety of ways, such as periodic self-assessments that outline what they believe they have learned, or the setting of new goals. In multiage environments, teachers report that students also assist in assessing each other because of their deep and long-term knowledge of each other. More advanced students continually notice new skills emerging in their younger, less developed peers, and they praise the progress as well as bring it to the teacher's attention. Assessment in such an environment is necessarily embedded into everyday experiences in multiple ways.

Inquiry-based learning suits multiage environments. The diverse abilities of class members can be utilized in forming multiage committees who designate jobs or roles based on individual strengths and preferences. Less developed learners are readily mentored into new skills and roles, with more advanced learners as models. The open-ended nature of group study encourages the community's most gifted and advanced learners as well, because of the need for leadership roles and the opportunity for self-initiated endeavors within the topic. In short, no one is bored.

Inquiry-based learning also suits multiple intelligences and multiple ways of knowing. The diverse experiences that take place are more apt to meet individual needs than are more uniform experiences. Inquiry classrooms use a great deal of hands-on experiences, art, and student-led formats that draw on a wide variety of intelligences.

One example from our own teaching days took place in an in-depth study of nutrition, propaganda, and advertising. Having already learned about the nutritional values of foods in conjunction with the needs of the human body, the intermediate-age learners then examined whether nutrition was at the core of television and radio advertising of food and food-related products. Naturally, after examining current ads, students discovered that foods were more likely sold based on the propaganda techniques they had studied, including *transfer, testimonial, bandwagon, plain folks,* and *glittering generalities.* Once students concluded that substantive scientific information was typically excluded from the food product ads they had reviewed, they formed small groups, each of which created its own product and designed its packaging, labeling, and television advertisement.

The conclusion of this line of inquiry was the performance of the television-like ads that students had created for their products. Other class members had to decide, for each performance, if they could determine the propaganda technique being used, and they looked for inclusion of facts about the product. Not surprisingly, most groups chose the technique they had most frequently observed in the media: transfer. In fact, the specific transfer they had concluded to be the most common was to associate products with glamorous and sexy lifestyles.

The entire food and propaganda study appealed to students with a variety of intelligences. Food packaging required artistic and spatial strengths. Many ads featured jingles (musical intelligence). Nearly all projects required some writing (linguistic intelligence), measuring (mathematical intelligence), designing covers and labels (spatial intelligence), and presenting or acting out the ad (linguistic and bodily/kinesthetic intelligences). In terms of assessment by the teacher, evidence of student work was documentable from multiple sign systems, including art, drama, and music. Throughout this project, selected students who did not normally stand out had the opportunity to take the limelight. Often, those whose strengths did not lie in linguistic areas were the most talented actors and composers. This gave those students the opportunity to see themselves differently and more fully as learners, and it gave their classmates a chance to learn their strengths. In fact, one young man whose comedic acting skills were most memorable in this project later became the star in the class play. Opportunities to exert his strengths changed his perception of himself and his image among his classmates. His teacher became informed of his abilities through multiple ways of knowing and could utilize this knowledge for his benefit in future learning and assessment.

A Partial Inquiry-based Model

Not everyone has the permission or confidence to tackle an inquiry model as Ostrow has done. Nonetheless, teachers who feel constrained, to varying degrees, by district guidelines, mandates, or other circumstances can still integrate a good deal of inquiry into their multiage classrooms.

"I think the biggest change in my teaching is that I have hardly any whole-group time compared to when I was a straight grade teacher. The students are almost always working in small groups, pairs, triads, or individually. I find myself each year trusting the students more and more. I have become an expert 'kid watcher' and classroom facilitator. My role has changed in that regard. I am also less nervous about the idea that the child has to be ready for the next grade level. The longer I have taught multiage, the more assured I am that each child will become a reader, writer, thinker, and problem solver when he or she is ready. They will all get there."

—Nancy Norman
Palmer, AK

Box 6-1

The most common manner we have observed for doing this is for teachers to predesign units of study using what is known about the typical age-level interests of the children. Units of study may be determined somewhat by district expectations, with an allowance for either individual students or small groups of students to pursue an area of focus. The teacher supplies the information required by district mandates, perhaps as a miniskills lesson. Students have access to many books and materials as they generate questions about the unit. After immersion in the unit, students choose their inquiry questions and begin their research.

For example, the concept of interdependence of people and places might be required, and students may select famous men and women on whom they will become experts. Although these men and women might be limited to the 19th century, for example, there is still a relatively large list from which to choose an interesting biography to pursue. Or, within a study of interdependence of nature, students might select to learn more about a marine life form and its dependence on other things in nature.

These independent study projects can lead to a variety of outcomes. Some classes have reports written by individuals, pairs, or small groups. Others construct informational books (sometimes a big book) to be shared with younger children, using the knowledge they have gained to design the book, plan graphics to enhance the writing, and even bind the books by hand or by machine. Other outcomes can include games, simulations, drama, multimedia presentations and dioramas. Students in Jackie Robbie's intermediate multiage class in

Colorado studied the Middle Ages; each student learned about something in depth as a result, such as the plague, medieval music, or medieval architecture. The culmination of their study was a presentation in a computer multimedia approach. Using programs such as Hyperstudio, Power Point, and Lotus Free Lance, students included written text, sound, imported and original graphics, and presented their product to classmates in the school computer laboratory.

This type of partial inquiry model can be accomplished in nearly all circumstances, no matter what particular constraints exist. Constructing this model from existing course materials, texts, and graded courses of study is addressed later in this chapter.

> "Our philosophy of student needs has changed from all students learning the same skill at the same time to students learning at their own levels. Assignments are given at many different levels with various expectations. We work with students individually, in small groups, and as a whole group. We use many volunteers in our classroom to give students even more small-group and individual practice. All children need to be challenged in their learning. We recognize that some students will move more slowly and others will move beyond the traditional primary curriculum. We do a tremendous amount of individual assessing. It is our job to motivate, encourage, and challenge each student."
>
> —Sue Beth Arnold and Barbara Kidwell
> Findlay, OH

Box 6-2

The Integrated Thematic Model

Some multiage teachers organize their classrooms around themes that are either teacher-initiated, schoolwide-initiated, or student-initiated. In an integrated thematic model, all or nearly all classroom experiences are integrated into the study of the theme, including reading, writing, literature, mathematics, science, social studies, art, music, and physical education (the latter with the help and cooperation of special-area teachers).

In understanding this model, *theme* is the key word. Unlike a topic, a theme represents a broader concept that has multiple applications into topics. For example, *dinosaurs* is a topic. *Extinction* is a theme or concept, of which dinosaurs might be a part. While the former might focus on information, facts, names of dinosaurs, and the epochs in which they ruled the earth, the latter focus serves to draw connections that make dinosaurs relevant to life today and other areas of study. As the earth has changed, some species have become extinct. Humanity has caused changes on the earth that have resulted in the extinction of species, such as habitat destruction.

Thematic teaching, like inquiry-based teaching, provides opportunities for sustained engagement with interesting concepts and ideas—something that rarely occurs in the teacher-centered industrial model of education (Barell, 1995). Deeper engagement with themes and concepts stimulates higher order thinking and allows for multiple intelligences and multiple ways of knowing for a diverse spectrum of learners. It is also more stimulating for both students and teachers.

Themed units begin in different ways and last varied amounts of time. Sometimes themes begin because of current events (such as during and after Operation Desert Storm, when study of the Middle East became a popular idea). Student interest can begin an area of inquiry; for example, one multiage primary class in a coastal community wanted to learn more about marine mammals and the dangers they face. Sometimes a piece of literature initiates study; for example, a teacher's reading aloud of *Number the Stars* (Lowry, 1989) led to a curiosity about World War II and other international conflicts.

Although it takes practice, it is not difficult to integrate other subjects into the theme of choice. For example, let's assume that a multiage class of children who are very interested in animals, and especially larger animals such as predators, became interested in wolves, mountain lions, coyotes, and other North American predators that once roamed the continent in abundance. Let's say this interest began with a harmless, entertaining story such as *The True Story of the Three Little Pigs* (Scieszka, 1989), which proposes the notion that people are prejudiced against predators such as wolves.

If we were to teach this as a *topic*, we might only study wolves or the food chain. But a thematic approach requires that we examine the larger picture, which in this case is that animals who shared the same place in the food chain as humans competed with us for food in early times, interfered with agriculture, and were viewed as dangerous, harmful (although this concept is disputed), and expendable. Bounties were placed on such animals to ensure their eradication, which resulted in some becoming endangered species.

This theme contains both science and social studies elements. The study of the food chain, the place of predators, the nature and lives of predators, and their habitats are all science topics within the theme. The same predators have affected humans in their environment by frightening early settlers and sometimes interfering with livestock (not, as popular tales suggest, by eating grandmothers, children in red capes, or little pigs in houses made of straw and sticks). The dilemma of competing rights—those of the animals to live, those of the farmers to earn their livelihood—are the debates of social studies education.

Such themes afford ample opportunity to explore mathematical concepts. What was the *time* line when all this happened? *How much money* were bounty hunters paid for wolves or mountain lions? *How many* animals were destroyed each year? *What year* were these species placed on the endangered species list? *How long ago* was that? Can we *graph* the decline of the species in this century? Can we also *graph* the results of their gradual return? How can we use the Internet to find out where radio-collared wolves are living at this precise time? Before wolves were released into Yellowstone National Park, rangers had to know *how many square miles* it takes to support one pair of wolves. *How much* is that? *How many* wolves could Yellowstone support? *How many* deer does a wolf eat in 1 year? What else does a wolf eat? How do we know for sure what wolves eat? Students might plan and *calculate costs* for a field trip to the nearest zoo or other wildlife facility that is involved in the reintroduction and captive breeding of an endangered species. They might even investigate the *funding* of such facilities.

We can similarly develop language arts skills throughout this unit. Students might write for information from the International Wolf Center (Ely, Minnesota) and other institutions for information on wolves and their restoration. Students might compose debates between the naturalists' and farmers' points of view on restoring wolves to public lands. Students might interview, by phone or by World Wide Web, scientists and science educators who work with wolves and other predators. Students might assemble literature and nonfiction on wolves and might evaluate some of that literature for scientific accuracy. They might compare and contrast multiple resources that provide similar information on predators. They might write and illustrate books about their favorite predators for younger students or future students to enjoy.

> "I have changed considerably as a multiage teacher. By eliminating textbook use, I have become more creative. I also am more aware of and concerned about what skills students are actually learning, instead of letting the textbooks do it. I have students do more comprehensive projects involving many subjects and more time."
>
> —Jackie Robbie
> Colorado Springs, CO

Box 6-3

The Partial Thematic Model

Some teachers feel too constrained by local, state, or provincial rules or perceived rules to be comfortable teaching completely thematically. Yet they appreciate the rigor and opportunity for sustained engagement that a thematic unit affords. In these situations, teachers continue to keep certain areas of the curriculum separate, such as reading and math, but they find extended periods of time in their schedule (all afternoon, 3 afternoons per week) to teach thematically. In our experience, these units are still theme- rather than topic-based. Although some language and math-related activities are included, their schedules still feature separate times for intensive reading or math instruction.

We have had opportunities to observe settings like this, and many teachers have found this model comfortable. Often, they feel this model is a compromise between their sense of the expectations and accountability placed upon them and their need to bring their teaching closer in alignment with cutting-edge practices. For other teachers, this model serves as a transition to more inquiry-based or entirely thematic teaching.

Classrooms involved in such a model would look fairly similar to the one mentioned earlier if one were to visit during the time period designated for themed study. Areas of study still feature universal concepts that can easily be applied to other learning. Instruction proceeds with a combination of some larger group lessons (such as introducing the concept of the food chain and where predators are on that chain), learning centers with meaningful sustained activities that enhance content and skill development (a math center for graphing statistics; a computer center for searching the Internet for information for reports; a listening center with related literature on audiotape; an art center where students design and make a mask of a predator with an array of provided materials; a writing center where students work on their personal books about predators), and individual projects.

Sometimes individual projects in such a setting are student-initiated. At other times, teachers may require students to find a related topic of personal interest for in-depth examination. Often, contracts between teachers and students for individuals, pairs, or small groups provide project parameters, due dates, and basis for later assessment.

> "We both feel that our philosophy of teaching and of children have not changed. We have always worked hard at meeting the needs of every child at his or her own level. We do feel that we continue to implement ways to provide the best environment for all our children to work together. Our themes have broadened to accommodate a two-year curriculum."
>
> —Marybeth Phelps and Gloria Morrison
> Danielson, CT

Box 6-4

The Topical Unit Model

The topical unit model is the easiest to implement and one that teachers often try out before attempting more complex models in order to gain a sense of the management. Topical units are, as the name implies, on topics. Popular topics include the rainforest, the tundra, Australia (or any other country), butterflies, insects, penguins, mammals, the solar system, the sea, endangered species, bears, dinosaurs, the Civil War, and inventions.

The principal difference between a topical unit and a thematic unit is that topical units teach many facts related to the topic; the topic is more typically teacher-chosen; the topic is planned for a finite time period; the subsequent topic is not necessarily related to the one in progress; more teacher-centered instruction is included; and fewer opportunities for flexibility and individual investigations are provided. Typically, teachers repeat a topical unit they have previously taught in a highly similar fashion.

A topical unit, taught in lieu of separate subjects such as science and social studies from published textbooks, is a big step toward more integrated learning. Highly preferable to the artificial delineations of disciplines, topical units are rarely taught all day but generally supplement other teaching, as in the partial thematic model. Often, teachers using this model will integrate selected areas of math and language arts into the topic, such as related spelling words, a novel or picture book related to the topic of study, or writing assignments on the topic.

Figure 6-4 shows a model that was first proposed by Libbie and has been modified by Libbie and Wendy for this chapter. The models are presented in the figure opposite to the order in which they have been discussed in the text, from the most teacher-centered, minimally integrated to the most student-centered, most integrated. The figure lists the models, their definitions, some features, and examples, in order to indicate the possibilities.

Figure 6-5 gives some guidelines for getting started in planning a thematic or topical unit if the process is still somewhat new.

Finding Your Own Model

The models we have shared are based on our many visits to and observations of multiage settings. We are not suggesting that these are the only ways in which to teach. Every teaching situation has unique characteristics, and we cannot possibly anticipate each and every circumstance. Consequently, we hope teachers reading this will be able to use these models to reflect and design their own. At the risk of sounding like a broken record, we remind readers that there are *no recipes*. Nor are there simple things you can buy and plug into multiage classrooms that will substitute for thoughtful, thorough planning and quality teaching.

Curriculum Models

Topical .... Partially Thematic .... Thematic ...... Partially Inquiry-Based .... Inquiry-Based

Somewhat integrated, child-centered .... Highly integrated, child-centered

Definition	A unit of study used part of a day on a topic. Lessons on facts, information concepts, and issues taught in a sequence determined by teacher; may include large- & small-group work. Experiences & activities a combination of teacher-centered & child-centered.	Conceptual or issue-based themes that apply to multiple contexts or topics. May be teacher-initiated when community is new, likely, direction theme takes is dependent on community interest and reactions; seamless between subtopics within theme; may be focal point over entire year or more.	Conceptual unit of study based on district requirements, seamless between subtopics. Usually lasts 9 weeks at least.	Generative curriculum, entirely planned as a result of teacher & student discussion & negotiation, centered around a problem or context, skillful teacher-posed questions with no right answers. Seamless.
Planning	Generally teacher-planned, may be student or teacher choice, most planning in advance of beginning study. Time period more defined.	Some teacher planning may initiate unit, especially seeking resources, including books, people, technology, field trip options, taping of books, finding related media. Flexibility for individual projects, investigations. Written plans may vary from groups & individuals. Content is rigorous, academically intriguing.	Teacher planning by using known student interests, and district requirements. Seeking resources.	Planning focused on assembling materials, productive discussions, flexible to context; written plans vary for groups or individuals. Rigorous.

Figure 6-4

| | Topical .... Partially Thematic .... Thematic ...... Partially Inquiry-Based ..... Inquiry-Based | | | |
	Somewhat integrated, child-centered .... Highly integrated, child-centered			
Continuity	Continuity within unit of study, not necessarily between units of study. Based on district requirements.	Varies, but continues for the duration of the unit, and often subsequent units are offshoots of previous one. Based on district requirements.	Usually follows 2-year cycle in multiage classroom. Some delineation between end of study and next study as dictated by district requirements.	High degree or continuity, few delineations between end of study & next, progress noted by segments of study. Based on district requirements.
Integration	Content-area study such as science & social studies integrated; some math, arts, language arts.	Varies, according to teacher comfort, sense of outside restrictions or limitations, or lack of scheduling conducive to sustained study.	Total, but based on district curriculum.	Virtually total.

Assessment	Students typically assessed on products (worksheets, stories, reports, tests). Might use some authentic assessments, some more traditional.	Varies according to nature of teaching. Might use evaluations of student products (reports, stories, hands-on projects), might include group self-assessment, student self-assessment, peer assessment, or any combination of those. Process might be part of evaluation valuing, social skills of group membership. Most assessments authentic. May use contracts.	Same as inquiry-based.	Highly embedded with instruction & daily activities; may include contracts, group-process evaluation, individual artifacts that demonstrate new skills (stories, reports) self- and peer assessments. Necessarily authentic in nature.
Examples	Dinosaurs, Wolves, Butterflies, Volcanoes, the Rainforest.	Extinction; food chains & the place of humans and other predators; metamorphosis in nature; the changing earth; specialized habitats and their effect on biodiversity and the environment.	Unit on systems—teacher teaches components of systems—students generate questions and determine what type of system to research, such as the solar system or ecosystems.	No formal texts. All areas integrated. Curriculum is negotiated between teacher and students. Extensive individual and small-group research occurs.
Cautions	Can get too cute, lack rigor. Can be superficial. Remember expectations for individuals vary.	Need to relinquish some control to students. May require staff development. Teacher needs to know skills to be integrated into content. Requires communcation with parents.	Can be too teacher-centered. Teacher needs to understand inquiry process.	May not be appropriate for newest teachers. Requires *confident* teacher, administrative support, communications with parents.

Figure 6-4, continued

Getting Started on Planning Thematically

Consider planning a thematic unit with a colleague in order to share resources, ideas, and make better use of planning time.

Gather all kinds of materials related to the theme, regardless of their "level" of difficulty. These might include but are not limited to:
1. Nonfiction trade books
2. Fiction with applicable themes
3. Poetry
4. Folk tales
5. Nonprint media such as films, videos, computer programs, posters, charts, maps
6. Artifacts related to the topics (bones, shells, microscope slides, specimens, chemicals, historical artifacts, old documents, photographs)

Consider what materials might serve to be read aloud to the class, be used as teacher resources, be on display in the classroom library for browsing.

Review the materials.

Decide which materials are best suited to
- large-group lessons
- small-group lessons, learning centers, or cooperative learning groups
- work in pairs or individually

Review graded courses of study to determine which needed skills are suitable to be taught through the theme.

Involve students where possible in constructing posters, diagrams, bulletin boards, decorations.

Plan some lessons or centers, but don't overplan. Allow some flexibility to continue some aspects while disbanding others as experience determines the relative success of each part.

Make introductory lessons that draw upon student knowledge in order to assess what is known before proceeding and that simultaneously serve as review and background for class members less experienced in the topics within the theme.

Assess throughout learning rather than only at the conclusion. Value the processes, such as working together, as part of the assessment in addition to student-produced works.

Figure 6-5

Designing Curriculum With Existing Texts and Guides

The models we described above are based on our long-term observations of multiage classrooms. Even within those models, teachers are accountable for certain kinds of skills, experiences, and outcomes that will need to be woven throughout the topics, themes, or inquiry. Here we'll describe some practices and adjustments that we have participated in or observed.

One multiage teacher of 7- to 9-year-olds who taught partially thematically still felt responsible for the content of the district's adopted texts, even though she was supported in not using them. She reviewed all the materials available to her that would normally have been used in grade-level classes for second and third graders. She outlined the content and skills from both sets of materials the summer before starting the multiage composite 2–3.

One of her first discoveries was that the existing texts and courses of study for grades 2 and 3 overlapped by more than 30%. Third-grade materials spent a great deal of space reviewing concepts that had been presented at the previous level. This was true in her district curriculum guides as well. Most "third-grade" skills or concepts either repeated or built upon those covered in previous books.

Using this information, she laid out the scope of both the content and the skills that she would most likely want to make plans for throughout the year. She organized the skills from least difficult to most difficult. For content, she decided on a logical progression of concepts that could be dealt with through themes. For example, the guides suggested "communities" as a topic for second grade and "structures of governments" for third grade. She decided she could address both topics through her plans to study one ancient culture, which also came up in the district-adopted social studies texts for third grade.

After surveying her class and giving them some options about ancient cultures, the group voted to study ancient Egypt. As this teacher gathered trade books, films, and project ideas for studying ancient Egypt, she also made a study of the ancient Egyptian forms of community and government structure as objectives.

Sometimes teachers use this sort of materials review to do some long-range planning, looking ahead to how units and themes might fit together over a 2- or 3-year period (since they will not have an entirely new class each year). One intermediate multiage teacher knew that his district typically had fourth graders study their state and local history. Fifth graders traditionally learned about national history. Furthermore, he anticipated that knowledge of these topics would be tested on a state-mandated proficiency test targeted at fourth graders.

The first realization in his planning was that *local history* is a subset of *national history*. Consequently, these are not separate topics. Instead of teaching one for an entire year and the other for a subsequent year, he collapsed the two topics and integrated them. History became his topic under the theme "Lessons from the Past." By creating a time line to organize the study, the focus each year was a particular time period (first year, pre-1900; second year, 20th century).

Within this structure, the content was organized around studying the large picture—what was happening in the country—followed by studying the smaller picture—what was happening locally. Since this American teacher taught in a midwestern state, American history from colonial times through Reconstruction was the focus for one year. Embedded into this time line were the particular events, impact, and changes in the part of the United States that eventually became their state. This enabled those students who would be tested as "fourth graders" to be well prepared and also to understand the relationship between state and national events.

Consulting his district curriculum guides, this teacher could meet many objectives that were set out for students in this age group (listed under grade 4 and grade 5 in the documents) as well as ones that would be tested. Some of these included understanding past, present, and future; using time lines; examining and using historical artifacts; recording community changes; raising cause-and-effect questions; conducting interviews about local history; using maps; comparing customs of different ethnic groups; and recognizing the diverse needs of societies with different characteristics.

Students in the younger half of the group would learn their history more chronologically. Students who entered the class in a subsequent year as new "fourth grade" equivalents would study the 20th century before studying earlier times. As long as quality curriculum and instruction are implemented in meaningful and rigorous ways, everyone will learn good history lessons, even if they learn them in a different sequence.

Other teachers handle the distributions on content topics somewhat differently. In a multiage class with 7- to 9-year-olds (grades 2 and 3, traditionally), where second graders had studied dinosaurs and third graders had studied the solar system, teachers noted that these old decisions were arbitrary. There is no educational reason why the solar system study is more suited to 8-year-olds and dinosaurs to 7-year-olds. She decided, as a result, to focus on dinosaurs (as well as other topics) during one year and focus on the solar system the subsequent year in order to avoid repetition of topics. Into these topics were incorporated concepts suggested in the district guide for either or both "grade levels." Using this format, district objectives could be met by embedding them in these areas of focus, such as exploring the nature of changes in scientific discoveries, how the history of a planet (Earth) relates to the history of the living things that thrive at different times, and how scientists learn about matter and energy through tools and exploration. These concepts can be applied to both dinosaurs and astronomy.

Other teachers have described how getting a handle on planning for a multiage curriculum involved working through these processes and decisions with another teacher. Two teachers who were each starting a class of 5- to 7-year-olds accomplished their task together. Their process, as they described it, involved laying out all the curriculum guides, tables of contents from grade-level materials, and developmental checklists (such as those that outline behaviors associated with emergent literacy) on the living room floor. As in the previous example, these teachers melded content, concepts, and skills by deciding on a unit of study as a starting point (assuming subsequent units would grow out of the earlier one by taking student interests into account). A study of the smallest living things on earth—insects—was their starting point. Believing the topic to be of high interest to their age group, they organized the concepts from science (metamorphosis, life spans, adaptations in nature), social studies (communities, the meeting of individual needs, resource use, societies, cause-and-effect questions), and mathematics (relative size, numbers, more than–less than). Other student activities included reading picture books by Eric Carle and poems about bugs, having a classroom ant farm or hatching fruit flies, reading nonfiction sources on all the bugs being studied, writing about their experiences with insects, writing about what they would be learning (in learning logs or theme books), acting out bug stories, and building vocabulary. Thus, objectives in reading, writing, and language development could also be developed through insect study. Even traditional skills, such as letter names and vowel sounds, could readily be developed with words from bug books—there are enough insects to create an alphabet book of bugs: aphids, beetles, caterpillars, dragonflies, earwigs, fleas, gnats, hornets, insects . . . you get the picture!

Planning a multiage curriculum can be a daunting thought at first, but it is a very rewarding experience. The opportunities that the diverse group affords for learning new things, accomplishing projects, and developing leadership in students are different from and more exciting than teaching to age mates. While these attributes might not be clear during planning, the comments of teachers throughout this chapter may better demonstrate the rewards that come with watching students learn from and with each other and then seeing them grow for a longer period of time. Implementing the curriculum will bring out more possibilities for maximizing the dynamic multiage environment.

Clipboard

Planning the Curriculum

1. With whom can I plan?

2. What resources should I consult to meet expectations? How can I keep track of these expectations?

3. Have I read and studied guidelines from learned societies, considering the suggested cutting-edge practices for implementation in my classroom?

4. How can I provide for multiple intelligences and multiple ways of knowing with my students without making the theory into a series of "cute" activities?

5. How can I involve students in planning decisions?

6. What is my level of comfort and expertise with integrated learning? Is one of the models presented appropriate for me?

7. Am I comfortable with the technologies available in my school? Do I understand how to use technology as a tool for learning?

To: Teachers & Principals

From: Libbie & Wendy

MEMO

RE: Planning for an Integrated Curriculum

Planning is different when curriculum is integrated. Making a graphic by subject area can help ensure that you're including everything and meeting course of study objectives. You might design a planning sheet something like this.

Theme Outline

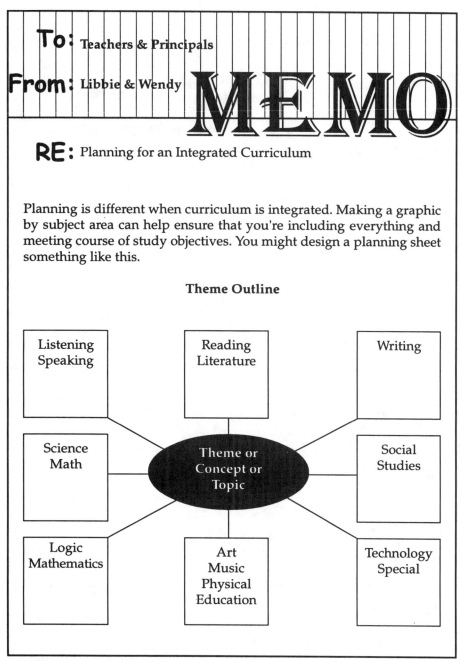

Listening Speaking	Reading Literature	Writing
Science Math	**Theme or Concept or Topic**	Social Studies
Logic Mathematics	Art Music Physical Education	Technology Special

Memo 6-1

To: Multiage Faculty & Principal

From: Wendy & Libbie

MEMO

RE: Assessment and Evaluation of Theme Study

Here's a form that Jodi Kinner and Beth Bonner use to involve students in self-evaluation after a theme. You can adapt this to suit your needs by changing the questions or adding questions, especially for older learners.

Name _____ Theme Topic _____

	Student Comments	Teacher Comments
How were you as a group member?		
How did you keep track of what you learned?		
What kinds of predictions did you make?		
How did you connect this topic to your own life?		
What are three things you discovered about this topic?		
What were your favorite centers? Why?		
What would you change about these centers?		

Memo 6-2

Implementing Your Curriculum in the Multiage Classroom

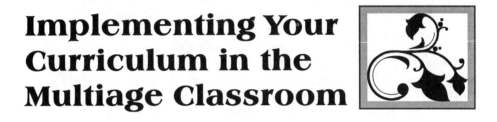

By this time you may have already made some determinations about how you will teach in a multiage setting. However, other practical decisions may still remain, including how (or if) to group students for instruction within the classroom, which strategies work in diverse settings and which do not, and daily or weekly scheduling to make it all happen smoothly. These are the topics we address in this chapter.

Grouping for Instruction in the Multiage Classroom

Lessons for the Whole Class

Sometimes teachers think that having a multiage class means that you can never teach a lesson to the entire class. Quite the opposite—many times it's appropriate to work with the class as a whole. In fact, these times can help to build feelings of community and group identity. As you consider designing your curriculum, here are some ways that large group lessons might occur.

Reading aloud to the whole class is still part of a multiage model (and should be part of every school day for every age group). When selecting a book to read aloud, remember that most children watch adult television programming. Although there are television programs just for kids and others just for adults, there are still many programs and movies that families view together. Not everyone gets the same impression from a movie or show, but everyone can enjoy it and benefit at his or own level.

Also remember that readers of all abilities are accustomed to listening to adult language far above their reading ability. Consequently, choose stories that will hold students' attention regardless of their reading ability. A quality piece of children's literature can be enjoyed by students of various ages, interests, and backgrounds. One of us had a graduate student go to Papua, New Guinea, to teach for 2 years. In her classroom there, students spoke 11 different home languages in addition to being from a variety of ethnicities and nationalities. There were few things that all the children had in common as reference points for comparison when learning a lesson. Yet a truly good story appealed to everyone, no matter what their backgrounds.

Whole-group lessons are part of many multiage classes we have visited. One primary multiage, for example, begins each day with the 5- to 9-year-olds on a carpeted area of the floor. Using a *shared book experience* format (see the strategies section later in this chapter), the teacher reads either a selection of nonfiction related to the themed study, a picture book that represents a folktale or story related to the theme, or a text composed by the class or part of the class in an earlier lesson (*language experience lesson*). These sessions can last up to 45 minutes and include the story as well as many skills that are embedded in the lesson to suit individual needs. A letter-sound relationship might be highlighted for emergent readers in the group, whereas quotation marks might be brought up briefly for fluent readers and writers. Everyone in the group enjoys learning and discussing the day's topic, such as manatees as part of a study of endangered species and the environmental factors influencing their demise. These sessions end by giving directions for the small-group work that follows and reviewing any announcements or expectations for the rest of the day.

An intermediate teacher of 10- to 12-year-olds uses a yearlong theme of environmental studies with many subtopics under it. She teaches many lessons to the entire group, especially at the beginning of a new part of the content. She states that in teaching such a diverse group, she must start further back in her explanations, taking less for granted, giving more examples and time for discussion before building on those concepts. By the time her lesson is completed, she has spanned a larger continuum of learning, realizing that the first part of the lesson is new to some and a review for others. The last part of the lesson is suited to more advanced learners and may go over the heads of others, but it serves as a first encounter to less experienced students. Since all learners need multiple encounters with concepts, this process works well in the long run.

Another teacher of the same age group had an overcrowded classroom of more than 30 pupils. Because of space constraints, no learning centers could be arranged and left for extended periods of time. Student desks, one table, and a sofa were all the room could hold (the teacher even got rid of her own desk to make space). Her innovative use of scheduling led her to arrange her lessons by the week instead of by the day. Hence, all large-group lessons took place on Monday. These would include concepts, miniskills lessons, and anything that might come up for the rest of the week. Large-group lessons set the stage for the rest of the week, which consisted largely of small-group work. Centers were housed in plastic tubs or pails, and student desks had to double as work areas for everything from editing the school newspaper to creating story maps of the reading material related to content study.

Another multiage intermediate teacher relegated all content teaching to students. Committees learned and presented parts of a topic to the entire class, who were instructed to take notes and ask questions of their teaching peers. The committees prepared visual aids to enhance their instruction and homework to follow their presentation. The teaching students were responsible for assigning and grading the homework. Students of all ages in the class thus developed teaching and oral presentation skills as well as confidence.

In any age group, there are appropriate times to have the class together as a single group. The degree to which this is used varies as much as any other aspect of one's individual teaching style.

Small Groups

Small groups work well in diverse settings. Sometimes students with similar needs or strengths are grouped for a period of time. Students who need help with place value, for example, might be grouped for a few days or weeks to strengthen their understanding of it. This *developmental grouping* lasts until the need is fulfilled. Similarly, most advanced students in math might be grouped for some challenge or for more advanced study of mathematics. In this way developmental grouping meets the needs of students at any place on the spectrum.

Grouping across abilities is very common in multiage classes. Placing students with different abilities and strengths at the same center or in the same group helps more advanced learners in that particular concept to become leaders, and less advanced learners in that particular concept can benefit from the models. Since this type of grouping cannot be done in grade-level classrooms, it is important to make good use of the diverse setting to spur more learning. This is the notion of the "zone of proximal development" and has powerful learning potential.

The opportunity to teach other students is an extremely powerful feature in groups that are deliberately mixed. Students proficient in a particular skill have an opportunity to review that skill with a less proficient student, causing an awareness and a synthesis of their own learning on the subject.

This feature of multiage environments is one of its best benefits and should not be overlooked in planning.

"Upon entering my classroom, you would first notice 'hello' written in five different languages on the outside of the door, and a sign that says 'Come into our beautiful room, come and find us,' written by one of my students. Student-generated environmental print is on the walls, shelves, desks, and chalkboard. Depending on the time of day, children could be working individually at centers or at a cluster of desks (they can choose where to sit), busy with an activity related to our theme. This may be in a small group facilitated by me or receiving direct instruction as a whole group. The environment is definitely not quiet."

—Jodi Kinner
Iowa City, IA

Box 7-1

For example, one primary multiage class has learning centers structured for mixed ages in reading, writing, art, math, listening, and computers. In the listening center and the computer station, the teacher ensures that there is at least one student placed there whose knowledge of the equipment enables the experience to run smoothly, without technical glitches. The teacher, then, does not have to deal with mechanical issues when her time is better spent giving small-group or individual attention.

For centers that have specific directions for an activity (art, math), a student who has finished using the center is required to give instructions to arriving class members before moving on to the next activity. Thus, the class members who completed the task reviewed the material and got an opportunity to explain it in clear language. Arriving students received instructions without teacher intervention being necessary.

Sometimes one center, such as writing or reading, was so ongoing that the instructions there were nearly always the same. Students at the writing center worked on their writing at their own individual pace and level but wrote on a similar topic (such as endangered animals). Expectations for products were in keeping with the best work that any individual was capable of, and the students knew well their own strengths. The presence of better writers at the writing center provided models for newer writers as well as a resource for occasional questions. Less experienced writers worked harder in the presence of more experienced ones.

At other times, students can be *grouped by interest*. For example, a group may read the same novel, share an interest in poetry, or work together on a project. Such a group can include students of more similar or less similar abilities, depending upon the circumstances; either is appropriate, depending on the project or task at hand.

Small groups are common in a diverse setting because of their inflexibility and efficacy. Many types of small groups can be used at different times. Figure 7-1 displays some different kinds of small groups that may be used (and perhaps there are some we haven't even thought of!).

Pairs

Sometimes the best plan is to have students work in pairs. Working with one other person means that no one can remain inactive. The combination takes advantage of the "zone of proximal development" (Vygotsky, 1978) when two heads can do better than one. Even students who are fairly similar in ability or experience will challenge each other when directions or decisions have to be discussed. Each will benefit from the other's perspective and understanding.

Adult learners make good use of pairing. For example, how many times can you think of something you explored or learned with a friend? Maybe one of you is better at taxes, and you worked out some income tax forms together. Perhaps it was primarily one friend who taught you to play golf or racquetball, took you to your first square dance or aerobics class, or suggested you take a class together on low-fat cooking. Whatever the situation, learning with one other individual is safe, comfortable, and very effective.

Sometimes it will suit teacher goals to pair a student with someone highly similar. At other times, pair members may be somewhat or even highly disparate in experience, depending on the goal of the lesson or activity. Most students enjoy working in pairs. Members of the pair monitor each other. Individuals are less likely to slip by without understanding the task at hand. *Paired reading* and *written conversations* are two popular strategies that make use of pairing and will be discussed later in this chapter.

Triads

Teachers of older students (10 and up) sometimes insist that *three* is the best way to group students. According to these teachers, triads have an advantage that is lacking in pairs—to stay "on task" rather than socialize. These teachers insist that in triads, "off-task" socialization is minimized and more work gets done.

Even in younger classes, occasions may arise when trying out certain lessons in groups of three would be a worthwhile experiment. Different group-

Grouping Patterns

Type	Size	Reason/Description	Examples
Whole Class	All class members	Sometimes there are concepts that need to be known by everyone. Sometimes the community needs a sense of togetherness. Sometimes you can teach a concept or idea or present an assignment, but execution of it and follow-up will vary by ability or age.	Reading aloud to class Classroom meetings Introduction of new unit and brainstorming topics & ideas Author's chair Announcements Shared book experience Sustained silent reading
Small Groups Needs group	3+	Teacher-initiated, led to meet developmental needs and teach a particular skill. Meets until objective is met. Similar abilities.	Grouping emergent readers to ensure they know alphabet Grouping for math to practice counting Introducing an advanced skill to more advanced learners needing challenges
Child-initiated group	3+	Child-initiated. Children make a valid request to work on something. Makes use of zone of proximal development. Various abilities, perhaps.	Several students ask to write a book or play together. Several students ask to study sharks on their own

Figure 7-1

Cooperative group	3–5	Teacher-structured and -initiated but not led with specific goal or objective. Makes use of zone of proximal development. Various or similar abilities.	Problem solving in math Creating an excitement map based on class story Asked to design a community for social studies & math Committee for class play
Project group	3–5	Teacher or student-initiated, not teacher-led. Students collaborate on projects related to a theme, read a book in order to incorporate hands-on learning and application. Various abilities, usually.	Asked to create a product, package, & design commercial to advertise Learning about a country or regions & designing and executing mural, diorama, or skit to show what they've learned
Book group	3–5	Reading together enables various abilities in members, creates a special group experience, builds vocabulary, causes deeper engagements with books. Varied abilities usually, but sometimes similar. Teacher- or student-initiated, student-led.	Literature circles Book clubs
Pairs	2	Working in pairs is comfortable for students. Easy to take risks. Requires participation of both, makes use of zone of proximal development. Varied or similar abilities.	Written conversations Problem solving Coauthoring works, reports
Individuals	1	Student- or teacher-initiated. Sometimes individuals have personal interests and agendas to pursue. Creates good sense of independence and confidence. Helpful for assessment and portfolio evaluation.	Independent contracts and independent study

Figure 7-1, continued

ing patterns are better suited to certain groups of children, teachers report. Also, the patterns and systems that may have been successful at one time are sometimes unsuccessful with a different mix of students. Teachers need a good repertoire of systems to meet the needs of various situations.

Individual Work

Every multiage classroom we have visited has provided time for students to work alone, perhaps on individual investigations. Typically, these are parts of the larger theme in the classroom, but sometimes they are spurred by other events. An addition of a new wing to a school stirred one young girl's curiosity about architecture. Her teacher arranged for a visit with the architect who was designing and overseeing the project. The visit was exciting for the student and caused her to want to read nonfiction books about architecture and engineering. No one else in her class expressed interest in this topic, but she pursued it nevertheless with the support of her teacher.

Sometimes individual students negotiate contracts for independent study with the class teacher. The contract usually contains some parameters as well as choices that need thought and planning before starting the study. Such a contract can be helpful for assessment when the study is completed and can even include evaluation criteria appropriate to the age and ability of the learner.

Some multiage teachers make use of a great deal of individual work. One teacher we interviewed keeps an Individualized Educational Plan (IEP) on every student, much as is done in the United States for students qualifying for special services. This plan outlines periodic goals as well as objectives for meeting them. These plans help this teacher to keep track of individuals and their progress and ensures that no one is forgotten in the business of everyday life at school.

Individualization has an important place in multiage classrooms, but that place varies as much as teacher styles do, and it manifests itself in many ways. Again, there are no recipes here, only a plethora of ideas from which to construct the multiage learning environment.

Strategies That Work in Multiage Settings

The theme of hands-on, developmentally appropriate experiences and child-centered approaches will permeate this section (for reasons which should by now be obvious). Where strategies are more complex than can be thoroughly explained here, references will be cited for further reading. This section is divided into literacy strategies and general strategies, although there is some overlap.

Literacy Strategies

Literacy is one of our areas of specialty. Wendy is a former reading teacher and teaches with the literacy faculty at her university. All the strategies listed here are constructivist, whole language ones, since strategies of this sort allow students to work at their own levels. All these strategies are appropriate for nonmultiage classrooms and represent sound, cutting-edge practices. We will indicate whether each strategy is suited to primary grades (K–3), intermediate ones (3–6), or any age level. (The overlap is deliberate.)

Also, since we aren't talking about grade levels in school, it's also not appropriate to talk about grade levels in reading and writing. Here we will use the three categories used by New Zealand schools. They are as follows:

1. *Emergent—Making a Start*

The emergent reader (coded as *em* in the following descriptions) is learning about books and their function. This reader shows an interest in books and in being read to; may discuss the stories with others; can make some predictions about what will happen when adults are reading to him or her; and may recognize some words or letters in context. (Note: We will not use terms like *nonreader, preliterate,* or *reading readiness* because of our constructivist viewpoint, which holds that all readers are eventually successful and that development is a continuum).

2. *Early—Becoming a Reader*

For the early reader (coded as *ea*), the habit of reading for meaning is established. Children who are early readers use their background experience, take risks and use approximations, begin to understand some print conventions and how they work, use texts to predict and confirm, begin simple reading (which is close to the actual text but may not be exact), and begin to self-correct.

3. *Fluent—Going It Alone*

Fluent readers (coded as *fl*) integrate semantic, syntactic, and phonetic cues, read for increasingly longer periods of time, include a variety of genres of texts, adjust their reading rate to suit different situations and needs, and reduce their need for print detail. Fluent reading may begin in primary grades, but students continue to grow as readers through their adult lives.

For more in-depth discussion of these periods in the life of a reader, see Mooney, 1988; Renwick & Department of Education, 1985; and Smith & Elley, 1994. The following strategies will work in multiage and nonmultiage settings and are coded for reading level.

Shared Book Experiences (em, ea, fl)—Originally developed by Holdaway (1979) for New Zealand schools, and now popular for emergent and early readers, shared book experiences (also called *Shared Reading*) are well suited to a diverse group. Generally, a book with enlarged text is placed on an easel for all to see, whether *all* includes an entire class or a group within the class. The text may be literature, in which case it is a generally predictable text (a story or poem), may be informational for content study, or may be from materials previously produced by students.

> "A visitor in our classroom would see an environment rich in print, tables arranged in groups of six or eight, materials accessible to children, open-space work areas, lots of busy children chatting and working—totally focused on their task. Teachers would be working alongside a child or on the floor with some children. Parent volunteers are working with children. Many types of activities would be occurring simultaneously. The classroom is cheerful, warm, respectful, and hard working."
>
> —Marybeth Phelps and Gloria Morrison
> Danielson, CT

Box 7-2

The teacher or student leader uses a pointer to follow the text at a comfortable and natural reading rate while reading the text to students and allowing students to join in chorally when they are ready. The choral reading permits more advanced readers to read and the struggling readers to join in wherever possible. Through repeated readings of the text, older students gain fluency, and less advanced readers learn the story and can eventually do a voice-print match (being able to tell precisely which words are being read and when).

The follow-up activities and skill lessons are an important part of the shared book experience. Activities that highlight comprehension (such as acting out the story), content (learning more about the characters in the story), graphophonemic skills (letters and sounds), and more advanced language arts skills (contractions, quotation marks, exclamation points), are used as needed. Some teachers also highlight interesting vocabulary, talk about the interesting words and brainstorm synonyms for them, and use *literature-extending activities*.

Let's say that we are using a big-book version of a popular folktale, such as *The Little Red Hen*. The story is entertaining, predictable, and has good learning potential. First, the teacher might read the story to students, using the pointer to follow along the text naturally (not in a stilted, choppy way).

The second time, students might be invited to read along with the teacher. On the third reading, some of the class may remain seated on the floor near the easel to be the "readers" while others are assigned the parts of the hen, the dog, the cat, and the mouse. Perhaps a few props are available, such as character labels for each actor (an index card on string that reads HEN, DOG, CAT, or MOUSE and is hung around the appropriate actor's neck). The actors then pantomime the story as others read aloud.

Because the story is short, this might be done a second time with a new set of actors, which allows for more students to participate and provides for repeated readings as well. As another comprehension check, the teacher can lead a *structured retelling*, asking someone to tell how the story began, asking someone else what happened next, and so on until the story retelling is complete. Perhaps the teacher has decided to compare and contrast the animals in the story. How many are mammals? How many are not? What are some of the characteristics of these animals?

For the least advanced readers, the teacher may decide to review *h* and the sound it makes, or perhaps the *r* from *red*. Or, because the story title contains two short *e* sounds, the teacher could introduce or review that as well. For more advanced students, the contraction in the sentence "Then I'll have to do it myself!" could be reviewed. The use of the quotation marks and the exclamation point are other possible skill lessons. The end result may be that the class will research different cake recipes, see if they contain similar or different ingredients, and then plan for how much flour, butter, or milk might be needed (math) and perhaps eventually bake a cake together. The shared book experience is full of possibilities and is aptly suited to the various reading abilities in the class.

Guided Reading (ea, fl)—This term is also from the New Zealand model of reading (but it has other meanings as well; see glossary). Guided reading lessons enable a teacher and a small group of children to purposefully think their way through a text, making possible an early introduction to silent reading (Renwick & Department of Education, 1985), in order for children to realize that the process of reading is one of constructing meaning and not just decoding. First, the teacher selects a text that is interesting and of a manageable length for the readers. Second, the teacher is clear about the selected purpose, which may be to develop a specific skill, to read for enjoyment, or to reteach a strategy, such as *predicting*. Next, the teacher introduces the selection through a discussion that prepares students for what is to come—noting the title, its possible meaning, the author, and the illustrator—and poses one or two questions related to the content or topic. Potential new words may come up naturally in the discussion but are not pretaught so as not to rob students of opportunities to learn how to deal with new words they meet on their own.

Next comes the actual reading, which for the newest readers might be only a small portion of the text. Sometimes the teacher reads to the children first and asks them to follow along with a finger in their own copies, or sometimes the students read silently. The teacher may lead an immediate retelling or discussion, but not so as to interfere with the enjoyment of the experience. After the reading, teachers may pose open-ended questions to engage students in a discussion about what they read. These procedures vary according to the type of text, the group of children, and their response to the reading. Comprehension is central throughout the process and is not left until the end.

Repeated Readings (em, ea, fl)—As in shared book experiences, there are many occasions and reasons to have a text read multiple times; one reason is to help develop fluency (Rasinski & Padak, 1996a, 1996b). Books, including big books, that have been read to the entire group might subsequently be read by individuals, pairs, or small groups just for fun. In fact, sometimes we have observed this happening spontaneously during free reading or other free-choice classroom times. Some classes take books read previously in a group or by the teacher and read them to each other (see *Buddy Reading*). Sometimes students reread plays many times to increase their expression and then listen to themselves improve on a tape recorder. In a study by Kasten, Clarke, and Nations (1988), even 4- and 5-year-olds voluntarily took big books from their classroom out onto the playground and sat on top of the slides or other playground apparatus reading to each other (or making approximations of reading, if they were still emergent readers).

Reading Aloud (em, ea, fl)—We can't emphasize enough our belief that every teacher should be reading to students every day. Furthermore, although this is critical and popular with younger children, the experience should continue for *all* grade levels because reading aloud has a strong impact on literacy even for older children (Trelease, 1995).

Reading aloud can take many forms. Even with younger children, teachers can read books with multiple chapters over a period of days or weeks. Trade books are read for pleasure or because they relate to what is being taught. Poetry is read aloud to develop student interest and enjoyment and because it may relate to other learning. Informational books are also read as they relate to content. Student-authored works are read either by students or by the teacher.

Reading aloud contains many lessons. Some of these include learning story structure, learning how good language and literature sounds, introducing and reviewing vocabulary, and developing listening skills. Even reading comprehension is enhanced in such classes. Students can listen to stories above their own reading level, so more advanced texts are stimulating academically as they also help to build vocabulary and schema. Wendy has her preservice students take an oath that they will read to their future classes every day. Reading aloud is appropriate for all ages and ability levels.

Sentence Pocket Charts (em, ea)—These involve taking a text, either a story from a reader or one written by the class on an earlier occasion, and writing it by hand onto sentence strips (strips of heavy paper that is generally sold on rolls). Placing each sentence on one strip, the familiar story can be reconstructed as a large group, small group, or even individually. Some companies make handy charts from nylon or plastic that have long, thin, clear plastic pockets where sentence strips fit nicely. This enables the story to be reread easily once it is reassembled. In the absence of such a nice prop, the sentence strips could be placed on a chalkboard with tape or a magnetic board with magnets to achieve the same effect. This strategy is most commonly used with early readers or newly fluent readers. This strategy strengthens comprehension and is generally not assessed formally (although it is very informative to observe students doing this).

"A second grader from another classroom stopped by last week to drop something off for another teacher. She had never been in our classroom before. After handing me the paper, she said, 'You know, this looks like a class of happiness.' [If you entered our room], you would see twenty-five 5-, 6-, 7-, and 8-year-olds working together in pairs or small groups or individually; some sitting at tables, some on the floor, some standing or walking to get something, some in chairs, some with adults, some alone, and some with other children. You would see students engaged in meaningful reading, writing, math, and science—children often choosing what they want to read or write and with whom they want to work—and most of the children would be 'on task.' You would see lots of parents and other adult visitors dropping in all through the day to visit with their child, or to compliment another child's work, or to listen to their child read."

—Nancy Norman
Palmer, AK

Box 7-3

Story Cut-Ups (fl)—Similar to the sentence pocket charts, a variation is to take short pieces of text, whether in a standard print format or enlarged onto a chart, and cut up the text by paragraph. Whether done individually, in pairs, or in small groups, students reading the paragraphs are forced to think about semantic logic in order to decide what paragraph most likely began the text, how the middle proceeds, and what chunk sounds like a logical ending. This strategy is mainly for fluent readers, but less proficient readers may participate by listening to the parts being read by others. As with many of these strategies, the complexity of the text, not the task (cutting it in various numbers), determines the age appropriateness of the strategy. This strategy is also best assessed informally or used mostly for practice.

Literature Circles (em, ea, fl)—This alternative to teaching with basals and reading groups is both a literature-based reading strategy as well as one consistent with whole language philosophy. Literature circles can be implemented in a number of different ways (Daniels, 1994; Kasten, 1995; Peterson & Eeds, 1990; Roser & Martinez, 1995), but the methodology here will be mostly based on Kasten (1995). Teachers should consider adapting *any* strategy for their own unique instructional program.

Literature circles involve small groups of students (three to five) reading quality children's trade books together, journaling in response to the selection, discussing the selection in depth, and eventually presenting to the whole class (or other classes) a creative expression of what the book has meant to them. Unlike conventional reading groups, the teacher is not present in the circle but acts as a facilitator as multiple book groups meet concurrently. No preconstructed questions, worksheets, or other materials are included. Participants in literature circles are generally fluent readers, but talented teachers have found ways to adapt this strategy to early readers by having texts read to students in advance, by peer tutors, by parent volunteers, or as part of class instruction.

Quality picture books, novels, or short stories might be used as long as the selection is sufficiently engaging and interesting, providing genuine food for thought. The example that follows here is based on intermediate-age fluent readers, although less proficient readers can participate readily with these groups by taking more of a listening role. These are presented as steps but are explained more fully elsewhere (Kasten, 1995).

1. *Select novels or picture books* for a first round of literature groups. Multiple copies (three to five) of five or six different selections are suitable for starting. For example, perhaps initially the teacher selects *Bridge to Terabithia* (Paterson, 1977), *Number the Stars* (Lowry, 1989), *The Lottery Rose* (Hunt, 1976), *Across Five Aprils* (Hunt, 1964), *The True Confessions of Charlotte Doyle* (Avi, 1990), and *Sounder* (Armstrong, 1969). All these selections are highly regarded titles that will provide a great deal of material for reaction and discussion. Having read these books previously, or relying on recommendations from a knowledgeable librarian, the teacher "book talks" each selection briefly. Listing the titles on the chalkboard or dry erase board, the teacher allows students to indicate a first, second, and third choice of book group in which to participate. From this information, book groups are con-

structed with three to five students each, with nearly all students getting one of their choices (with assurances that if they did not get a first choice, the title will be available to them at a future time). The teacher is responsible for ensuring that the resulting groups are balanced and workable (which sometimes means moving students around a bit or having veto power over certain students in the same group; it also means having a balance of more and less proficient readers).

2.   With groups in place, larger blocks of time are set aside two to five times per week (30, 45, or 60 minutes) in which *students read aloud together* on a voluntary basis, so the selection is mostly shared aloud. This aspect enables students with a wide variety of abilities to participate; someone in the group will know most of the words (and you may need to set guidelines for not prompting others too quickly), and less proficient readers may mostly listen with the text in front of them. Group members need to practice courtesy as others read, and they should understand that occasional minor miscues may not be worth bringing up. In other words, the readers should support each other. Guidelines may be set for the amount of time to read (perhaps half of the allotted time).

3.   When reading is concluded (determined by time or the end of a chapter), *students respond in a journal,* based on whatever they are thinking about in relation to the reading. This is difficult at first because students are predisposed to teachers requesting summaries or retellings (which is not the goal here). Three guiding questions for responding include, "Write something you notice about the story," "How does this story make you feel?", and "What does this remind you of in your own life?" (Borders & Naylor, 1993). Writing may be designated for 5–10 minutes prior to any discussion.

Some intermediate teachers have found that many students want to make journal entries short and effortless. A system of awarding points for journal entries based on effort and thoughtfulness may remedy this and also aid in later assessment of the group.

4.   When writing is concluded, *discussion* proceeds either by students volunteering to read what they have written or to talk about their entry. Teachers should allow flexibility here for student discussion to take off on occasional tangents that are stimulated by the entries. The roving teacher-facilitator might stimulate a lagging discussion by posing interesting questions of an open-ended nature to act as a catalyst for discussion. Many of these selections contain ethical dilemmas for the characters or difficult decisions that teachers might prompt students to think over in more depth.

Steps 2–4 are repeated until the novels are concluded. Variation in length of books can be accommodated in several ways. Some groups may need additional time to read; some groups may get additional time to plan step 5; groups with all proficient readers may read some of their selections during sustained silent reading times.

5. *Presentation* is the last step in the literature circle and is critical to its success. Students in the group meet to discuss how to share the book they have read with the class and what it meant to them. Presentations may use art, music, drama, media, computers, or anything else that students design. Finished presentations will most likely require a time limitation and the criterion that the story not be divulged too much, since other students may wish to read the book at another time.

Planning a presentation becomes a powerful learning opportunity. Students must consider the story carefully, will often need to reread, may discuss the characters in more depth, and will perhaps write their plans or scripts. Presentations may be shared with other classes or videotaped for future groups. Often, the results are priceless and should be archived. One group, for example, composed a rap based on their novel. Complete with music, words, and dance steps, they arrived in costumes appropriate to their story for a fairly breathtaking performance. Another group constructed a television talk show based on their novel. One student was designated host while the others were characters who were guests on the show and were being interviewed about their unique lives and experiences. Another group videotaped their rehearsed scene on the school grounds and presented their product with a VCR. Another group created puppets of their characters and presented a key scene. The possibilities are endless. Literature circles can be assessed for student understanding of books by examining student journals or evaluating presentations.

Reader's Workshop (ea, fl)—Reader's workshop may consist of several different aspects of reading. Typically, sustained silent reading is a major part of this format, in which all class members, student or adult, take time for self-selected individualized reading. Sometimes teachers conference with students about books, and at others times sharing about the completed reading takes place. Students often keep personal records about books completed or number of pages read during a day or a week. These records may become part of student portfolios. Reader's workshops generally also include minilessons related to the reading material.

Literature-Based Board Games (ea, fl)—Literature-based board games are teacher- and student-made games, sometimes using leftover boards, tokens, spinners, and remnants of commercial games, or sometimes the teacher constructs them on poster board, file folders, or matte board. Groups of students then play the game following their sharing of a book (Kasten, in Watson, 1987). Three kinds of activity cards accompany three colors or shapes of spaces on the board, so that players are signaled by the space they land on what activity to do. The first activity is *vocabulary cards*. On these, a sentence from the story is written (by hand or with a computer), and an interesting or challenging word is underlined. Players landing on this type of space pick a card from the top of the vocabulary card deck, read the card to the other players, and explain the meaning of the underlined word. The second type of activity is *cloze*. A sentence or part of a lengthy sentence is written on a card with one word deleted, and players landing on that type of space pick a card from the cloze deck, read the card to the other players, and fill in an acceptable word for the one that has been deleted. The third type of activity is the *sentence set*, in which a sentence from the story has been written onto a strip of paper, omitting the capitalization of the first word of the sentence and the punctuation at the end of the sentence. The sentence has been cut into two, three, or four pieces, each of which contains several words. The player who lands on this type of space must read the pieces and put them together to form an acceptable sentence.

Making these games from quality picture books or short stories for up to four players at a time is recommended. Generally, if games are made with similar rules and structures, students will need no further directions for completing the games on subsequent occasions. Less proficient readers can participate by having the book read initially to the group by the more proficient members, and having the cards or sentence sets read together with the help of a friend. Varying the complexity of the book makes the games suitable to a wide range of students, from primary- through intermediate-age readers. Game directions can be written in a variety of ways, but ending the game when everyone reaches the "finish" space is more productive than declaring a winner based on who gets there first. These games are based on a whole language reading model, and they require students to use semantic and syntactic cues to determine lesser known or unknown words in order to complete the activities. These strategies are especially helpful for students who need comprehension strengthening. Playing these types of games is generally a practice activity and needs no formal assessment. These games work well as learning centers or stations.

Literature-Extending Activities (em, ea, fl)—Often, in conjunction with reading a story, lessons or activities are prepared that enhance or extend some part of the story. After reading about Johnny Appleseed, for instance, students might make applesauce or plant apple seeds. After reading about a desert in a picture book, students might learn about the particular desert in question. Reading a story in which a food was made or a song was sung, the class might then spend time finding out more about the food, actually cooking it, or learning a song. Literature-extending activities, whether they take place before or after a story, enhance schema and comprehension in some active way. Literature-extending activities are especially important when the content or theme of a book is unfamiliar to students but is appropriate on any occasion and for any age level.

Book Corners (em, ea, fl)—Book corners aren't really a strategy; they are a structure within the design of the classroom, but they deserve mentioning here. It's so simple to devote a corner of a classroom to books, yet many classrooms we have visited haven't done this yet. Some reading corners are set off by freestanding bookshelves or racks that hold classroom titles or books on loan from the school media center or public library. Some corners are enhanced with inviting places to sit, such as pillows on a carpet, beanbag chairs, or even an old sofa. Whatever the design, the presence of the book corner and the opportunity to use it sends a strong message that books matter in our lives. Sometimes we teach by example, and this is one of those times, so it is a strategy in that sense.

Some items in the book corner stay the same, whereas others may change with the units of study. Some of the books are categorized by reading level for specific use in individual independent reading, whereas others are available to everyone for browsing. All kids can browse through books that are still too difficult for them to read. We have met many little children who love to browse through reference books, even encyclopedias, long before they can actually read them. This is okay. For now they will enjoy the photos and diagrams while developing a taste and appreciation for reference books.

"When you first walk in our room, you would see a double-size classroom with the west wall being all windows. There are lots of plants, a couch, two aquariums, two bird cages, and many polar bears and penguins (toys). On the end walls each student has an individual bulletin board. The north pole is where we have our calendar area and room for whole-group instruction. A stage, computer center, and several tables for small-group instruction are also in the north pole. In the middle of these two rooms, at the equator, are two tables and our desks, This is where we have our individual conferences. On the south pole side there is a blackboard, the students' tables, and their cubbies."

—Sue Beth Arnold and Barbara Kidwell
Findlay, OH

Box 7-4.

Book Talks (ea, fl)—Replacing the old and timeworn book report, book talks are an oral and somewhat dramatic presentation of a book to entice others to read it. Similar to the short talks used on public television's *Reading Rainbow*, students compose their own talks in advance. They may choose to share some highlights or what the book meant to them, but the format varies according to the creativity of the presenter. One popular notion is to dress up as one of the characters in the book and talk from the character's viewpoint. Book talks might be likened to a movie preview or an advertisement for a book and may include a picture or poster as part of the presentation. Book talks may be assessed based on criteria predetermined by the teacher or based on best effort.

Again, as with many strategies, the suitability of this varies not by age group but by the complexity of the text used. Five-year-olds can do book talks on books that have been read to them before they are fluent readers. Book talks are equally popular in high school English classes.

Dramatizing Books (em, ea, fl)—Some books beg to be dramatized, either wholly or in part. Bill Martin, Jr., author and educator, advocates putting on productions of quality picture books just like plays. These productions can be simple and spontaneous, such as a group pantomiming the words to *Where the Wild Things Are* (Sendak, 1963) while a narrator reads it aloud, or acting out *Abiyoyo* (Seeger, 1986) while the teacher or a more advanced reader in the classroom acts as narrator. At other times, groups may be charged with the job of deciding how to act out a book or a scene from a book, and these might be performed for other classes or as part of a celebration of books the class has read. Simple clothing, puppet props, or masks might be utilized. *Who's in Rabbit's House?* (Aardema, 1977) uses masks in the illustrations. Brown paper bags can be used to make these masks for the actors of this story, and others can combine literature and art. This strategy can be adjusted for a variety of grade levels, depending on the story being used. Even emergent readers can participate in some way with more fluent readers through acting, art, saying lines, and contributing ideas to the production. Students will most likely never forget a book they have acted out. While acting out books may not need to be assessed generally, student reactions and behavior during such projects are an excellent context for *kidwatching* and accumulating substantive information about student strengths.

Computer Story Presentations (fl)—A variety of software already exists with which students can create stories or plays importing existing characters, sceneries, and properties. This is a very productive and creative use of the computer. Students can write and present their stories individually, in pairs, or in small groups. The ability to see the story or play performed on the screen, complete with sound clips and people or animals speaking the lines written for them, is very satisfying. These presentations may be assessed on criteria set up by the classroom teacher appropriate to the student's age and ability.

Radio Plays (fl)—Radio plays are audio dramatizations, rehearsed and then performed behind a screen, sheet, or other barrier. As with real radio broadcasts, some sound effects may be added for flavor. Radio plays can be performed using existing plays, students' original productions, or adaptations from children's literature. These plays can be adapted to all age levels. Assessment will vary, depending on the intent of the lesson, but it may range from assessing the script, the performance, or the degree of group cooperation (early or emergent readers could help with production, sound effects, etc.).

Listening Center (em, ea, fl)—The listening center is a staple in many primary- and intermediate-age classrooms. Using an audiotape recorder, headsets, and prerecorded children's books (picture books or novels, either commercially produced or teacher-made), selected students attend the listening center to hear a book read aloud while having a copy of the text in front of them. The listening center suits a variety of learners, depending on the complexity of the books on tape. The potential for strengthening vocabulary and comprehension is similar to that of reading aloud in general. Sometimes, accompanying activities are completed after the listening experience, and at other times the listening is for practice only, with no formal assessment of any kind.

Language Experience Approach (em, ea, fl)—This has been around for a long time and is still a good strategy that is consistent with contructivist, whole language principles. Basically, language experience refers to one student or several students dictating a story or other piece to someone who writes it down. A student being tutored, for example, might dictate a journal entry about his or her weekend. A group of readers might invent a story together as a teacher or parent volunteer writes it down. Several guidelines are generally connected with this strategy. First, students need to be able to see the writing that results from their dictation so they can make the connection between their language and the written piece. Second, their language is written down verbatim, so their contributions are honored despite any language variation of nonstandard English. Honoring learner language helps learners to feel accepted and enables them to later reread. Third, the emerging texts are reread regularly throughout the process with the students so that they understand that their utterances are now reading material. Finally, the materials that result from the episode are used for instruction with the same readers who generated it.

This strategy can be effective for emergent and early readers who still don't have the capability to write on their own. It's also especially good for older, at-risk learners, even adult ones, for whom appropriate and engaging reading materials are limited or absent. Second-language learners can also benefit from this strategy, as it ensures that the texts they produce are within the scope of their understanding in the new language. Often these student-dictated texts are bound and saved for future students, whose interest is piqued by the presence of student-produced work.

Buddy Reading (ea, fl)—Also called *Paired Reading*, this strategy is very easy because it requires no special planning and no follow-up. Students are simply paired off and then read back and forth to each other. Sometimes it makes sense to pair students of fairly similar abilities and at other times to pair them across abilities. There is no rule that you have to do this the same way each time. Most students thoroughly enjoy reading to each other, and often they are even willing to read to each other stories that they have already read (so as to get in some repeated readings). You may consider setting guidelines for how to tackle words that neither reader can identify, such as going back to the beginning of the sentence to reread, making joint guesses of words that would make sense, and confirming or disconfirming their predictions with phonetic clues. This strategy focuses on practicing a skill and is not formally assessed (although observations for anecdotal records are appropriate).

Theme Books (em, ea, fl)—This is another popular New Zealand strategy that is used during content-area study or themed study. Each student in the primary-age classroom has his or her own booklet, usually handmade with scrap or art materials such as construction paper, newsprint, and covers made of discarded wallpaper. Each day, during a designated period of time, such as when visiting the writing center, students are instructed to draw and write about what they have learned in the theme. Younger students might have less detailed drawings and less writing than more proficient students, but everyone must do his or her best to write and draw something related to the theme, and everyone adds a new page to the theme book. Theme books might be saved for student portfolios; one may last for several weeks, and a combination of two or more in the portfolio will provide documentation for assessment and student growth. Theme books are similar to learning logs, with more of a balance between art and writing.

Journaling (em, ea, fl)—Writing freely (first draft only) is usually the main purpose of journaling. Many teachers use various types of journals in their classrooms, such as journals that are sent home periodically, journals for science observations, journals for math, dialogue journals (writing between students and teachers), or buddy journals (writing between students). Journals should provide students with an opportunity to write for themselves. Although journals are a useful assessment tool for following student development in writing and spelling, the journals themselves are generally not graded in a formal sense. Nor are corrections generally made by the teacher (although modeling spelling and conventions within the response is an excellent way to impact student writing development). Too many uses for journals within the same classroom can lead to overkill and cause students to feel as if journals are a dull, repetitive chore rather than an expressive or creative outlet for writing (Bonila, 1991; Fulwiler, 1987).

Story Rewrites or Story Parodies (em, ea, fl)—New Zealand may have been the first source of rewriting known stories, but language experience guru, Roach Van Allen, advocated using known stories as models in the United States 20 years ago.

Using popular, sometimes predictable story patterns, teachers and students think of a way to rewrite a text on a slightly different premise. For example, with young children, stories like *Brown Bear, Brown Bear, What Do You See?* (Martin, 1967) might be revamped so that each child contributes a page of his or her own animal or object, perhaps using the colors of the original story or perhaps using shapes and sounds. Each child contributes a page, creating a new story that can be bound and saved for future reading. These books are enormously popular for rereading.

The complexity of this strategy can be adjusted by changing the complexity of the text being used. *Brown Bear, Brown Bear, What Do You See?* is suitable for emergent readers, and *If the Dinosaurs Came Back* (Most, 1996) is slightly more complex. Other books can make this strategy suitable to fluent readers, even at the intermediate level. For example, *What Do You Do With a Kangaroo?* (Mayer, 1973) has more text and a more difficult vocabulary and requires a greater amount of writing on each contributed page (which can be done in pairs or small groups). For more fluent readers, a story such as *Traveling to Tondo* (Aardema, 1991) can be rewritten using four other animals who all share the same habitat (to get a little science in there), who are going someplace else (other than Tondo) for a different reason (other than the cat's wedding), and who encounter different obstacles along the way. Writers in small groups can decide on their own moral for their tale and can even write, rehearse, and perform their new versions.

In a diverse group, this strategy enables group members of different abilities to contribute in their own way. More capable members might be the writers, but less proficient readers will have ideas to contribute and a willingness to act out the story.

Story Comic Strips (fl)—We're not sure where this idea originated. One of us has used it in her classroom, however. At the end of a picture book, novel, chapter, or other text selection, students divide a piece of drawing paper into four (or any number of) sections. Using comiclike characters and speech balloons, students represent four scenes of their choice from whatever they read, as long as the scenes are in the sequence in which they actually occurred. This is a very revealing assessment tool, and we have discovered that it shows persistent misconceptions as well as understandings and provides the teacher with the information to correct misunderstandings. For example, in one multiage primary class, more advanced readers read *Sarah, Plain and Tall* (MacLachlan, 1985). One student who appeared to understand the story very well placed characters in the same frame who never actually met in the book. Another student drew scenes implied through Sarah's letters to and from Jacob (a rather sophisticated level of understanding!). This strategy can be social studies–oriented, drawing events in a time period that is being studied. The strategy can be used with readers of a variety of abilities, depending on the complexity of the selection.

School-Based Publications (ea, fl)—Students write for a variety of purposes in a good reading and writing classroom. Some student works should be published in a product that others can read and enjoy. Some schools have a place set up within the building, sometimes staffed by library aids or volunteers, where supplies and equipment are available for bookbinding. Listed below are four types of publications that might be included.

1.   *Individual Books* (ea, fl)—Individual students will sometimes include stories, collections of poems, or informational books connected with theme study and with writer's workshop (described below). Ideally, all children should have an opportunity to "publish" something on a school level. The quality of the works—as well as the execution of the art, the proofreading for spelling and punctuation, and the length and breadth of the actual writing—should vary with the individual's age and ability. Books produced by 5-year-olds should look different from those done by 8-year-olds, which should in turn look different from those done by 11-year-olds. Generally speaking, we adjust our expectations (and assessment) according to whether or not an individual child has done his or her personal best.

Schools that lack bookbinding machines often use simple and multiple types of bookbinding, employing a variety of kinds and sizes of paper, stapled bindings, sewn bindings, or ones adhered with library tape. Bookbinding machines, however, are not very expensive at a large office supply store.

Many librarians will display student-produced books on a regular basis. Having a real audience for one's work is extremely motivating and rewarding and serves as a model for others. Students enjoy reading the works of their peers.

2.   *Class Books* (em, ea, fl)—Many occasions occur for classes to produce books together. As a group, students may rewrite a favorite fairy tale, changing the characters, setting, time period, or premise. Each group can contribute several pages, or pages can be planned and divided up among class members in small teams. Songs that children love to sing may be written, one line at a time, on big chart paper as a book, with a group illustrating each page. One class did this with Louis Armstrong's "It's a Wonderful World"

and used magazine pictures to illustrate each line. Students reread and resang the songbook often, both with and without accompanying music on audiotape.

Still other classes have made content-area books that summarize learning on a topic or from a field trip. After the students decided which text to place on which pages and who would illustrate each page, these books became part of the classroom materials. These large class books, made from chart, poster, or art paper, last longer if laminated.

3.   *Student-Produced Newspapers* (fl)—Communication in any school is enhanced with a student-produced school newspaper. Some multiage classes, usually intermediate-age students, are in charge of school publications. Different students apply to be editors, reporters, illustrators, marketers, or proofreaders. Teacher-devised tests and applications make the process more authentic when, for example, to be a part of marketing and selling, students must do well on a math test. Once a month, students may indicate that they wish to resign from a position, leaving it open for new applicants who are interested. Throughout this process, authentic language arts skills are utilized as students conduct interviews, write copy, edit, revise, design, produce, and sell their work (for a nominal fee to recover paper costs to the school).

4.   *Mailboxes* (ea, fl)—Mailboxes certainly aren't a new idea, but in some places they have become an institutional practice. Some schools have placed mail pick-up points around the campus or building. All classrooms and, in fact, all areas of the school have addresses. Anyone in the school can write to anyone else within the school, including the office and custodial staff. Selected students are responsible for mail delivery, or sometimes different classes rotate the responsibility. Obviously, this reading and writing strategy is highly authentic. Students are encouraged to do more writing, and recipients must be able to read what they have received (or get help from a friend). Postal carriers must read many names and addresses. Sometimes this is done only within a classroom rather than throughout a building.

Minilessons (em, ea, fl)—Minilessons meet curricular objectives or benchmarks whether presented to small or large groups. These lessons are typically short in nature (10–15 minutes), perhaps followed by discussion, practice, or application. In some classrooms, several minilessons may take place in one day and may be math, reading, writing, theme, or content specific.

Written Conversations (fl)—This strategy is very popular in New Zealand and Australia. Students are paired and write to each other on a common piece of paper or a notebook in front of them. Sometimes the conversation in writing is related to readings done earlier, and sometimes it is purely social and open-ended. A little like "passing notes" (something kids used to get in trouble for!), this requires students to understand their partner's writing in order to respond. This ensures that comprehension is taking place. Students may not talk during a written conversation, but two students in Australia confessed that they sometimes need to whisper if they can't read the other person's handwriting.

Dramatic Play Center (em, ea, fl)—In primary grades, dramatic play centers are places that children can go during designated times to use materials that lend themselves to dramatic play. As children act out scenes with each other, they use language from a variety of contexts, use their imaginations, interact with others in appropriate ways, and even create stories. These opportunities utilize multiple intelligences, as children have a variety of contexts over time. Nancy Norman from Palmer, Alaska shared a list of props that she assembles in these centers. Her *house center* includes aprons, brooms, mops, sponges, a clothesline, a high chair, bowls, silverware, pots and pans, a pot holder, play food, colored water in unbreakable containers, salt shakers, a baby bathtub, dolls, containers for baby powder and shampoo, diapers and pins, balloons, streamers, dishes and cups, a fake birthday cake, candles, ribbons and bows, scarves, a toy telephone, boxes, paper with which to make greeting cards, and dress-up clothes. Her *fire station center* includes fire hats, raincoats, boots, garden hose lengths, a bell, boots, squirt guns, and a large box as the firetruck. The *circus center* includes hula hoops, costumes, hats, wigs, a chair, clown make-up, and cages (refrigerator boxes). Sometimes an *airport center* is available, which consists of suitcases, backpacks, a blue blazer (like the ones pilots wear), oxygen masks, seats, earphones, magazines, pillows and blankets, and a large box for a cockpit. An occasional *medical center* is set up with smocks, white shirts and jackets, doctors' kits, a telephone, a cot, a blanket and pillow, an examining table, growth and eye charts, bandages, medicine bottles (empty, of course), tongue depressors, cotton balls, surgical masks, gloves and hats, leashes (for a vet), stuffed animals, chairs and magazines for the waiting room, a clipboard and pencils, a scale, and some dolls. The *science center* is stocked with magnifying glasses, microscopes and prepared slides, plastic test tubes, calibrated cylinders, scales for weighing, lab coats, measuring tools and cups, picture books of insects and animals, clipboards, paper, and pencils. At times she might also have a safari jungle center, a grocery store, a florist shop, a theater center, a restaurant center, a zoo center, an office center, a pirate theme center, a service garage, a beach, a hair salon, a spaceship, a laundromat, a boating/fishing/camping center, a post office, a symphony, a castle, or a magician center.

Spelling and Punctuation Committees (fl)—Once students are writing connected text, strategies that help students take responsibility for their own learning of spelling are preferable to those that rely on teacher correction. One intermediate teacher we met had formed committees in his classroom as part of a writer's workshop (described below). When student writing was nearing completion, committees scheduled meetings. There was one committee for spelling, one for punctuation, one for grammar, and perhaps others. All pieces of nearly completed student writing had to circulate through all committees to be carefully examined. Committee members had to "sign off" after they had edited for the skill in question, making them accountable for being thorough. Committees would stay intact long enough for their members to become proficient at what they were doing. It was also the responsibility of each committee to research its spelling, punctuation, or grammar questions in classroom or school reference books.

Committee membership was rotated several times throughout the year to ensure that all students would have an opportunity to focus on each skill. In a multiage classroom, these committees are comprised of students who vary in age and writing ability in order to make use of class expertise and to mentor newer experts toward eventual leadership.

Spelling From Literature (fl)—Some teachers have experimented with arranging class spelling lessons to be connected to the novel that is being read aloud to the students. Rather than assembling a list of words, the teacher selects (or has students select) a passage from the book in question (maybe 50–75 words) and puts this passage on a chart or overhead transparency. Early in the week, the teacher presents the passage, and the students identify interesting words that may warrant further study, both for spelling and word analysis (prefixes, root words, etc.). These words are highlighted or underlined in context. On a subsequent day, other features of the passage are the focus of language study, such as the use of quotation marks (in dialogue), unusual punctuation (such as a colon or ellipsis), or interesting word features (contractions, compound words, very descriptive verbs).

Language study continues on the passage until the students are tested by having the teacher dictate the entire paragraph for students to write down, keeping all the words in context. Scores, if required, are obtained by computing the number of words spelled conventionally over the total number of words in the passage (which can be computed by students who need practice in math computation and percentages!). This strategy for fluent readers and writers has the advantage that the spelling words are in context, they are student-selected, and the passage is relevant to the students. The disadvantage is that the words aren't necessarily ones that students need in their writing.

Spelling From Writing: Group (fl)—Some teachers who still wish to use weekly spelling lists create them from combined student writing errors. In a multiage situation, however, in order to meet the needs of a diverse group, the list would have to have at least two parts: (a) certain words for everyone (high frequency words, or words everyone may need to know, such as the name of the city, county, or school) and (b) selected additional words for advanced spellers. The overall principle here is that everyone needs to do his or her best and learn as many words as possible and still be successful.

Spelling From Writing: Individual (fl)—Probably the most effective strategy we've seen for teaching spelling is for teachers to choose spelling words from an individual's own written work. Starting from the premise that the words the student has used are also the ones that he or she needs to know, teachers will ask students to identify some misspelled words in their own works to learn how to spell and to study. The actual number of words varies according to the age and ability of the learner. Then the teacher may suggest up to three additional words for the student to add to the list. Students study their words with a classmate during the week, and the classmates test each other on a given day. This strategy is consistent with constructivist, whole language principles and can be adapted to nearly any age group. We would not, however, recommend formal spelling until students are fluent (as opposed to early and emergent) readers and writers, which varies with age. Spelling is, after all, a subset of the writing process, not a prerequisite.

Sketch-to-Stretch (em, ea, fl)—First developed at Indiana University by Carolyn Burke and researched by Marjorie Siegal, sketch-to-stretch is an easy strategy that suits a wide range of learners. After reading or hearing a thoughtful story, students are asked to "draw what the story means to you." These deliberately open-ended instructions leave possibilities wide open for students to draw a picture relating to the story or one that reflects their understanding of the story. These sketches are then shared voluntarily as each artist explains the sketch and how it relates to the text. These pictures can be used to assess student understanding and are well suited to individuals whose stronger learning modes are in visual media. Leland and Harste (1994) use this technique with unusual stories such as *Sylvester and the Magic Pebble* (Steig, 1969).

Story Maps (em, ea, fl)—This is yet another reading and comprehension strategy that is very popular in Australia and New Zealand, and it allows for multiple ways of knowing through art. Students who have read a short story, picture book, or folktale, for example, use large paper, perhaps poster size, to draw the events of the story or represent in art the major parts of the story without using words. Generally, these are completed in small groups so that group members must discuss how to depict their text and make joint decisions about how to represent their story. These story maps are then used by group members to share the story they read with others through an oral retelling. Retelling is an opportunity for teacher assessment and evaluation of group understanding of the story. Story maps can be used at a variety of age levels by varying the complexity of the story being mapped. Early readers can draw maps of stories read to them before they can read the stories independently.

Excitement Maps (fl)—Excitement maps are similar to story maps in that a small group reads a story and, cooperatively using large paper, designs a graphic that segments the story into major events, and then draws some type of bar graph that rates each segment of the story on the level of excitement it generated in them as readers. The graphic illustrates a profile of the story's plot. This strategy can be used on shorter or longer texts, including novels, and suits a variety of ages of learners by varying the text difficulty.

Webbing (em, ea, fl)—Webbing begins with a book that a group or the class has read. Using large paper, a chalkboard, or a white dry erase board, students brainstorm areas of interest and study that the book or story suggests. Originally used as a teacher planning tool for integrating literature with the curriculum, webbing is sometimes used by a teacher and an entire class to brainstorm areas of study the class might like to pursue. One class we visited used a large portion of the wall to create this web. Books are webbed by themes to help determine or negotiate the directions that study might take (see Figure 7-2).

Writer's Workshop (ea, fl)—Like reader's workshop, writer's workshop is time devoted to the development of longer written pieces in a variety of genres by individual students, with a focus on the process. Like real writers, students are working on pieces that may be in various stages of development toward completion, including multiple drafts of self-selected writing. While the general topic might be directed by the teacher (such as researching and writing about local history), the specific topic is left to the writer. The context of the actual writing is the impetus for the teacher to teach minilessons from time to time on writing conventions and mechanics to large groups, small groups, or individuals. In writer's workshop, conferences consist of teachers guiding individuals or small groups and peers guiding each other after some training and experience. The teachers are also writers in writer's workshop, occasionally working on pieces of their own to act as strong models of writing. Sharing emerging and finished works happens often, and publication is a natural consequence of some of the writing of each student. Writer's workshop techniques and procedures are more fully outlined in a number of references (Atwell, 1987; Calkins, 1994; Graves, 1991).

General Strategies

The following general strategies may be applied in any subject area, theme, or type of classroom that is suited to diverse settings.

Individual Contracts (fl)—These can be used to further individualized research or projects or to enhance research and study skills. These contracts

Sample Web

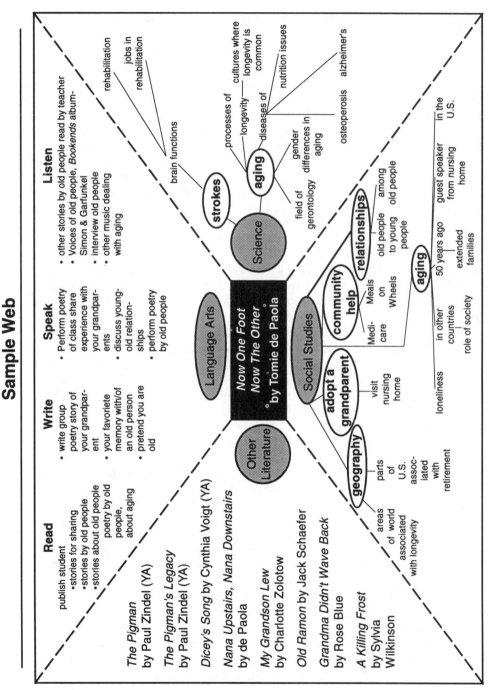

Figure 7-2

are jointly developed by the child and the teacher based on teacher parameters. Contracts list specific expectations as well as required products. Sometimes teachers design forms to facilitate this process (see Figure 7-3).

Projects (em, ea, fl)—Products that permit assessment of student learning are frequently in the form of projects. Projects are scored through the use of a rubric that can be created by the class or the teacher alone. Each project is directly related to the individual student's research or inquiry. The parameters for the projects are the same; however, the product is different based upon the chosen topic and interpretation of the rubric criteria. Projects are completed in class during designated time and can be in the form of dramas, presentations, technologically enhanced presentations, games, art products, simulations, and so on. More information on projects is available from Ward (1988), including involving parents and dealing with possible plagiarism.

Games (em, ea, fl)—Some schools or classrooms set aside time either daily or occasionally for students to engage in games that require critical or strategic and speculative thinking or problem solving. During such times, students may choose to play chess, checkers, selected card games, "battleship," "Othello," and so on. During these times, kidwatching may take place to collect valuable information about learners' strengths and potentials. This information may be utilized to make curricular decisions and to enhance personal development, and it is consistent with utilizing multiple intelligences.

Learning Centers/Stations (em, ea, fl)—Learning centers or stations are activities designed for implementation with small groups without a teacher present and without a formal evaluation. The experiences designed by teachers for centers or stations may vary in the degree to which they are structured with specific or open-ended instructions, but they are always active, hands-on experiences. Typically, centers relate somehow to themes or content study. Some centers may be more or less permanent, such as a listening center, art center, or writing center, where the procedures do not vary but the specific materials do. Other centers may be temporary, lasting within the classroom for a period of weeks and then terminated, such as a specific experience related to a theme that would not apply to other areas of study. For example, during a study of the Middle East and Operation Desert Storm, a particular science center was constructed where students could experiment with the effects of oil on different animal-related substances (because of the extensive oil spills that were created during the war). Substances such as fur, feathers, bone, and shells were provided to be dunked into a shallow pan containing motor oil. Students were then provided with a variety of safe substances with which to attempt to clean the oil, including paper towels, cloth, ordinary soap, and dish detergent. Students later wrote about what they learned. This center was terminated once the study of the Middle East was completed. Generally speaking, any paper-and-pencil tasks produced in conjunction with centers are designed to be self-checking or peer-checked.

Sample Individual Contract for
Independent Study

Name _____ Date _____

Topic/Theme/Concept _____

Requirements

1.   One written report of two to three pages.

2.   At least three references other than encyclopedia.

3.   At least one on-line source.

4.   Options—Circle one letter
     a.   a bulletin board depicting what I learned
     b.   a diorama depicting what I learned
     c.   a computer presentation with graphics, sound clips, and charts
     d.   a mural depicting what I learned
     e.   a skit that I will present to the class that will inform them about
          my topic
     f.   other (to be discussed with teacher)

This contract will be completed by _____
                                                      (date)

Assessment

Student comments (Explain how I went about completing my contract,
what I think I did best, how I think I could have done better):

Teacher comments:

Figure 7-3

Cooperative Learning (em, ea, fl)—A strategy that is appropriate at times in all classrooms is cooperative learning. Johnson and Johnson (1987) suggest that cooperative learning is more than putting students side by side and having them complete work together. Conceptual cooperative learning is a long-range means of creating interdependence and individual accountability rather than the quick gimmicks often associated with cooperative learning when low-level tasks are the focus. Children are taught how to be interdependent group members as well as individuals accountable for work and information. Groups are often created that stay together for long periods of time and are used as the context for many different types of activities. However, other groups are used on a short-term basis so that children become familiar with everyone's ideas in addition to those with whom they work most often.

Cross-Age Tutoring (em, ea, fl)—Crossed-age tutoring was discussed extensively in chapter 1, since studies on it provide insights into learning dynamics in a diverse setting. However, it's also a strategy, and a very powerful one for both tutor and tutee.

Learning Logs (ea, fl)—Learning logs (or *Writing to Learn*) are essentially journals except that they are geared specifically toward writing about a content-area lesson, such as math, science, or social studies. Generally, writing is designed to follow up the lesson with a general prompt (such as "Write what you have learned" or "Write an example of what was just learned") or a more specific prompt (such as "Discuss the most difficult problem you did today and why it was hard") (Countryman, 1992). Learning logs take advantage of writing as a powerful learning tool for students because of the cognitive demand that writers present and synthesize in words what they are thinking (Emig, 1981; Flower and Hayes, 1981; Perl, 1980). For teachers, learning logs create an invaluable assessment means. Examination of learning logs helps teachers to know what students understand, what misconceptions exist, and whether a lesson was successful. Many teachers report that this assessment aspect is as valuable for self-assessing teaching as it is for evaluating student learning. Generally speaking, learning logs are not formally assessed, although feedback for the effort put into them might at times be appropriate. Teachers may examine entries for evidence of understanding in order to evaluate individual student progress, and they can note it accordingly for portfolios or classroom record-keeping systems.

Cooking (em, ea, fl)—Cooking is real-life math, science, and social studies that forces the application of fractions (using measuring cups and spoons), science (changing properties of substances with heating and cooling; adding ingredients such as yeast; understanding mixtures, nutrition, and properties of substances), and social studies (foods from different cultures, nationally and internationally). Although cooking usually requires additional supervision (such as an older student or trained parent volunteer), the experience is academically grounding and memorable. One of us used cooking extensively in her teaching experience, dividing the class into groups ahead of time, having the group assign responsibilities for ingredients and equipment (Who will bring the flour? Who will bring the mixing bowl?) days before the actual cooking would take place. Baking schedules were arranged with the school cafeteria personnel when necessary. Experiences with cooking rarely receive formal evaluation, since even things that go wrong can be tremendous learning experiences (such as the time when one group forgot to put yeast in their pizza crust and another group accidentally doubled theirs). However, the cooperative, interpersonal skills of working together may be part of an evaluation, as we continue to value social development more in elementary teaching.

"We are in an outside portable and our door is usually open. If you would look in, you would see students seated in pairs or foursomes. Because students are encouraged to discuss work with each other, the room is often not quiet. Students are allowed and encouraged to move around when appropriate. Students are also seen going from room to room. Perhaps you would see third-, fourth-, and fifth-grade students reading with their first- and second-grade buddies. Theme displays and student works cover all the wall space."

—Jackie Robbie
Colorado Springs, CO

Box 7-5

Student-Led Instruction (ea, fl)—We have observed this being used in multiage classes very effectively. Content-area study was divided into subtopics in either science or social studies themes. Each subtopic was adopted by a heterogeneous committee within the class. Students' responsibilities were to teach themselves the necessary content through the use of texts and other informational sources and then teach the material to their classmates. Presentations of content included appropriate visual aids (posters, overheads, diagrams), guided practice (group-constructed worksheet or activity, sometimes in the form of student-assigned and student-evaluated homework), and evaluations (test questions to be used later, student committee evaluating homework results for student assessment and self-assessment of lesson). Assessment of the process might be accomplished through a rubric describing teacher and student expectations, group self-assessment (How well did we do? What would we do differently next time?), and class assessment of the presenters.

Experiments (em, ea, fl)—Experiments have long been a mainstay of science teaching but may be appropriate in other areas as well. One advantage in the multiage setting is having some of the more responsible students placed in each group where experiments are being conducted. This grouping can help procedures to go smoothly and may require somewhat less direct teacher supervision. More is accomplished in experimenting if everyone participates in some manner, perhaps by having stations with complete sets of materials and instructions (rather than one experiment being performed for the class). These stations can rotate if, for example, there aren't enough microscopes to go around for every group to conduct an experiment of some kind concurrently. Both the process (working together) and the product (an explanation, observation, diagram, chart of computations) are available for assessment as necessary.

Drawing to Learn (em, ea, fl)—One rather simple way to add a "hands-on," experiential element to lessons is to have students draw something in conjunction with their lessons. In science teaching, for example, drawing can enhance concepts and better anchor student understanding. If the group is studying insects, then drawing the insects and labeling their parts will reinforce the terms and ideas. Wendy visited a multiage intermediate class in Australia that had just been studying streams and estuaries. Students in all age groups were designing a scene of an estuary that had certain requirements set by the teacher. Several different kinds of flora and fauna that had been studied had to appear in the scene. Those items had to be drawn as well as each student could, with correct features and colors to demonstrate their understanding of the key elements taught. Part of each scene had to be under water and part along the water's edge. Blue acetate was cut and placed over the water portion of the picture to make a finished product for display. Theme books, mentioned earlier, also use drawing to learn ideas.

Strategies That Don't Work in Multiage Settings

Understanding what doesn't work in diverse settings will be described generically rather than by strategy names or labels. It should be obvious that strategies that are contrived for grade levels don't work for multiage settings. We will mention these by categories.

Because part of the multiage model is making diversity a strength, and in that model students readily forget their grade-level designations, then one counterproductive move would be to split the class by grade level for whatever purpose (except, perhaps, standardized testing). In other words, since we have emphasized the value of having learners of mixed abilities together, it would be nonsensical to divide these same class members by grade levels for math, reading, or spelling instruction.

Jodi Kinner and Beth Bonner, who have team taught for several years, were happy with their math program, which was integrated into content-area themes and featured manipulative, concrete, real-life mathematics experiences. Children were developmentally grouped at times for specialized instruction in a particular math skill, but these groups were temporary and fluid. As in most multiage classes we have visited, the lines between grade-level designations became extremely blurred. Often, students have to think hard to remember their "grade level" because it is not relevant in everyday life.

These two teachers, who were in the same building as some traditional, nonmultiage intermediate teachers, succumbed to pressure from their peers to get their students "ready" for the subsequent grade. Consequently, they split their multiage family into grade levels for math instruction for an entire year. They were extremely sorry that they did this, and they have vowed to never again compromise their own quality program for the sake of teachers who are less knowledgeable about developmentally appropriate instruction.

In addition to taking away the powerful role models conducive to more learning, the split caused students to begin to notice grade-level issues more readily. Whereas they could once include a struggling older student in the group with younger students for reading or any other subject-area instruction, under this system students began to notice when they were the "only second grader" in the group. Previously such distinctions had been seamless and consequently were not an issue. Splitting the group for math was a big mistake in hindsight. These teachers learned a valuable lesson, including a need for confidence in their own teaching!

Departmentalization is another structure that does not work in a multiage setting (nor is it developmentally sound in any grade-level setting). For example, among several multiage classrooms, the teachers might decide that one of them teach all the math while another one teaches only science or reading. This structure places the requirements of a curriculum over the needs of the children. Furthermore, it breaks up the community and the benefit of the predictable and stable environment that multiage classes enjoy.

Tag teaming, which is similar to departmentalization, is another structure to avoid. Where two teachers work as a team, there are four eyes always in the room and on the children. Tag teaming means that one teacher takes a break while the coteacher teaches, creating a turn-taking sort of system. Even in a good team, one teacher is generally teaching at a time, but the other teacher is not off somewhere on a break. He or she is serving in another capacity but is involved and observing students nonetheless.

Having the same expectations with the same paper-and-pencil activities in a classroom is also inappropriate in a multiage class. Actually, it's inappropriate in *any* classroom, as even grade-level membership does not imply equal ability or achievement. In a multiage class, however, it is even less workable.

Whatever tasks teachers have students undertake, the expectations for each student should always be commensurate with age and ability. In other words, everyone should always do one's personal best.

Similarly, using grade-level texts with the expectation that students perform in similar ways is inappropriate for multiage classes. Textbooks may certainly be useful in the multiage classroom, but they can't be used in the same way they would have been in a traditional grade-level class. Some teachers find useful information and resources in their existing texts. They may be used for ideas, overviews of topics students are studying, maps and graphics, and ideas or examples for follow-up guided practice on certain kinds of skills.

We have already discussed that multiage classes still have time for whole-group instruction. However, a steady diet of whole-group, lecture-style instruction all day long (which we wouldn't recommend in *any* classroom), or for extended periods of time, would be dismal in a multiage setting. Whole-group experiences, when they are used, should be presented in such a way as to accommodate individual differences. For example, lessons might begin with a review, include examples to suit different learners, or be more far-reaching in scope to challenge higher achieving students. In any case, the expectation that all students get the same benefit from any lesson is not appropriate (nor is it in any class, actually). That is simply a throwback to the factory model that we have been trying to abandon with multiage teaching and learning.

Assessment will be discussed in Chapter 9, but it should be readily apparent by now that no single assessment with the same expectations or benchmarks is appropriate in the diverse classroom. In other words, if there were to be a test on a unit of study, even one that all students could handle, different scores should at least be expected for different students based on their abilities. The multiage environment is conducive, however, to more authentic and multiple assessments for both short-term and long-term goals.

By now the theme should be obvious. An academic assembly line is not conducive to a diverse classroom (and even grade-level classrooms are diverse). Anytime that developmentally appropriate experiences are implemented and assessed accordingly, instruction and assessment are both suitable for multiage teaching and learning.

Scheduling for Success

Scheduling the school day will vary greatly from building to building; it has much to do with time constraints, imposed by the busy agendas we try to accomplish in elementary and middle school settings. The general goal for scheduling in a multiage class, or any class where inquiry and sustained engagement is the goal, is to try to find the largest blocks of time possible with the least number of delineations or borders between subjects or experiences. Because of the difficulty of finding enough quality time in any one day, many teachers have taken to scheduling by the week instead. For example, rather than having writer's workshop every day for a short period of time, have it less often for a longer period. Instead of having math every day, concentrate it into longer blocks of time with practice, manipulatives, or problem-solving games.

Here we attempt to describe and share some actual schedules from multiage classes we have visited, or schedules that have been shared with us by multiage teachers that we have met or with whom we have worked. We hope that the array of ideas will assist anyone in coming up with alternatives that are more suitable for sustained engagement. We present a generic schedule from a primary multiage, one schedule from an intermediate, and two from our interviewees.

The classroom where Wendy and a colleague did their multiage research had the advantage of having the same time every day scheduled for one of the "specials," such as art, music, library, or computer. This schedule was the same when this class was a K–1, a K–2, and later a K–3. Their day looked like this:

8:30–9:00   Arrival, attendance, lunch counts

9:00–10:15   Large-group instruction (centered on the theme, generally around a big book or class-generated story, with content and skills embedded into the reading and study of the text, and sometimes language experience story on what was learned).

10:15–10:30   Directions for rest of the day, especially the centers. No one was allowed to ask the teacher these directions afterwards; questions not raised during this time period had to be directed to classmates.

10:30–11:35   Centers: writing, listening, art, math, reading corner, and other occasional centers. In this time period, the teacher pulled aside any small groups that needed instruction (minilessons) in any subject. Centers are all student-managed concurrently.

11:35–12:30   Lunch, recess

12:30–1:10   Specials

1:10–2:15   Miscellaneous. This time could be used to complete centers, catch up from previous lessons, or write in journals, but it was left without a particular designation for flexibility.

2:15–2:30   Group sharing, debriefing. Everyone gathered in the same place where they had started the day. Students shared how their day went, something they had learned, announcements, reminders of things to take home or bring back to school, and previews for the following day.

2:30   Buses begin to arrive for dismissal.

One valuable aspect of this schedule is that it's simple and flexible. Three major time blocks are allotted, one for whole-group instruction and two for "other." Plan books are not made too far in advance so as to allow for necessary changes when lessons or activities take longer than originally planned. Another classroom Wendy visited, of intermediate and inclusion multiage students, also had this simple and flexible element. Most teaching was thematic, so a generic schedule like this appeared on a chart on the classroom wall. Their day looked like this:

8:30–9:00   Opening activities

9:00–9:45   Center 1

9:45–10:30   Center 2

10:30–10:45   Break

10:45–11:30   Center 3

11:30–12:15   Specials

12:15–1:00   Lunch, recess

1:00–2:15   Center 4

2:15–2:30   Clean-up

In this daily generic schedule, "center" could mean several things. Themes alternated between a social studies–based theme and a science one. At the time of our visit, the class had just completed an in-depth study of the Civil War and was currently starting a study of the human body. The class was divided into committees. For the human body study, each committee was charged with the task of becoming resident experts on one system of the body, making plans to teach it, assigning appropriate homework or follow-up work, and writing several test questions for a later examination. Consequently, some center times were used for small-group research, planning, and preparation, whereas another center time might be devoted to students teaching their classmates content material. Some center time was also used for the teacher to pull aside small groups or individuals who needed instruction in a concept or practice in a skill. This might be language, math, or anything else.

This schedule allows fluid movement from one part of the day to another. Some days might consist of rather intense study and research; others might involve more presentations. Often, the beginning of one center time might be a continuation of activities from the previous center time.

Individual Schedules

Some of the teachers we interviewed shared their schedules. Jodi Kinner and Beth Bonner have a schedule that may appear fractured at first glance. Special subjects such as music and art are staggered rather inconveniently throughout the week—a feature the two teachers don't control. They have labeled different parts of their day with different terms despite the fact that all parts relate, whenever possible, to their theme. During the time that we interviewed this team, they had just completed a conceptual unit they called "Soil, Sand, and Silt," which addressed concepts related to geology, geography, topography, and soil science, as well as many other topics. "Inquiry workshops" might be whole-group lessons where new questions about the concepts would be explored. "Theme centers" would be small-group, hands-on experiences related to the inquiry. "Literature choices" were titles of fiction and nonfiction that related to some aspect of "Soil, Sand, and Silt." Similarly, "read aloud" time was thematically related to the content. The only parts of the day other than "specials" that might not relate directly to the integrated content would be the "D.E.A.R." time (Drop Everything and Read), which was a free-choice individual reading time scheduled on most days. Figure 7-4 lays out their weekly schedule.

Nancy Norman also shared her integrated schedule with us. It doesn't, however, fit neatly into a figure, so it is listed as follows:

8:55 a.m.: Buses arrive, coats off, sign in, lunch count, handwriting practice. Some students then play math games. Children who are able copy a daily message from the board that also needs some editing for punctuation and spelling.

9:05 a.m.: Tardy bell rings. Students play math games, which are usually chosen by the teacher and focus mostly on operations. Students share their strategies for problem solving with their partners. The teacher meets with small groups to work on new strategies or reinforce old ones. The teacher records observations about student development on a clipboard and in a notebook.

9:40 a.m.: Stop math games and do one of the following:

1. *Roll and Write*—Students roll teacher-made numeral dice appropriate for their ability level for 5 minutes and write the problem and record the solution. One day a week the children do an addition roll and write; one day is "doubles" roll and write, and one day is subtraction. The goal of roll and write is to increase the number of total problems that can be worked in 5 minutes.

Sample Weekly Schedule				
MONDAY	**TUESDAY**	**WEDNESDAY**	**THURSDAY**	**FRIDAY**
8:00–8:25— Planning	Planning	Planning	Planning	Planning
8:25–9:00— Settle in & News	Settle in & News	Settle in & News	Settle in 8:35–9:25—Art	Settle in & News
9:00–9:45— Theme Centers	Math	Theme Centers	News	Theme Centers
9:45–10:00— Recess				
10:00–10:15— Math	10:00–11:10— Inquiry Workshop*	10:00–11:10— Inquiry Workshop*	10:00–11:10— Inquiry Workshop*	10:00–10:40— Math
10:15–11:10— Music	* Science or math workshop or theme-related activities			10:40–11:05— Physical Education
10:40–11:10— Math				
11:10–11:45— Lunch				
11:45–12:15— D.E.A.R. (Individual conferences)	11:45–12:20— D.E.A.R.	11:45–12:15— D.E.A.R.	11:45–11:55— Read Aloud 11:55–12:20— Music	11:45–12:00— Read Aloud 12:00–12:25— Media Checkout & D.E.A.R.
12:15–12:45— Literature Choices (small group instruction)	12:20–12:45— Physical Education	12:15–12:45— Literature Choices	12:20–12:45— D.E.A.R.	12:25–12:55— Literature Choices
12:45–1:00— Read Aloud	12:45–1:15— Literature Choices	12:45–1:10— Physical Education	12:45–1:15— Literature Choices	12:55–1:35— Literature Study Groups
1:00–1:30— Literature Study Groups	1:15–1:30— Read Aloud	1:10–1:25— Read Aloud	1:15–2:00— Writer's Workshop	
1:30–1:45— Recess	1:30–2:00— Literature Study Groups	1:25–2:25— Writer's Workshop (minilessons)		1:35–2:00— Reading Buddies
1:45–2:25— Writer's Workshop	2:00–2:25— Music		2:00–Early Release— (Building/ District Meetings)	2:00–2:25— Author's Chair
2:25–2:50— Oral Literature	2:25–2:50— Writer's Workshop	2:25–2:50— Media		2:25–2:50— Oral Literature
3:00—Dismissal				

Figure 7-4

2.   Two days a week, for about 15 minutes, students copy a set of four problems, appropriate to their developmental level, from the chalkboard onto paper, solve the problems, and check their solutions with a calculator. As they finish, the teacher writes two or three more problems for each child that are appropriate to his or her developmental level.

3.   Two days a week, for about 10 minutes, students work in a whole-group setting with the teacher posing problems of various difficulty on the overhead or chalkboard; students solve the problems "in their heads" and then share their strategies with the other students.

4.   Once a week for about 20 minutes, students work individually or with a partner on open-ended problem solving; the last 5–10 minutes, they share strategies as a whole group.

10:00 a.m. or so: Guided reading and response groups, independent self-chosen reading, listening center. Children record a written response to a book once a week. About once a month, after children have established good strategies, the teacher conferences individually with students and records observations on a clipboard and in a notebook. Children are regrouped frequently depending on the strategies with which they need help. Students read books appropriate for their instructional level chosen by the teacher and books that they choose themselves for independent reading time. About once a quarter they do several "Readers' Theater" productions for a whole week. Children also practice writing their spelling words during this time. The teacher uses a special spelling program that she has developed for this purpose that reinforces spelling patterns and reading skills.

10:20 a.m.: Kindergartners arrive, sign in, do handwriting practice. Teacher checks handwriting, assigns a few letters to practice, and records observations about development on a clipboard; children begin reading from individual book boxes, then independent self-chosen reading.

10:40 a.m.: Begin kindergarten reading conferences, which are individual; teacher records observations about strategies used on a clipboard and in a notebook.

11:00 a.m. or so: Class meeting begins with a "Book Commercial" (students sharing books they've read) and then a read aloud by the teacher. Reading strategies and personal response are modeled. A variety of reading materials and genres are used. Discussion includes topics such as author's and illustrator's style or purpose. Once or twice a week the whole group contributes to a concept web, story map, or Venn diagram about the book(s). Sometimes they dramatize the story. Following the story are some routines, which may include phonics (2 minutes), calendar, newspaper reporter, show and tell, rote counting, reading strategies, and modeling of personal response. Activities may also include "Author's Tub," a shared reading from big books and/or chart paper (sometimes students dramatize big books), snack bucket,

"Mystery Bag," and other take-home math, science, and writing bags. Reference strategies are modeled (using indexes, atlases, globes, maps, encyclopedias, and dictionaries). Some, but never all, these things are done.

11:30 a.m. or so: More math activities, which are chosen by the teacher and usually focus in an interdisciplinary way on measurement, estimation, problem solving, geometry and spatial relations, patterning, sorting, and graphing. Math games involving operations may also be included during this time. Children almost always work with a partner or in a small group. The teacher observes and records student development on a clipboard and in a notebook. On some days, this math time is skipped and writing time continues instead.

11:45 a.m. or so: Writer's Workshop, using the writing process. The teacher conferences with the children individually as needed and records observations in a notebook and on a clipboard. Children choose a topic and write about it in a spiral notebook in order to keep a record of their writing development in one place. Completed writing products are published (teacher word processes for students), illustrated by the student, shared with the class via the "Author's Tub," and then sent home or filed.

12:10 p.m.: Children eat lunch in the classroom. Teacher uses this time to check in homework reading books and to check out new ones. Children are expected to have someone in their home read to them each evening. More experienced readers are expected to read *to* someone at home each evening.

After the children finish lunch, they go outdoors for recess. When they return, they have 5–10 minutes together for "shared spelling" time, where the teacher models spelling generalizations based on words that the students generate and spell.

1:15–1:45 p.m.: Special classes—music, physical education, and library classes.

1:45 p.m.: Study time (integrated science, social studies, and health instruction). This period is devoted to developing an understanding of basic science, social studies, and health concepts centered on a theme or topic unit. The teacher uses a constructivist lesson planning model that she has developed that allows children to explore with real materials and generalize their understanding of the concept for that day. Each of the concepts helps the children to be able to produce a product at the end of the unit called "unit tests." In order to demonstrate "mastery" of the material in each unit, students create a product with a team of other students in the class. The products are evaluated using a rubric that the students and teacher design together to describe what an exemplary performance will be. Sometimes the lesson for the day is done in small groups with the teacher while other students work on other projects; at other times the students work in small groups, but all students do the activity at the same time.

Independent project time is chosen and directed by the students. On days when the children do not go to physical education, they either go out for a short recess, do some type of creative movement activity, or dance in the classroom. There is no art activity on Fridays; beginning in October, the children cook instead. If the children would like a snack, they may eat it during this time. Children take turns bringing a snack from home for the whole class.

3:10 p.m.: Clean up the room. It's usually a mess by this time of day, and the students can actually clean it in 5 minutes! Sometimes they stop 5 minutes earlier if some students have a special project they want to share with the rest of the class.

3:15 p.m.: Singing is done many times during the day, but there is a special singing time as the children put their coats on and get ready to go home. They leave the classroom singing every day.

3:25 p.m.: Dismissal

The two individual schedules we have presented here are vastly different because local situations vary greatly. Yet both feature a great deal of integration of subject matter and aspects that create a community. Schedules for multiage classes will vary as much as schedules in any setting. The particulars will vary, and there will be some aspects that teachers most likely do not control. However, for the parts of the schedule that are in one's control, two guidelines may be useful. The first is to work towards longer blocks of time that are conducive to sustained engagement. The second is to allow for flexibility. For example, sometimes it's best not to schedule every single block of time in advance. Often, the unpredictable demands of everyday school life will result in not getting things accomplished as originally intended. Having some open space will allow for flexibility throughout the week and enable the class to bring closure to particular lessons and activities.

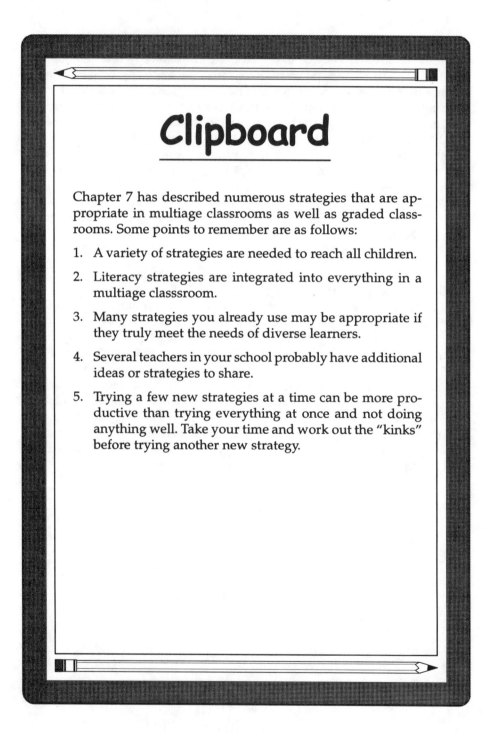

Clipboard

Chapter 7 has described numerous strategies that are appropriate in multiage classrooms as well as graded classrooms. Some points to remember are as follows:

1. A variety of strategies are needed to reach all children.

2. Literacy strategies are integrated into everything in a multiage classsroom.

3. Many strategies you already use may be appropriate if they truly meet the needs of diverse learners.

4. Several teachers in your school probably have additional ideas or strategies to share.

5. Trying a few new strategies at a time can be more productive than trying everything at once and not doing anything well. Take your time and work out the "kinks" before trying another new strategy.

To: Teachers & Principals

From: Wendy & Libbie

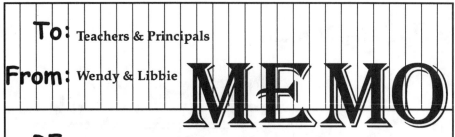

RE: Meeting District Requirements and Proficiency Tests

One strategy outlined in chapter 7 is literature circles. Sometimes we worry that when we innovate, we won't meet district guidelines or we won't be preparing our students for state proficiency tests. Following is a list of objectives met using literature circles based on the Cleveland City Schools' study guides. The indication "P4" means it's tested on the Ohio Proficiency Test at grade 4. "P6" means it's tested at grade 6. You can construct a list like this for your district or state.

Literature Circles

Identify various literary forms. (P4, P6)

Compare and contrast elements of works of various authors. (P4, P6)

Analyze story elements of fiction selections. (P4, P6)

Infer meaning from daily reading. (P4, P6)

Choose probable outcomes using clues contained in fiction. (P4, P6)

Determine reasonable conclusions using details in fiction. (P4, P6)

Determine the best summary of fiction or other genre. (P4, P6)

Summarize or retell fiction or other genre. (P4, P6)

Identify similes and metaphors in fiction. (P4, P6)

Distinguish between literal and figurative expressions. (P4, P6)

Select fiction or nonfiction in response to a theme. (P4, P6)

Compare and contrast story elements. (P4, P6)

Memo 7-1

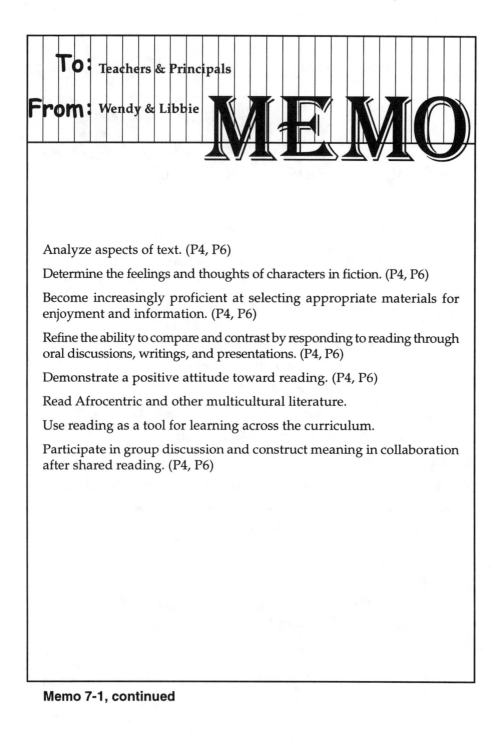

To: Teachers & Principals

From: Wendy & Libbie

MEMO

Analyze aspects of text. (P4, P6)

Determine the feelings and thoughts of characters in fiction. (P4, P6)

Become increasingly proficient at selecting appropriate materials for enjoyment and information. (P4, P6)

Refine the ability to compare and contrast by responding to reading through oral discussions, writings, and presentations. (P4, P6)

Demonstrate a positive attitude toward reading. (P4, P6)

Read Afrocentric and other multicultural literature.

Use reading as a tool for learning across the curriculum.

Participate in group discussion and construct meaning in collaboration after shared reading. (P4, P6)

Memo 7-1, continued

Math in the Multiage Classroom

In a multiage intermediate classroom that one of us has visited often, students produced the newspaper for their elementary school. *The Moody Express* at Moody Elementary School in Bradenton, Florida, was published monthly and was student reported, written, designed, illustrated, edited, marketed, and distributed. Inside the school, it was sold for 10 cents a copy. Obviously, within the process of producing and selling a publication from beginning to end, a great deal of authentic language arts and mathematics learning took place.

One feature of *The Moody Express* was a Letters to the Editor column written by students and staff. On one occasion, an intermediate-age student wrote a letter that provoked hours of genuine mathematical learning. The letter writer levied an accusation against the school (and schools in general) that the distribution of space was unfair. Younger students, the letter writer alleged, have larger-size rooms and fewer students in their classes. Consequently, individual younger students, who are themselves much smaller people, have more relative space allotted to them in the school building. The letter writer further explained that older students in the school are not treated fairly. In addition to having larger class sizes, their classrooms are smaller, and since older kids are bigger, they need more space than younger students.

This surprising accusation caused a flurry of activity among *The Moody Express* staff. Was the letter writer correct? How could they find out? How should they respond in the next edition?

Students had to gather long measuring tapes, measure the classrooms to determine their area in square feet, find out the population of each room, and calculate the amount of area allotted to each class member. The process was lengthy in this school of almost 600 pupils. When they were done, they had to organize their data by rooms designated for "lower grades" and "upper grades," interpret their figures, write a response for the next edition, and present their findings to the principal. (The letter writer was correct, by the way; older students in the school had less relative space than younger ones.)

Mathematics teaching has undergone a revolution in recent years similar to the revolution in language arts and reading known as the whole language movement. Paper-and-pencil skill-and-drill computations, once the sole math curriculum, have been reconsidered. The National Council of Teachers of Mathematics (NCTM) has offered meaningful and specific guidelines for a mathematics curriculum (see Appendix G) to help students construct an understanding of mathematical concepts and use those concepts to solve realistic, practical problems like the students at Moody Elementary School did. These kinds of interesting, engaging, and relevant experiences have breathed life, enjoyment, and rigor into the teaching and learning of math.

Math as a Language and a Tool

For many years, students of all ages have performed operations, row by row, example by example, both in school and for homework. These abstract exercises, which were decontextualized from problem solving, have been a mainstay in math teaching. Students memorized formulas and multiplication tables and could perform computations, but they were often unable to apply these mathematical concepts when they were not neatly contrived for them or written in a tidy manner on a work sheet. The result of years of this was frustrating for many learners, who ended up disliking math education and even felt extremely apprehensive about their abilities in math (Bickmore-Brand, 1990; Countryman, 1992; Gawned, 1990; Mills, O'Keefe, & Whitin, 1996; Parker, 1993; Rowan & Bourne, 1994).

Today, a different attitude toward mathematics has replaced those time-worn practices. Mathematics is viewed as both a language and a tool (Bickmore-Brand, 1990). As a language, there is a recognition that mathematics is a process that relates to everyday life. Many of the principles applied to language learning also apply to math education. These include teaching math in context for relevant, meaningful learning; utilizing the interests of learners and beginning with areas with which they can relate; modeling mathematical thinking and problem solving by others in the environment; building learner scaffolding; building metacognitive strategy; helping students take responsibility for their own learning; and teaching math within a supportive learning community (Bickmore-Brand, 1990).

"One way I deal with mathematics instruction in my multiage setting is by organizing center-type activities that the students rotate through. This allows me to work with individuals or small groups. Just as in literacy, I feel that children need to have a balanced math program. They need experiences with classification, ordering, patterning, measurement, geometry, fractions, and numeration. Some instruction is given to the whole group depending on the need. This year, for example, our whole group benefited from direct instruction in time, fractions, and geometry."

—Jodi Kinner
Iowa City, IA

Box 8-1

As a tool, mathematics is now viewed as something that is only truly meaningful to learners when the concepts are applied to solving meaningful, real-life problems and can be used by the students to construct their own, lasting meaning. (Will those students at Moody Elementary ever forget how to calculate *area*?) Today, teachers are charged with the challenge of helping students to experience math in ways that make sense to them at their age and developmental level. The idea is that math is part of everyday life and can be integrated into other areas that help students make connections between areas of learning.

The NCTM guidelines listed in Appendix G can be implemented into classrooms of all age groups. In addition to these standards, NCTM lists five instructional goals to guide student learning. These include the following: learning to value mathematics; becoming confident in their ability to do mathematics; becoming mathematical problem solvers; learning to communicate mathematically; and learning to reason mathematically (Rowan & Bourne, 1994). The real-life experience of *The Moody Express* newspaper staff helped to fulfill all these goals.

Why Is Math Teaching More Difficult?

Throughout our consultations with schools that are already multiage, starting to be multiage, or thinking about becoming multiage in the future, the most common concern we found was about teaching mathematics. Persistent questions posed to us all over this country and elsewhere have led us to several possible conclusions. First, as a group, elementary teachers are less well prepared in teaching mathematics than other subjects. Second, elementary teachers are less confident in their math teaching abilities. Third, elementary teachers are themselves less proficient in mathematics as a skill.

As is usually the case, reality lies somewhere among these possibilities. Recently, one of us was teaching a short course on multiage teaching. Knowing that the group was relatively confident about their teaching of reading and writing, when the topic of math came up, we asked our students this question: *What is the same in teaching literacy and teaching math?*

As a group, the teachers in the course constructed the following list:

1. Both math teaching and literacy teaching are developmental.
2. Both involve critical thinking by students.
3. Both literacy and math are language processes.
4. Both literacy and math are symbol systems.
5. Neither literacy nor math is as sequential as we all once believed.
6. Both literacy and math relate to everyday life.
7. In both subjects, the abilities of students will vary greatly.
8. Both literacy and math are best taught through experiential approaches.
9. Both literacy and math are best assessed authentically.
10. Both involve the development of concepts.
11. Both require practice in order to become proficient.
12. Both can be taught using journals.
13. Both literacy and math learning should be developmentally appropriate.
14. In both literacy and math, learners must construct their own meaning.
15. Both literacy and math can utilize technology such as computers.

After the construction of this list, the opposite question was posed to the class. *What is the difference between math teaching and literacy teaching?* Initially this question was met by minutes of silence as the graduate students thought carefully and searched for differences. After what seemed like an eternity, they finally offered the answer that *the difference between literacy teaching and math teaching is teacher confidence!*

Perhaps it is not surprising that the list constructed by our graduate students who are practicing teachers is remarkably similar to the NCTM list of basic standards, which outline some key issues for implementation for grades K–4 (although these notions apply to older learners as well).

1. The understandings that children bring to the classroom should be built upon in classroom experiences.
2. The curriculum should be developmentally appropriate (as listed in the appendix).

3. The quality of content and instruction is more important than the quantity.
4. Children should build confidence in themselves as mathematical learners and not feel inadequate or intimidated by mathematical situations.
5. Children must be actively involved in doing mathematics with hands-on, manipulative, relevant experiences.
6. Mathematics should be integrated into other areas of content so that children see how math is applied in subjects and situations.
7. A broad range of content should be taught (in addition to computation).
8. Calculators and computers should be used appropriately as both computational and instructional tools.

One of the most important things to understand here is that the essential elements for successful literacy teaching also apply to mathematics teaching to a great extent.

The next thing we did with the multiage class was to ask the graduate students to list all the logical and mathematical concepts that belong to that domain but to omit the obvious ones—the operations of addition, subtraction, multiplication, and division (because everyone thinks of those right away, and sometimes we forget how much else there is). The intent here was to revisit the breadth of topics and concepts that constitute mathematical thinking and teaching. These are some of the words that ended up on their list:

Estimation, probability, symmetry, geometry, tangrams, proportion, percentage, ratio, money, place value, decimals, fractions, whole numbers, temperature, negative numbers, time, clock use, speed, distance, linear measurement, metrics, counting, volume, area, perimeter, problem solving, graphing, calculator use, story problems, rounding, nonstandard units of measurement, prediction, weight, patterns, data tables, shapes, dimensions, perspective, diameter, radius, pi, circumference, lines, intersections, associative properties, commutative properties, unknowns, equations, more than, less than, equals, inequalities, congruence, interest, banking, mortgages, loans.

After 20 minutes or so of brainstorming, the graduate students were reminded that mathematical thinking is not only a vast array of topics and concepts, but that many of them relate to other subject areas (graphing in science and social studies) and to real everyday life (banking, stock market, estimation, loans and mortgages).

Key Points to Consider

Here we'd like to reiterate the points we have made over and over in workshops for multiage teachers. Even though they are clearly stated in the NCTM standards, they bear some discussion in reference to multiage teaching specifically.

More Than Computation

The domain of math teaching spans the entire gamut of logical and mathematical thinking. As the list compiled by our class suggests, this is a large domain that touches on many concepts, and many of those concepts seep into everyday life.

"Math is an important part of the structure of our day. Counting, place value, fractions, and reading graphs and thermometers are all part of our morning activities. Along with having a math time every day, we integrate math into other subject areas. Math activities are done as a full group or as small groups. When we meet as a large group, we generally do an activity together and then each student continues to work at his or her own level. When we use small groups, students are divided in many ways. Every Wednesday, students make an entry in their math journals. This gives them another opportunity to explain various math concepts. Two days a week we have parents come in and help us, and we have math groups. The class is divided into four groups to do hands-on math activities. These groups rotate every 15 minutes. The variety of math activities and the hands-on approach that we use in our classroom enables us to reach every student."

—Barbara Kidwell and Sue Beth Arnold
Findlay, OH

Box 8-2

For example, many mathematicians believe that the most commonly used mathematical skill is estimation. People estimate all day long in everyday life. We estimate the time to which we set our alarms to get up in the morning, what time to leave in order to get where we have to go, whether we have enough gas in our car to get there, whether we have sufficient money with us to meet our needs, what tasks we will have the time to complete, how long each task will take, how many groceries we'll need, how many bills we can pay with our paycheck, how much we can afford to save from our paycheck, how long we'll have to save at this rate to meet a financial goal, whether or not we can afford the dress, tool, or computer program we've seen on sale, what time we need to start cooking dinner, what time we need to get to bed to get sufficient sleep, how long we'll take the next morning to get ready, and, consequently, how to set our alarm clock again.

Estimation is therefore a skill that becomes almost unconscious to some and continues to be a challenge for others. Yet we spend little time teaching it in school, for this is one skill that must be learned in realistic settings. A work sheet simply won't get a child to work on time when he or she grows up.

A useful exploration for any classroom would be brainstorming all the ways that logical and mathematical thinking is used around the house. Math is an integral part of cooking, baking, sewing, using tools and nails, hanging pictures, paying bills, telling time, setting clocks, using the telephone, setting the table (counting the implements needed), doing the laundry (measuring the detergent), using the microwave (estimating the time needed), and many more things. In other words, math is an important part of everyday life!

Math Is Developmental

Just because teaching math has been basalized into neat and tidy sequences by publishers does not mean that it is a strict sequential process. Like literacy learning, math is developmental. As learners, we construct our own meanings, build on our own understandings, and are able to handle increasingly complex tasks as we progress. Although there are some things that one needs to know in order to understand others, more often than not there are many things for which the sequence is not critical.

The process by which different learners develop will vary greatly, even among students of the same age. Some students come to logical and mathematical understandings readily, and others struggle and develop more slowly. This has little to do with overall learning capability. Both of us know well-educated, smart adults who developed slowly in either math or reading and today have advanced degrees.

Teachers of younger students have long understood development and have generally known that their students will vary greatly in their development of math (and other) concepts. Teachers of older students are sometimes less informed about developmental issues. Consequently, when learners are very different, teachers have a tendency to blame the students, previous teachers, or the curriculum.

Goodlad and Anderson (1987) remind us that the developmental gap widens rather than closes with age. Upper-grade teachers often deal with more issues of diverse learners and are more likely to have to amend instruction to accommodate individuals than has been previously thought. The same principles that apply to creating developmentally appropriate experiences for younger students apply to intermediate-age students as well.

For example, one of us taught sixth grade for a number of years. Among the 11- to 13-year-olds in that grade level, students who still had difficulty adding a list of six numbers could be found. Others, in the same class of 26 students, had mastered all concepts traditionally taught at that level and were quite ready for simple algebra. Having similar expectations for all students in this classroom would be just as inappropriate as it would be in a multiage class. No matter what the age or circumstances, we still teach learners by starting where they are.

Math for Diverse Settings

In this section, we will outline a number of ways of teaching math that are conducive to learners who vary in their abilities. All these approaches will suit multiage classes and can be used in any combination based on the needs of the learners. Our examples are drawn from our travels. We are not specifically math teachers (although we both have taught elementary school and, as part of those jobs, math). Instead, we are drawing on the many talented teachers we have met in our travels who are having a great deal of success with math in multiage settings.

Math and Literature

Many children's books have been written that are quality literature and also contain quantitative concepts. Whitin and Wilde (1992, 1995) have assembled trade books by age-appropriateness and mathematical topics. They present books, for example, that include counting, classification, big numbers, fractions, geometry, and estimation. Also included with their list are ideas for classroom use.

The use of children's literature in math has several advantages. First, many elementary teachers are already comfortable using literature as a basis for lessons. Second, the concepts arise naturally as part of life situations, showing the relevance of math to everyday life. Pengelly (1990) cautions us that simply reading the books will not ensure an understanding of the concepts imbedded in the story. She suggests that the literature be followed up with concrete experiences that capitalize on the introduction provided by it.

Math Projects

Within other areas we've discussed, there are many projects that include mathematical dimensions. Some math projects might also relate to social studies or science. Franki Sibberson, an Ohio multiage teacher, sends "science challenges" home with her intermediate multiage students, which they must complete with their family over the course of the week. Students report that they like these challenges immensely and learn from them. Nearly all the challenges involve math.

For example, one challenge asked students to discover how far they can lean over without falling. No directions were given on how to find the answer, so students had to find their own way of collecting data. One student shared that he needed his brother to measure because he couldn't lean and measure at the same time. Then his brother helped him to construct a chart of his findings to present back to the class.

"Math has been a challenge! We are becoming more comfortable with our practices. We strive to address all math needs and not isolate as much as possible. We begin each math lesson as a whole group and end each lesson as a whole group. We teach in small groups according to instructional need, which constantly varies. Our math centers support our current math instruction and encompass multiage groups of children. We have found that the children who have been with us and have been exposed to many math concepts soar in their learning! We often wonder if this is due to being in a multiage math setting, or is it just delivery of instruction, or is it just the kids' abilities? Food for thought!"

—Marybeth Phelps and Gloria Morrison
Danielson, CT

Box 8-3

In another challenge, students had to discover the difference between walking and running. By running and walking alternately through water and soft dirt, they were able to note both the different patterns made in water by running or walking and the different depth of impressions made in soft dirt by walking or running feet. Math was used to determine these differences.

Another time the students were prompted to experiment with dropping substances of different masses to see if they would fall evenly or if one would hit the ground first. Again, no one told them how to construct their trials, and all of them realized that they needed an assistant, since their objects were weighed before dropping and trials were timed, recorded, and graphed for interpretation. Projects that explore truly interesting questions can provide opportunities for realistic problem solving.

Math and Social Studies

At the risk of being repetitive, we'll reiterate here what we have said several times already. When working with real numbers in trends, rises, declines, or patterns of information on charts and graphs, the topic has to be *something*, and this topic is either social studies or science material. Here is a good example of math as a tool to further understanding of content material.

Within theme study, both science and social studies issues come up with nearly every theme, and math is a tool for investigating information and questions. For example, the theme study on "Soil, Sand, and Silt" (see chapter 7), may appear mostly science-related. However, when one discusses the impact of housing developments on soil erosion or habitat destruction, social studies has also been addressed. Issues that confront municipalities making decisions between land use that supports human communities and that which maintains natural animal and plant communities is part of social studies. Similarly, the allotment of agricultural land for conservation efforts and the subsidies by governments to farmers to grow fewer crops are both social studies as well as science issues.

Math and Science

The relationship between math and social studies and its spillover into science has just been discussed above. No good, substantive topic belongs to one discipline only when the complexities of the issues, problems, and decisions are explored. This type of teaching blends the traditional disciplines in ways that make learning more meaningful and relevant. This type of teaching is also more intellectually stimulating for teachers and students as they discover questions and issues together. We have referred to science frequently throughout the last few chapters, so we will not repeat ourselves here. Science is a large part of the content we study in school, using the tools of math and language arts.

Math in Theme Teaching

Theme teaching is well suited to multiage classes, as we have discussed in earlier chapters. Within a well-developed theme, opportunities for logical and mathematical thinking have been planned as part of the unit. Sometimes these are experiences at a center or station. At other times there may be projects that require much mathematical application. Earlier we mentioned a theme unit on "predator and prey" with an emphasis on studying wolves. Within such a unit, the possibilities are vast for math, such as charts and graphs. These lend themselves well to small-group lessons as well as centers within an area of study. Every topic or theme study has number concepts that are related. Every topic or theme has information that can be turned into a graph, chart, or time line. Graphing and charting are skills with which students need multiple encounters, and they are also heavily tested on many proficiency and standardized tests.

Consumer Math

One boy in Franki Sibberson's multiage intermediate class decided to compare brands of raisin bran cereal to discover which had the most raisins. Another youngster graphed and charted packages of M&Ms to see if there were equal numbers of red, orange, yellow, blue, green, and brown pieces. Someone else, who was annoyed by the amount of air in bags of potato chips, set out to discover exactly how much air was pumped into them. He wanted to know if they were weighed before or after being blown up to look fuller than they are and how much of the bag space is devoted to actual chips. Still another student decided to compare major dishwashing detergents and see which one's suds last the longest. Another investigated the effects of household products entering the water system on marine life such as snails.

Consumer math is both exciting and relevant. Students choose a problem, issue, or question to investigate. Their investigations may be mostly mathematical, but their experience spills over into social studies (marketing, manufacturing, advertising), science (collecting and interpreting data), and language arts (presenting their findings to the class and writing a letter to the company involved).

As each student pursues a real-life question for which the answer does not exist in any teacher's manual or at the back of any textbook, many decisions must be made that involve logical and mathematical as well as scientific reasoning. How will they find the answer to the question? How will they record their data? Will they need multiple trials to get reliable results? Will they have to control for other factors? How can their information be displayed graphically? What will they share with the involved company at the end of their project?

These mathematical experiences are extremely real and engaging. Students explore questions they care about and that relate to everyday life in some way. The processes are real and require critical thinking as well as a variety of practical skills, like graphing, writing, and presenting. These tasks, we have discovered, are very popular with students, who realize the depth of their learning in such situations. In fact, these types of experiences implement the NCTM standards very well.

Math Journaling

Two teachers in the Kent State University graduate program have chosen to investigate math journaling as a way to enhance math education and the abilities of their students to understand math and to communicate mathematical ideas. Vickie Tapp pursued math journals with her sixth-grade class because she herself had been so very terrified of math as a little girl. She noticed many of the same anxieties in her students, especially the girls. Lisa

Wood had students who all expressed "hating math" at the beginning of the school year, so she made it her goal to change their minds by the end of the year.

Although these teachers did not teach in multiage classes, they had the same issue that exists in multiage ones—students with very different abilities in math. Having expectations of success for all students, they decided to explore the value of math journals in elementary and middle school teaching. Their results were very interesting.

Vickie and Lisa, who both taught intermediate-age students, found that using math journals was effective. Most students reported feeling that the experience had helped them to learn math better. These journals were more popular with female students, who unanimously expressed enthusiasm for math journaling, whereas the boys' opinions were somewhat more mixed.

Math journals make use of the "writing to learn" idea we discussed in chapter 7. Students must think in order to put into language their understanding of something. Math journals force students to confront what they know and what they don't know. They also provide teachers with feedback of the efficacy of the lessons (did everyone get what we taught today?) and act as an assessment tool for understanding individual needs. Teachers direct students to write what they have learned after a particular lesson. Sometimes teacher directions are specific, such as when students are told to write an example of what they have just learned or to explain how what they have learned differs from something else. The important thing about math journals is the modeling that must take place. Mathematical thinking requires logical reasoning that is different from the type of thinking used in other writing contexts (Countryman, 1992).

One primary classroom, for example, was studying subtraction. Students were directed to both draw and write an example that used subtraction. After presenting something like a story problem that had subtraction as part of it, they would also write the resulting equation mathematically.

In the multiage setting, math journals are effective. Concepts taught either to a large group or a small group can be followed with instructions for learners to write about what they understood from the lesson and include an example to illustrate their understanding. Pengelly (1990) cautions that writing alone is insufficient in math journals. It wouldn't be helpful, for example, if students only wrote that they thought it was a really good lesson or that they loved learning about triangles. The writing needs to be specific to the lesson content in order for it to be useful and for the teacher to be able to gauge student understanding as a result.

Math Games and Centers

Manipulative math objects, such as unifix cubes, buttons, tangrams, measuring cups, Cuisenaire rods, and geoboards are featured as part of math centers (see chapter 7 for an explanation of centers or stations) and games. Games and manipulatives that are commercially available, and those that are teacher arranged, can provide the concrete experiences that newer math students need in order to practice and build understanding of whole numbers, counting, operations, place value, and other skills. As usual, activities in the centers are not formally assessed by the teacher and do not produce or feature paper-and-pencil work sheets (unless they are in conjunction with the concrete experiences).

One primary teacher used inexpensive toys as manipulatives to give students concrete assistance with story problems. Using cheap little plastic turtles (they were studying turtles, tortoises, and terrapins), she made a pond scene with fabric paints on a piece of fabric. There were about 25 plastic turtles in a container by the "pond." An assortment of story problems suiting both less experienced and more experienced students were available in a basket, written on file cards at the center. Students at the center were encouraged to work out story problems together that featured adding or subtracting turtles. By acting out the language in the problem, students could understand the necessary computations.

"This year, every one of my 11-year-olds picked math as the subject they do with the most confidence (with the exception of a student new to my room this fall). I give total credit to the multiage approach. I have all three levels (third, fourth, fifth grades) of students working on the same assignments with different expectations. I am required to use the textbooks, so I have modified the assignment to include work from all three levels, although the students don't know which problems came from which book. Younger students are exposed to more new concepts, and some work up to the level of the older students. The older students love to show the younger ones what to do. Putting their ideas into words helps the older students to retain the concepts."

—Jackie Robbie
Colorado Springs, CO

Box 8-4

Commercially produced math games might sometimes be appropriate at math centers. Each item used or purchased should be carefully evaluated.

Do the materials comply with NCTM standards? Are they developmentally appropriate for the ages of the children who will be involved?

Some math games are also available as computer software. As mentioned above, these possibilities should be evaluated for worthiness just as any classroom materials are. Does the math game on the computer comply with NCTM standards? It's neither logical nor economical to spend valuable school money on software that's little more than an electronic workbook page of abstract or inappropriate activities. And, as usual, the software must developmentally suit the ages and abilities of the learners in the classroom who might use it.

Using Existing Math Texts and Materials

While multiage teaching may have fewer requirements for textbooks than most of us have been accustomed to, there may still be a useful place for math textbooks in the multiage classroom. This, of course, depends on the quality and features of the particular text. Some texts, for example, have instructed teachers through the manuals to be used in very sequential ways, without exception. Others offer flexibility, and these can have value in multiage environments.

Jackie Robbie from Colorado Springs feels obligated to use her texts somewhat, although she teaches children ages 8–11. She finds practice examples and exercises in various texts that would have been used for grade-level teaching. She chooses examples or activities to suit her instructional goals regardless of which level of text she uses to get them. The students are not aware what "level" of book has been used. Jackie saves time by this method.

Math texts that already exist may contain excellent graphics, diagrams, and explanations that can be helpful in math teaching. For the study of geometry, metrics, or Roman numerals, for instance, examples, pictures, and diagrams can be helpful (see chapter 7, Nancy Norman's schedule, for some math games).

Classroom Banking

A teacher one of us met in Florida had her entire classroom set up in banking. She paid her students an imaginary salary for doing their work and attending school. She also charged them rent for a desk and school supplies to simulate real-life obligations. Each student had an account on paper in a plastic file box in the room. Bank accounts were brought up to date at the end of the day, initially by the teacher. However, this responsibility was gradually assumed by capable students. Discipline in the classroom was also tied to bank accounts. Students who disobeyed rules could face financial penalties: fines were levied depending on the seriousness of the infraction. This economic system, while primarily mathematical in nature, also included a great deal of social studies. Students began to understand not only banking but also economic structures of communities.

One interesting social studies issue arose from this economic system. Some students, because of poor money management and frequent fines, were bankrupt before more than a few weeks had passed. A class discussion followed that addressed what to do about individuals who could not meet their obligations. Naturally, this discussion included real-life circumstances when, for example, people declared bankruptcy, had their homes foreclosed by banks, or became homeless. Students had to vote to determine whether to levy a tax against themselves to create a welfare system for their struggling classmates, or they could try to think of a better solution to get classmates back on their feet, fiscally speaking.

Computers and Math

Computers have often been used as a means of mathematical practice, but the possibilities go well beyond the electronic workbook page. Computers can help to analyze simple data and create charts and graphs as part of content-area learning. Students can use spread sheets to organize their findings in projects or investigations. Using computers for any substantive investigation or application requires logical thinking and reasoning, which are part of instructional goals. Computer programs can also manage imaginary bank accounts like the ones mentioned above. New software hits the market almost daily. The key is to be critical and evaluate software for worthiness. Good software should help to implement NCTM standards and should be developmentally appropriate.

What Does a Math Lesson Look Like?

Once the decision has been made about what methods or strategies will be used in math, math workshops can be initiated. Math workshops are highly similar in format and principles to reading and writing workshops (Lolli, 1994).

Typically, the teacher has predetermined what focus lesson should be taught. The root of this decision might be a requirement that has yet to be met, or a need that was identified based on student conferences or observations. A minilesson, using manipulatives, models, or demonstrations, is presented to the entire class. Following this short lesson, students are asked to practice the new learning with the same sorts of materials that the teacher used in the lesson, such as unifix cubes, geoboards, or perhaps teacher-constructed manipulatives. As students practice at their own level, teacher observation takes place, perhaps by roaming the room while students work. These observations enable teachers to assess the growth of student understanding and to troubleshoot where needed.

The data that teachers gather during these types of sessions will guide decisions about future instructional needs. Teachers determine small-group lessons for selected students, as well as individual needs. As students complete their practice time, the use of many strategies previously mentioned might begin. Students move into workshop time completing tasks defined by the strategy.

For example, students engaged in consumer math activities might resume their individual or small-group inquiries; classes where banking is a focus might flow into time where students are required to bring their bank accounts up to date. Different groups may be doing different things that were previously started—everyone might pick up where he or she left off during the last math workshop time.

While these independent or small groups continue their activities and assignments, teachers might conduct conferences with individual students to check their understanding. Many teachers keep notebook binders with sections for every student. At the beginning of these personal conferences, the teacher calls up the individuals and starts by asking them about what they are doing and how they are doing it. The teacher listens for understanding or misconceptions. An instant correction with a minilesson where needed might remedy something on the spot, and the teacher notes the change and intervention in the notebook. While only a few individual conferences may be conducted per day, over time the notes on each student become good records of his or her development. Assessment information is readily available to fill out the necessary pupil progress reports.

The conclusion of math workshops might be math journaling, as described earlier. Sometimes oral sharing can take place, with selected students sharing their findings on an ongoing project or inquiry. Math workshop is a busy and productive time of the school day.

Conclusion

No matter what requirements are made of teachers for teaching math to a particular age group of learners, whether there is freedom to innovate or enforcement of strict adherence to curriculum guidelines, all the experiences in mathematical learning still must be adapted to be developmentally appropriate for the group or individuals in question. Written guidelines are not more important than the needs of the human beings whom we serve as teachers (Rowan & Bourne, 1994).

Basic principles still apply no matter what constraints exist. Learners need to be assessed, formally and informally, about what they know and what they can do. Teachers need to decide what students need and how to best teach it to them. Some considerations are the following: Which concepts will lend themselves to whole-group instruction? Which are best addressed through the hands-on experiential nature of centers or stations? Which concepts are most critical for the group or individuals in question? What sequence or strategies will be most effective and assist students in constructing their knowledge and understanding of math?

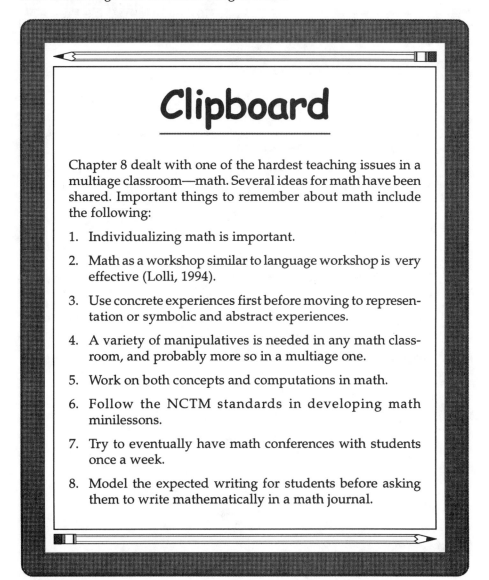

Clipboard

Chapter 8 dealt with one of the hardest teaching issues in a multiage classroom—math. Several ideas for math have been shared. Important things to remember about math include the following:

1. Individualizing math is important.

2. Math as a workshop similar to language workshop is very effective (Lolli, 1994).

3. Use concrete experiences first before moving to representation or symbolic and abstract experiences.

4. A variety of manipulatives is needed in any math classroom, and probably more so in a multiage one.

5. Work on both concepts and computations in math.

6. Follow the NCTM standards in developing math minilessons.

7. Try to eventually have math conferences with students once a week.

8. Model the expected writing for students before asking them to write mathematically in a math journal.

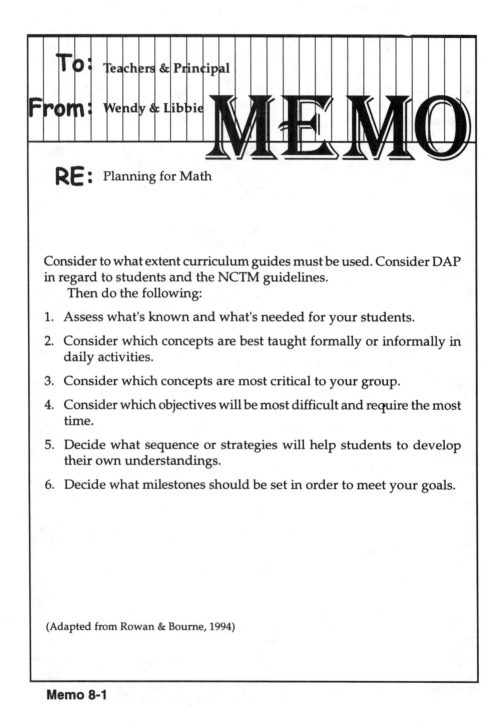

To: Teachers & Principal

From: Wendy & Libbie

MEMO

RE: Planning for Math

Consider to what extent curriculum guides must be used. Consider DAP in regard to students and the NCTM guidelines.
   Then do the following:

1. Assess what's known and what's needed for your students.

2. Consider which concepts are best taught formally or informally in daily activities.

3. Consider which concepts are most critical to your group.

4. Consider which objectives will be most difficult and require the most time.

5. Decide what sequence or strategies will help students to develop their own understandings.

6. Decide what milestones should be set in order to meet your goals.

(Adapted from Rowan & Bourne, 1994)

Memo 8-1

CHAPTER 9

Assessment in the Multiage Classroom

What Is Assessment and Why Do We Do It?

Assessment is the process of gathering and organizing data to fulfill a variety of evaluation needs (Hart, 1994). Throughout this book, we have tried to relate assessment to the discussion, such as in the strategies section of chapter 7. Assessment is not necessarily different because classrooms are multiage. The same common principles apply because assessment, including authentic assessment, should be part of every good school and classroom. We will therefore not discuss assessment extensively in this chapter. With so many outstanding books about assessment (Genishi, 1992; Goodman, Bird, & Goodman, 1992; Harp, 1994; Perrone, 1991), and more specifically about portfolios (Farr & Tone, 1994; Shaklee, Barbour, Ambrose, & Hansford, 1997; Tierney, Carter, & Desai, 1991), there simply isn't any reason to reiterate what our very knowledgeable colleagues have done. Our treatment of the topic will outline some key ideas with this in mind.

Earlier in this book, we discussed school visions and long-term goals. The purpose of assessment is to help us achieve these goals by using heuristic devices as tools in making instructional and curricular decisions for districts, schools, and individuals. Assessments are part of the teaching process, not something we do just before progress reports are due. Well-constructed assessments are helpful in looking at our teaching as well as at our students, no matter what the setting. The principal difference in the multiage class is that the expectation that students will be very different is paramount, and assessment will take place over a longer time period because each student remains with a teacher longer than in grade-level systems.

243

What Assessment Used to Be

When the factory model of education dominated, the sole assessments were standardized tests and report card grades. Standardized tests were an attempt at becoming "scientific" or objective about student performance—or so we all thought. Students were evaluated in similar ways with similar expectations. As we have noted, not all students were expected to succeed; just as in the factory model, we discarded "seconds" or "irregulars" in our "merchandise" along the way. Unfortunately, assessment and evaluation of this sort still persists, but change is clearly needed to break down the factory model so that we can serve all our students better.

Why Assessment Must Change and Is Changing

More recently, researchers have criticized standardized tests for their biases, limitations, and narrowly defined functions (Bertrand, 1994; Darling-Hammond, Ancess, & Falk, 1995; Gipps & Murphy, 1994; Harp, 1994; Hart, 1994; Kamii, 1990; Klitgaard, 1974; Perrone, 1991; Resnick, 1976; Valdes & Figueroa, 1994). In spite of the accumulated criticism and the general consensus in the field of education about the severe limitations and misuses of testing, extensive testing persists—often initiated, mandated, or encouraged by stakeholders outside the field who worry about education, distrust educators, or are simply ignorant of the implications of their demands. This situation is unacceptable, and change is urgently needed.

Today we know more about learning and teaching, and we also know more about testing. Although learning and teaching have become more constructivist, meaning-centered, and inquiry-based, testing has remained mostly the same. The structures of testing are no longer compatible with our teaching or the state of our knowledge about education.

Of course, the most serious problem with testing is that the public is not currently informed about its problems and limitations. Popular wisdom still equates test scores with absolute truth. After all, when scores are published— and no one ever thinks the scores are good enough when they are reported in the media—then who or what gets blamed? Generally teachers, schools, and students are held accountable. How often is the validity of the tests questioned publicly? How often is the appropriateness of testing held accountable?

Problems With Letter Grades

Before the two of us knew each other, each was working with a school district in a different part of the country that had set in motion the process of changing reporting methods from letter grades to more descriptive and developmentally appropriate methods. Although each district's research into alternatives was exemplary, it neglected to include parents in its discussions about how to change. Consequently, when changes were nearing implementation in one of the districts, a small group of very noisy parents hired a lawyer and threatened to sue the school board if changes were made and letter grades were taken away! In the other district, parents showed up en masse at a school board meeting demanding input.

> "Assessment is done continually. It is much easier in a multiage class because I know the students better. I appreciate the gains I see over the 3 years. I like to have the students work on self-assessment and have them lead frequent student-parent conferences."
>
> —Jackie Robbie
> Colorado Springs, CO

Box 9-1

Both districts had to back up and have "town meetings" about assessment and possible changes. Each of us was a speaker at such a meeting, attended by at least one of the very noisy parents. When the question was put to parents, "What exactly does an 'A' mean?", they were hard pressed to respond. They only expressed that to them it meant there was nothing with which they needed to be concerned. Others contended that letter grades would be needed for determining college admission.

To investigate the latter claim, one of us called two colleges with extremely rigorous admission standards and inquired about how letter grades are used in college admissions. An immediate response was that letter grades were insufficient and unreliable as predictors of college success because, one admission director stated, no one knows what an "A" really means. He cited as support the fact that honors courses might be more rigorous in high schools than other courses, and they could not treat all "A"s as equal. He outlined a procedure that uses a composite of information in order to determine admission likelihood. He even added that colleges were already learning to deal with high schools that do not use letter grades, and that they had determined ways to evaluate portfolios.

Another objection the few noisy parents had to deleting letter grades was that such grades would be needed for students to get jobs after high school. To address this concern, one of us called the area's major employers and asked the personnel directors if letter grades were considered for employment. This director emphatically stated no. He claimed that for positions requiring college degrees, high school records were irrelevant. For hourly wage jobs, the information they were most interested in was school attendance.

Both districts finally did change report cards in the primary grades. In one district, after the first semester of implementation, a parent survey indicated more than 98% parent satisfaction with the newer, more descriptive reports without letter grades.

"We have a goal sheet, and at the beginning of each grading period or at the end of the previous one, we sit down with the child and the parent and we set goals for that grading period, and we continually assess those goals. Once the child meets those goals, then we set new ones, depending on where he or she is developmentally."

—Diane Kittelberger
Massillon, OH

Box 9-2

Letter grades as an assessment are outdated in K–12 education. Although many districts have already changed, for the most part changes are in flux now and will be so in years to come. In some areas of the world, change will be slow, and the topic of assessment will be around for a while. The bottom line is this: *Letter grades don't communicate any information.* They represent a rating and not an assessment. Their use is inconsistent among teachers, and there isn't one good reason for continuing them (except "tradition," which is also the argument for grade levels).

New Ways of Looking at Assessment

"Assessment is the gathering of data, usually quantitative in nature and based on testing, that provide the information for evaluation to take place" (Bertrand, in Harp, 1991).

As practices in the classroom continue to change, so must the manner in which children are assessed. A major problem that we encounter across the country is that schools have moved to a nongraded philosophy in the classroom yet maintain the required evaluation procedures. Authentic assessments must eventually replace any evaluation that is purely quantitative. This section will describe the principles of assessment, some types of assessments, reporting student progress, and some options to help teachers get by before changes in assessment have been completed.

Principles of Assessment

Several principles that support assessment practices can be found in the literature. Among these are those identified by Herman, Aschbacher, and Winters (1992). They maintain that common characteristics of authentic assessments

- ask students to perform, create, produce, or do something;
- tap higher level thinking and problem-solving skills;
- use tasks that represent meaningful instructional activities;
- invoke real-world applications;
- use people, not machines, to do the scoring;
- require new instructional and assessment roles for teachers. (p. 6)

Each of these characteristics allows for qualitative data to be gathered and valued as a mechanism for planning instruction through watching the processes involved in completion of a task.

Anthony, Johnson, Mickelson, and Preece (1991) suggest several additional characteristics of assessment. Assessment must be *data driven*. Collection of data enables teachers to look for patterns in the learning and to view the processes involved. Interpretation and use of these data drive curricular and instructional decisions. Assessment must be *dynamic* as it responds to classroom needs. For instance, grading as a means of evaluating students remained stagnant over time even though conditions in classrooms had begun to change. Assessment, on the other hand, *continually changes* in an effort to be fair, consistent, and worthwhile. As with other topics we've discussed, assessment is based on understanding the goals of the school and the curriculum. Without knowing what is needed in a child's education, any other information is relatively worthless.

Harp (1991) describes the following characteristics in teachers who effectively assess:

- Looking for patterns in the learning process
- Knowing how to get the behaviors necessary so observations can occur
- Listening to children
- Allowing for self-evaluation in the classroom
- Advocating for students by focusing on the process and respecting the product
- Using assessment to immediately influence instruction

- Emphasizing process and what students can do (pp. 47–48)

The assessment notions presented by these authors have common themes that can guide assessment practices in both multiage and nonmultiage classes.

Types of Assessment

In a multiage classroom, as in any classroom, one single form of assessment is inadequate. Just as children have a multitude of intelligences, their assessments must reflect a multitude of ways of being assessed. Equally important is not overdoing the types of assessments used in the classroom. Assessment is a seamless part of the instructional process. If it becomes cumbersome for the teacher or noticeable to the student, it loses authenticity, becoming contrived like many timeworn evaluations.

Assessment drives the instructional process in multiage classrooms. In one graded classroom in a district we visited, we heard a story about the state testing that was done once a year to determine whether children were proficient in their learning. A teacher was very frustrated because a child who had received all good grades had a test score that indicated he was not competent. When further questioned, the teacher indicated that on all the end-of-the-chapter tests and quizzes, the student seemed to understand. Clearly, assessment was not driving the individual instruction for the student or for the classroom lessons. This teacher tended to give information, assign rote work to students, and test. She then moved on to the next chapter, continuing this pattern. Unlike this classroom, authentic assessment drives the instructional and curricular decisions in a multiage classroom.

In several of the multiage schools in which we consult, an assessment plan for the school, classroom, or team has been developed. The teachers talk about what they already use to assess and what they know about other forms of assessment, and then they determine what they will use as the main assessments in their classrooms. We recommend that no more than three new forms of assessing student growth be used each year. Assessment planning can help to control the impulse of adding additional ideas in midyear. Figure 9-1 shows one school's formal assessment plan.

An uncontrollable part of the assessment plan for many teachers is required testing, often in the form of state proficiency tests or competency tests. Although these tests give only one picture of one day in the child's life, they are mandatory. Multiage teachers often have to split their children in grade levels for the administration of these tests. We have discovered that children in multiage classrooms, where authentic forms of assessment and process-based learning are used, do well on these types of tests *if* they are taught the test procedures, such as how to fill in the bubbles on the answer sheet.

Roosevelt Multiage Assessment Plan

All classrooms will utilize the following types of assessments:

Observations or anecdotal records—form determined by teacher

Working portfolio—container determined by teacher and students

Showcase portfolio—given at end of the year; parent volunteers make portfolios on school-arranged work day

Chosen work samples—when and what determined by teacher

Videotaping—each child to have at least one example from each quarter

School assessments include the following:

Standardized achievement and ability tests—given in March

Audiotaping of all children reading—three times, completed by parent volunteers; training to occur before beginning of taping

Cumulative portfolio—items as determined by staff to be placed in folders before end of school

Customized goals for each quarter—designed by teacher, parent, and student

Narrative reporting—on school form

Individual conferences with parents and children—three times each year on district-designated days

---

Figure 9-1

We have also consulted with an extremely innovative school that lies within an otherwise conservative district. This innovative school has made various wonderful changes toward DAP in all subjects, theme teaching, and multiage classes. The rest of the district has yet to change, and the administration refuses to entertain any changes in school assessment. So the innovative classrooms, teachers, and principals are stuck with outdated, graded reports. The best solution we have seen in this situation is for multiage teachers to create a supplementary report to accompany the required one. This might be a simple narrative sheet or an opportunity to pilot a more descriptive progress report created or borrowed from another school. In our experience, parents have responded positively to the additional information about their children. In fact, in some cases, these supplements helped to pave the way for eventual change by preparing parents to read more substantive reports.

"Our responsibility is to find out where children are developmentally, how they best learn, and move them on from there. In public education, we are continuing to be met with a diverse population, culturally and academically. Meeting the needs has become a greater challenge for all educators. We need to be constantly abreast of new research that helps us provide for this challenge. In our classroom, we are implementing centers focusing on our theme through the use of multiple intelligences. This is just one of the endless ways we can best provide for children."

—Gloria Morrison and Marybeth Phelps
Danielson, CT

Box 9-3

Portfolio assessment seems to be the most popular form of authentic assessment that we have seen. Most multiage classrooms maintain at least one type of portfolio. In Libbie's former school, teachers maintained three portfolio types based upon a study in a northeastern Ohio school district (Tierney et al., 1991). A cumulative portfolio included three writing samples a year, two math samples from a designated period of time, an artwork sample, and a reading attitude survey. These portfolios were kept in a central area and passed from age-level team to age-level team. Working portfolios were kept inside the classroom; they were, in essence, holding bins for student work. At the completion of a grading period, students would sit with the teacher and choose a specified number of pieces to save. The teacher did the same thing, and the parents were asked at the quarterly conferences to make their choices. Anything not chosen was sent home with the parent or child. All chosen pieces were placed in a showcase portfolio. This was not an assessed portfolio but simply a collection portfolio that the children received on the last day of school.

An assessed portfolio has different characteristics than a collection portfolio. Portfolio assessment is based on gathering and comparing data over time. This comparison occurs when teachers and students have the opportunity to reflect on the portfolio using set criteria. The standards by which the portfolio is assessed can be developed by the student, the teacher, or even by the district office. However, we suggest that jointly developed standards be used.

Portfolio assessment entails various steps in the process (Anthony et al., 1991; Clemmons, Laase, Cooper, Areglado, & Dill, 1993; DeFina, 1992; Tierney et al., 1991). Beginning portfolio assessment requires a gathering of identified baseline samples that can be written, taped, or even project-based. Samples are dated and stored until the reflection time arrives. Criteria for assessing the portfolios must be established and discussed with students prior to their own assessment of their work. Students are taught how to self-evaluate their work, understanding that the product may be completed or may still be "in process." As students finish the quarter, they are given time to reflect and assess their portfolio based on the predetermined criteria for evaluation. After this reflection occurs, teacher conferences can be held to discuss the teacher assessment as well as the student assessment of the portfolio. Goals for improvement can at first be generated by the teacher and student together, and as time passes, the student may be able to begin self-evaluation and reflection and set individual goals alone. Figure 9-2 provides a chart detailing one way to do portfolio assessment.

Steps in Portfolio Assessment

Teach children and parents about portfolios.

Share your professional portfolio with them (this is a good time to get one started!).

Set up standards for evaluating the portfolio.

Begin to collect baseline data.

Practice reflecting on work and self-evaluation.

Evaluate the portfolio (teacher and student separately).

Write up the results of the evaluation. Students can do so in the form of a letter to an audience. Teachers can do so in narrative form.

Conference with each child using the portfolio as a discussion tool.

Set new goals for learning by using what is known from the portfolio.

Share the results with everyone involved with the child through portfolio nights, displays, or during parent conferences.

Figure 9-2

Electronic portfolios are now available to classroom teachers. These can provide sound and image to the child's portfolio. Through the use of scanners, children's work can be added to a portfolio page; through the use of video cards and sound-recording equipment, student presentations can also be archived. In Libbie's current district, multiage teachers are working to record as many media into an electronic portfolio system as possible. Parents arrive for conferences, and children take them through their electronic portfolio, showing everything from handwritten samples to violin lessons to seeing a physical fitness routine to hearing the child present a project from a classroom concept unit. Several prominent companies sell these programs as well as the hardware required to run them.

Assessment in the Future

In this section, we will comment on assessment trends we have observed that are relatively new and those we anticipate.

Learner Responsibility in Assessment

One exciting trend that is catching on quickly is that the assessment domain no longer belongs only to teachers. As a profession, we have discovered that we can obtain good information by treating our students as informants about their own growth. Having asked simple questions of students, such as "How do you think you are doing?", we have discovered to our delighted surprise that the responses are neither simple nor superficial. Most learners take their growth seriously, and others who may not in the beginning are taught this new and responsible role.

"Assessment comes in many forms and styles in our classroom. There are one-to-one hands-on math assessments, the use of anecdotal records during our reading and writing conferences, observation during small- and large-group work, and some traditional paper-and-pencil types. Each student is viewed as an independent learner, knowing that everyone is going to master skills at different times and at different levels. When mastery of a specific skill is evident, then we mark that skill or objective as being met on the progress report continuum."

—Barbara Kidwell and Sue Beth Arnold
Findlay, OH

Box 9-4

As a result, we have seen a number of trends arise. First, we see classrooms where students write self-assessments periodically (Anthony et al., 1991). These might be monthly reports where students thoughtfully consider and list their newest accomplishments and goals. Although at first the goals may be unrealistic, students soon learn to set fair and manageable ones.

Second, student self-assessment might be by personal or peer reviews. Sometimes, groups of students in different contexts must assess each other. Often difficult at first, students learn to be honest and contructive in their comments. From this, they learn about themselves and others as well as how to be appropriately critical. Some teachers design forms on which students assess each other's participation, rubrics on which students assess each other's projects or presentations, or writing. The act of assessment is a strong learning tool. After having to evaluate others, it becomes easier to implement the learning into one's own work. We attend more to punctuation after having to edit the punctuation of our peers; we pay more attention to spelling when we've had to edit the spelling of our classmates.

A third way that students take responsibility for their learning is through student-led conferences (Little & Allan, 1988). We mentioned earlier how Jackie Robbie has students confer with parents at school on a predetermined evening. Conferences are all concurrent, so she roams around the room observing and facilitating the process as necessary. Other districts have implemented student-led conferences districtwide. Students bear the burden for preparing folders of their work, deciding what achievements to report, and offering their ideas for new goals. When the conference appointment arrives, students do a great deal of the talking, especially in the beginning. Parents and teachers ask questions of students, and vice versa. To document this event, the teacher records the information in a short narrative that is copied and given to parents.

This trend is very exciting, in our opinion. Students feel more in control of their own learning. Communication is increased among all parties. The mood and tone of conferences is constructive and productive. It's a win-win situation. Of course, there may be times that teachers and parents need to meet in private. Also, student-led conferences do not absolve teachers of assessment responsibilities, but assessment practices are now shared among teachers and learners.

Parent Responsibility in Assessment

The newest member of the assessment team is the parent. Obviously, parents know their children in depth. In the past, their knowledge was undervalued in the educational process. Parental input, while not always accurate, still needs to be solicited and valued. Parents are an integral part of the process. The resulting input from three sources (teacher, student, and parent) makes a better recipe for success—more information and more substance on which to base instructional decisions about serving our students better.

Changes in College and University Assessment

Although these changes have been taking place in elementary schools, and to lesser extents in middle and secondary schools, most colleges and universities have remained the same. Letter grades or number grades of various types still dominate higher education. For colleges of education, this position is often an uncomfortable one, as we preach about newer assessments in our classes and workshops but are required to assign quantitative grades no matter what our philosophy of teaching.

In recent years, it has been more common for portfolios to be required as part of the admission process, especially in the form of writing samples to help place students into freshman English classes. These first steps are big ones for higher education. One of our own graduate students noted during a class discussion about assessment that if universities changed, then K–12 education would be forced to respond. At this point, we aren't certain what the nature of these changes would be if we could create them. But it's clear that the issue is being raised more and more often. Now many education courses require students to assemble portfolios to reflect their understanding of course content. However, these portfolios must still be translated into a quantitative grade for the registrar's office.

We anticipate that in years to come, more discussions about assessment and evaluation of students in higher education will occur. We look forward to participating in these discussions and trying to be part of future changes.

> "[Assessment and meeting the needs of individuals] is really easy for me now because I have developed (what feels like a million) checklists and spreadsheet grids with different skills on them, which I keep on clipboards and check off as I notice children achieving the different targets. I have based these checklists on my own observations of the steps or stages children move through as they progress from being a beginner to a skilled learner in reading, math, handwriting, spelling, writing, etc. This is how I keep track of who is where. I also have several different folder systems to keep track of important student work and ability levels. I also rely on the students and their parents to tell me if I'm not meeting students' needs or if the work is too difficult. I communicate quite clearly to the students and parents that I expect them to let me know if I'm 'off base,' and they do let me know. I appreciate it tremendously!"
>
> —Nancy Norman
> Palmer, AK

Box 9-5

Clipboard

Chapter 9 has concentrated on the need for a more authentic form of assessment in the multiage classroom. Portfolios and student-led conferences tend to be the most common practices in multiage classrooms today.

Other types of assessments to consider include the following:

- Student interviews—talking to students about their learning; finding out about their likes and dislikes.
- Rubrics—generated by the students with teacher guidance; used to assess classroom projects or products; typically, several areas are identified and characteristics for them are generated.
- Narrative reports—instead of checklists, used to describe the success of each goal; written in paragraph form.
- Anecdotal records—brief, nonjudgmental observations; used to assess child's progress in areas of growth and development over a period of time.
- Surveys and inventories—information gathered from students about their interests and their comments on current studies; used to help make the learning more appropriate and engaging for the student.
- Customized learning goals—designed for a period of time, usually a quarter; jointly developed by parent, child, and teacher; individualized.
- Videotaping or audiotaping—record of children's progress throughout the quarter or year; indicate growth over time and can be specific to goal or all-encompassing.

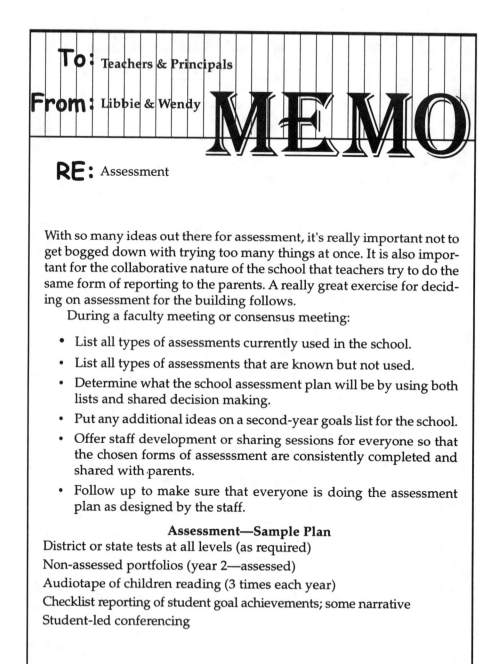

To: Teachers & Principals

From: Libbie & Wendy

RE: Assessment

With so many ideas out there for assessment, it's really important not to get bogged down with trying too many things at once. It is also important for the collaborative nature of the school that teachers try to do the same form of reporting to the parents. A really great exercise for deciding on assessment for the building follows.

During a faculty meeting or consensus meeting:

- List all types of assessments currently used in the school.
- List all types of assessments that are known but not used.
- Determine what the school assessment plan will be by using both lists and shared decision making.
- Put any additional ideas on a second-year goals list for the school.
- Offer staff development or sharing sessions for everyone so that the chosen forms of assesssment are consistently completed and shared with parents.
- Follow up to make sure that everyone is doing the assessment plan as designed by the staff.

Assessment—Sample Plan

District or state tests at all levels (as required)

Non-assessed portfolios (year 2—assessed)

Audiotape of children reading (3 times each year)

Checklist reporting of student goal achievements; some narrative

Student-led conferencing

Memo 9-1

APPENDIX A

Developmentally Appropriate Practice (DAP)

Definition: Activities and experiences should be both age-appropriate (suited to the development of the age of the learner) and individually appropriate (suited to individual style, background, culture, etc.).

A. DAP curriculum provides for all areas of a child's development: physical, emotional, social, and cognitive, through an integrated approach.

B. Appropriate curriculum planning is based on teachers' observations and records of each child's special interests and developmental progress.

C. Curriculum planning emphasizes learning as an interactive process. Teachers prepare the environment for children to learn through active exploration and interaction with adults, other children, and materials.

D. Learning activities and materials should be concrete, real, and relevant to the lives of young children.

E. Programs provide for a wider range of developmental interests and abilities than the chronological age range of the group would suggest. Adults are prepared to meet the needs of children who exhibit unusual interests and skills outside the normal developmental range.

F. Teachers provide a variety of activities and materials; teachers increase the difficulty, complexity, and challenge of an activity as children are involved with it and develop understanding and skills.

G. Adults provide opportunities for children to choose from among a variety of activities, materials, and equipment; and time to explore through active involvement. Adults facilitate children's engagement with materials and activities and extend the child's learning by asking questions or making suggestions that stimulate children's thinking.

H. Multicultural and nonsexist experiences, materials, and equipment should be provided for children of all ages.

I. Adults provide a balance of rest and active movement for children throughout the program day.

J. Outdoor experiences should be provided for children of all ages.

Bredekamp, S. (1987). *Developmentally appropriate practice in early childhood programs serving children from birth through age 8.* Washington, DC: National Association for the Education of Young Children.

Whole Language Beliefs

• •

- A holistic approach to the acquisition and development of literacy in all its aspects.

- A positive view of all human learners.

- A belief that language is central to human learning.

- A belief that learning is easiest when it is from whole to part, when it is in authentic contexts, and when it is functional for the learners.

- A belief in the empowerment of learners and teachers.

- A belief that learning is both personal and social and that classrooms and other educational settings must be learning communities.

- An acceptance of all learners and the languages, cultures, and experiences they bring to their education.

- A belief that learning is both joyous and fulfilling.

- A belief in the developmental nature of learning which builds on learner's prior knowledge and experience.

Based on the brochure for the Whole Language Umbrella, a confederation of teachers. The Whole Language Umbrella is an affiliate of the National Council of Teachers of English, Urbana, IL.

http://www.edu.yorku.ca/~WLU/WLUHome.htm

Staff Survey

Please fill out this survey and return it to the principal before January 15. Thank you for your honest self-evaluation and comments.

1. I believe that I understand the philosophical foundation of multiage grouping.
   Yes   No
   Comments:

2. I believe that I can discuss multiage grouping in a manner that indicates I understand and believe in it.
   Yes   No
   Comments:

3. I feel that the consensus team operates in a true consensus format.
   Yes   No
   Comments:

4. I believe that I am an equal member of the decision-making body on the consensus team.
   Yes   No
   Comments:

5. I believe that we as a staff are moving toward the vision that we created.
   Yes   No
   Comments:

6. I believe that I am meeting the needs of my students and their parents.
   Yes   No
   Comments:

7. I would really enjoy additional staff development in the following areas:

8. If I could give the principal advice about anything related to the school, it would be:

Parent Survey

• •

Please answer each question as completely as possible. Return to the box outside the office by January 31.

1. My child feels welcome in the school.
    Yes   No
    Comments:

2. My child feels welcome and liked by the classroom teacher(s).
    Yes   No
    Comments:

3. My child is achieving at the appropriate level.
    Yes   No
    Comments:

4. The teacher(s) keeps me informed regularly about my child's progress.
    Yes   No
    Comments:

5. The individual goals we jointly designed with the teacher(s) are being followed.
    Yes   No
    Comments:

6. The office staff is always helpful and courteous.
    Yes   No
    Comments:

7. I believe that the school is servicing children first.
    Yes   No
    Comments:

8. I am pleased that my child attends this school.
    Yes   No
    Comments:

Are there additional comments or suggestions that you would like to make? If so, please use a separate sheet of paper.

Thank you for your honest, constructive response to this survey.

Class List Form: Children Remaining in Classroom

Teacher Name _____ Year _____

Identify children who will remain in your classroom next year. Please tally the characteristics below and return to the office by May 15.

Boys	**Girls**
1. _____	1. _____
2. _____	2. _____
3. _____	3. _____
4. _____	4. _____
5. _____	5. _____
6. _____	6. _____
7. _____	7. _____
8. _____	8. _____
9. _____	9. _____

Tally Marks

Discipline problems _____   Social problems _____

Motivation problems _____   Emotional problems _____

"Low" academically _____   Motor problems _____

"Average" academically _____   Other concerns _____

"High" academically _____   Please List _____

Special needs _____   _____

    Please List _____   _____

    _____   _____

Class List Form: Children Moving On

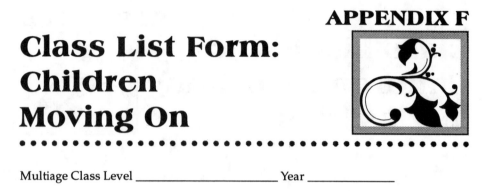

Multiage Class Level _____ Year _____

Identify children who you think will fit well together in the next-level multiage class. Please make sure the list is balanced; your colleagues will appreciate your thoughtful, careful groupings. Please tally the characteristics below and return to the office by May 27.

Boys	Girls
1. _____	1. _____
2. _____	2. _____
3. _____	3. _____
4. _____	4. _____
5. _____	5. _____
6. _____	6. _____
7. _____	7. _____
8. _____	8. _____
9. _____	9. _____

Tally Marks

Discipline problems _____	Social problems _____
Motivation problems _____	Emotional problems _____
"Low" academically _____	Motor problems _____
"Average" academically _____	Other concerns _____
"High" academically _____	Please List _____
Special needs _____	_____
Please List _____	_____
_____	_____

National Council of Teachers of Mathematics Standards

Curriculum Standards for Grades K–4

Standard 1: Mathematics and Problem Solving

In grades K–4, the study of mathematics should emphasize problem solving so that students can:
- Use problem-solving approaches to investigate and understand mathematical content
- Formulate problems from everyday mathematical situations
- Develop and apply strategies to solve a wide variety of problems
- Verify and interpret results with respect to the original problem
- Acquire confidence in using mathematics meaningfully

Standard 5: Estimation

In grades K–4, the curriculum should include estimation so that students can:
- Explore estimation strategies
- Recognize when an estimate is appropriate
- Determine the reasonableness of results
- Apply estimation in working with quantities, measurement, computation, and problem solving

Standard 6: Number Sense and Numeration

In grades K–4, the mathematics curriculum should include whole number concepts and skills so that students can:
- Construct number meanings through real-world experiences and the use of physical materials
- Understand our numeration system by relating counting, grouping, and place-value concepts
- Develop number sense
- Interpret the multiple use of numbers encountered in the real world

Standard 7: Concepts of Whole Number Operations

In grades K–4, the mathematics curriculum should include concepts of addition, subtraction, multiplication, and division of whole numbers so that students can:
- Develop meaning for the operations by modeling and discussing a rich variety of problem situations
- Relate the mathematical language and symbolism of operations to problem situations and informal language
- Recognize that a wide variety of problem structures can be represented by a single operation
- Develop operation sense

Standard 9: Geometry and Spatial Sense

In grades K–4, the mathematics curriculum should include two- and three-dimensional geometry so that students can:
- Describe, model, draw, and classify shapes
- Investigate and predict the results of combining, subdividing, and changing shapes
- Relate geometric ideas to number and measurement ideas
- Recognize and appreciate geometry in their world

Standard 10: Measurement

In grades K–4, the mathematics curriculum should include measurement so that students can:
- Understand the attributes of length, capacity, weight, area, volume, time, temperature, and angle
- Develop the process of measuring and concepts related to units of measurement
- Make and use estimates of measurement
- Make and use measurements in problem and everyday situations

Standard 11: Statistics and Probability

In grades K–4, the mathematics curriculum should include experiences with data analysis and probability so that students can:
- Collect, organize, and describe data
- Construct, read, and interpret displays of data
- Formulate and solve problems that involve collecting and analyzing data
- Explore concepts of chance

Standard 13: Patterns and Relationships

In grades K–4, the mathematics curriculum should include the study of patterns and relationships so that students can:
- Recognize, describe, extend, and create a wide variety of patterns
- Represent and describe mathematical relationships
- Explore the use of variables and open sentences to express relationships

Curriculum Standards for Grades 5–8

Standard 1: Mathematics as Problem Solving

In grades 5–8, the mathematics curriculum should include numerous and varied experiences with problem solving as a method of inquiry and application so that students can:
- Use problem-solving approaches to investigate and understand mathematical content
- Formulate problems from situations within and outside mathematics
- Develop and apply a variety of strategies to solve problems, with emphasis on multistep and nonroutine problems
- Verify and interpret results with respect to the original problem situation
- Generalize solutions and strategies to new problem situations
- Acquire confidence in using mathematics meaningfully

Standard 5: Number and Number Relationships

In grades 5–8, the mathematics curriculum should include the continuous development of number and number relationships so that students can:
- Understand, represent, and use numbers in a variety of equivalent forms (integer, fraction, decimal, percent, exponential, and scientific notation) in real-world mathematical problem situations
- Develop number sense for whole numbers, fraction, decimals, integers, and rational numbers
- Understand and apply ratios, proportions, and percents in a wide variety of situations
- Investigate relationships among fractions, decimals, and percents
- Represent numerical relationships in one- and two-dimensional graphs

Standard 6: Number Systems and Number Theory

In grades 5–8, the mathematics curriculum should include the study of number systems and number theory so that students can:
- Understand and appreciate the need for numbers beyond whole numbers
- Develop and use order relations for whole numbers, fractions, decimals, integers, and rational numbers
- Extend their understanding of whole number operations to fractions, decimals, integers, and rational numbers
- Understand how the basic arithmetic operations are related to one another
- Develop and apply number theory concepts (e.g., primes, factors, and multiples) in real-world nonmathematical problem situations

Standard 7: Computation and Estimation

In grades 5–8, the mathematics curriculum should develop the concepts underlying computation and estimation in various contexts so that students can:
- Compute with whole numbers, fractions, decimals, integers, and rational numbers
- Develop, analyze, and explain procedures for computation and techniques for estimation
- Develop, analyze, and explain methods for solving proportions
- Select and use an appropriate method for computing from among mental arithmetic, paper-and-pencil, calculator, and computer methods
- Use computation, estimation, and proportions to solve problems
- Use estimation to check the reasonableness of results

Standard 8: Patterns and Functions

In grades 5–8, the mathematics curriculum should include explorations of patterns and functions so that children can:
- Describe, extend, analyze, and create a wide variety of patterns
- Describe and represent relationships with tables, graphs, and rules
- Analyze functional relationships to explain how a change in one quantity results in a change in another
- Use patterns and functions to represent and solve problems

Standard 9: Algebra

In grades 5–8, the mathematics curriculum should include exploration of algebraic concepts and processes so that students can:
- Understand the concepts of variable, expressions, and equation
- Represent situations and number patterns with tables, graphs, verbal rules, and equations and explore the interrelationships of these representations
- Analyze tables and graphs to identify properties and relationships
- Develop confidence in solving linear equations using concrete, informal, and formal methods
- Investigate inequalities and nonlinear equations informally
- Apply algebraic methods to solve a variety of real-world mathematical problems

Standard 10: Statistics

In grades 5–8, the mathematics curriculum should include exploration of statistics in real-world situations so that students can:
- Systematically collect, organize, and describe data
- Construct, read, and interpret tables, charts, and graphs
- Make inferences and convincing arguments that are based on data analysis
- Evaluate arguments that are based on data analysis
- Develop an appreciation for statistical methods as a powerful means for decision making

Standard 11: Probability

In grades 5–8, the mathematics curriculum should include explorations of probability in real-world situations so that students can:
* Model situations by devising and carrying out experiments or simulations to determine probabilities
* Model situations by constructing a sample space to determine probabilities
* Appreciate the power of using a probability model by comparing experimental results with mathematical expectations
* Make predictions that are based on experimental or theoretical probabilities
* Develop an appreciation for the pervasive use of probability in the real world

Standard 12: Geometry

In grades 5–8, the mathematics curriculum should include the study of geometry of one, two, and three dimensions in a variety of situations so that students can:
* Identify, describe, compare, and classify figures
* Visualize and represent geometric figures with special attention to developing spatial sense
* Explore transformation of geometric figures
* Represent and solve problems using geometric figures
* Represent and solve problems using geometric models
* Understand and apply geometric properties and relationships
* Develop an appreciation of geometry as a means of describing the physical world

Standard 13: Measurement

In grades 5–8, the mathematics curriculum should include extensive concrete experiences using measurement so that students can:
* Extend their understanding of the process of measurement
* Estimate, make, and use measurement to describe and compare phenomena
* Select appropriate units and tools to measure to the degree of accuracy required in a particular situation
* Understand the structure and use of systems of measurement
* Extend their understanding of the concepts of perimeter, area, angle measure, capacity, and weight and mass
* Develop the concepts of rates and other derived and indirect measurements
* Develop formulas and procedures for determining measures to solve problems

Parent Volunteer Survey

• •

The school welcomes new committee members. We are eager to have you, the parents, involved as quickly as possible. With all the special things that occur in a school this size, we need your help. Please fill out one survey for your family.

Teacher's Name _____

Student's Name (s) _____

Parents' Names _____

Home Phone _____ Work Phone _____

Days and Times Available to Volunteer _____

Interest Areas:

___ Classroom Work ___ Technology ___ Special Events

___ At-Home Work (book making, cutting out, etc.)

If you cannot work in the school building, is there another person (grandparent, caregiver, etc.) who can volunteer? If so, please give name, phone, and relationship to your child. _____
_____

Do you have special talents or interests you can share with the school? _____
_____

Are there any parent or teacher inservices or classes that you would like to see offered through the school? _____
_____

What committee would you like to work on this year? ___ Fundraising
___Recognition ___ Inservice ___ Volunteer ___ Projects ___Public Relations

Please leave this with your child's teacher after your conference. Thank you in advance for your support.

© Adapted from Central Academy TEAM Survey, 1992

Southpoint School
News for the Week
January 10, 1999

● ●

This bulletin provides concise information so that fewer papers are sent home. Please retain this bulletin until the end of the week, as it serves as the announcement for upcoming events.

Announcements

- Art Club lessons begin on January 18. Please have your permission slips and paint shirts.
- Volleyball Team try-outs will be held for all 10- to 13-year-olds in the gym on January 25.
- No school on Monday, January 21.

Anticipated Minilessons for the Week: Unit—Around the World in 30 Days

Multiage 5- to 6-year-olds
Math: Introduce measuring
Content: Our city
Language Arts: Continue work with big books and interactive charts

Multiage 6- to 9-year-olds
Math: Introduce or review weighing and measuring
Content: Our city and county
Language Arts: Read graphic aids (maps and charts)
Projects: Weigh classroom items with various weights and tiles

Multiage 8- to 11-year-olds
Math: Fractions (adding and subtracting them; reducing to the lowest terms)
Content: Our state and region
Language Arts: Introduce or review expository writing
Projects: Begin research on state or region of choice

Multiage 10- to 13-year-olds
Math: Nonstandard measurement
Content: Regions of the world
Language Arts: Fact and opinion
Project: Begin research on region of choice
Speaker/Special Event: Visitor from Japan will share cultural information with classes

Physical Education
Continue work on ball-handling skills. Passing, dribbling, catching, throwing. Practice time will include ball games from area of world students are studying.

Music
Continue work on rhythm; introduce structured and unstructured movement. Practice time will include singing and playing music from area of world students are studying.

Art
Begin environmental sculptures related to what students are noticing within area of world they are studying.

Connecting the Work of Home and School

Volume 15, No. 2

November 5–January 15

This 9-week period will allow your children to explore the concept unit based on cycles. Many cycles exist in our universe, including the life cycle, water cycle, and seasonal cycle. Children will have the opportunity to learn what makes a cycle a cycle and then research a type (of cycle) of their choice.

Anticipated language arts tools to be taught include:

Early Primary
- Verbs
- Dictionary: entry word, guide word
- Commas in series
- Cause and effect
- Continued work on vowels
- Narrative writing
- Poetry

Early Intermediate
- Cause and effect
- Inferential information
- Extending material
- Adjectives used in writing
- Pronouns used in writing
- Research skills
- Reading graphic aids

Intermediate
- Dictionary: pronunciation key
- Fact and opinion
- Research skills
- Technical writing
- Extending material
- Relevancy of information
- Reading graphic aids

Some at-home activities to encourage literacy are listed below. Please do not feel you must do these every night or for longer than 20 minutes per night. They are simple yet effective ideas for parent-child study time.

- Research how the tides are affected by the cycle of the moon.
- Watch the moon move through its cycle throughout the month.
- Research how the water cycle works.
- Describe how the life cycle of a tadpole and a caterpillar are similar and different.
- Read to your child everyday!
- Write about the seasons and how they repeat.

Northfield Elementary Multiage Parent Survey

We are very pleased with how our first year has progressed. We believe that the hard work has been worth it. We would like some input from you as we move into our second year. We will use this information to adjust our program to better meet your child's needs.

Listed below are statements. Please read each statement and circle the number that best represents your reaction to the statement.

	Strongly Disagree	Slightly Disagree	Neutral	Slightly Agree	Strongly Agree
1. The multiage grouping helps my child to learn as much as possible.	1	2	3	4	5
2. The multiage grouping helps my child to learn to work well in a student group setting.	1	2	3	4	5
3. The multiage grouping helps my child to develop a strong positive self-image.	1	2	3	4	5
4. My child receives adequate individual attention in the multiage setting.	1	2	3	4	5
5. Adequate communication exists to keep me informed about my child's progress.	1	2	3	4	5
6. The atmosphere in the classroom is positive.	1	2	3	4	5
7. Our classroom helps students to learn to cope with a rapidly changing society.	1	2	3	4	5
8. Discipline is not a serious problem in our program.	1	2	3	4	5
9. The morale of my child is high.	1	2	3	4	5
10. I am satisfied with the academic progress in the classroom.	1	2	3	4	5
11. I have seen progress/improvement in the following areas:	1	2	3	4	5
reading	1	2	3	4	5
math concepts	1	2	3	4	5
writing	1	2	3	4	5
social interaction	1	2	3	4	5
12. I have enjoyed being actively involved in the goal-setting process with my child and the teacher.	1	2	3	4	5
13. My child has made progress in his or her personal goals.	1	2	3	4	5

The one thing that has really helped to make our multiage program a success is:

The one thing that would really help our multiage program be more successful is:

Please return this survey by Monday, March 24. There will be a survey box in each classroom.

Multiage Program Brochure

SOUTHWEST NONGRADED

Southwest Nongraded is an elementary building in the Madison City Schools. The Madison community offers a diverse population in an urban setting. The district is the 27th largest in the state and serves approximately 6,000 students in 19 schools.

Southwest was opened in 1993 as a nongraded elementary based upon Dr. John Goodlad's research of the early 1960s. The model is built upon the basic premise that all children can learn given appropriate instruction and time. The developmentally appropriate teaching strategies used at Southwest include literature-based reading, manipulative mathematics, cooperative learning, and authentic assessments.

The children are grouped in multiage classrooms with an age span of 2–4 years. All classrooms are heterogeneously mixed to assure appropriate socialization opportunities as well as academic opportunities. Children experience whole-group, small-group, and individualized instruction daily in the classrooms at Southwest.

The staff at Southwest is well-trained, experienced, and dedicated to children. Every staff member has more than 10 years of experience in education. The staff has restructured the district curriculum to develop schoolwide thematic units. The day is totally integrated around the theme.

Southwest assesses students through portfolios, the district standardized achievement tests, a standardized writing sample given three times each year, and an audiotape of the child reading three times during the year. The portfolios used include a working portfolio, a cumulative writing portfolio, and a showcase portfolio for parents. Various other authentic assessment instruments are used by individual teachers in the building.

Every 9 weeks, the staff prepares a narrative report on each child. The narrative focuses on the individual goals designed by the teacher and parents. Each report describes the progress the child has made throughout the 9-week period.

PARENT INVOLVEMENT

Parents are a vital part of the school community. At Southwest, parents help to write the individual education goals for their children in each 9-week period. The parents also are requested to attend a reporting conference each quarter. The school is proud of its 99% attendance rate at all conferences.

Doing your best at Southwest

Muldoon Elementary School Report Card Goals for 1996–97

● ●

<u>GOAL 1</u>—Students in grades 1–6 who have attended Muldoon for 2 or more years will meet grade-level standards for reading as demonstrated on the Title I Integrated Theme-Based Assessment and portfolio data collected by classroom teachers.

EXPECTATION—Seventy percent of the students in grades 1–6 who have been attending Muldoon for 2 or more years will meet grade-level standards for reading as demonstrated on the Title I Integrated Theme-Based Assessment and portfolio data collected by classroom teachers.

ACTION PLAN
- A schoolwide reading incentive program will be implemented by teachers and parents for October 1996–May 1997, including:
  - All students will set a personal reading goal.
  - Book-It Program with Pizza Hut will be implemented in October.
  - Reading Is Fundamental distributions will occur throughout the year.
  - Monthly Family Storytime in the library will be conducted throughout the year.
  - Schoolwide silent reading periods will be established in each classroom for 20–30 minutes daily.
  - Battle of the Books
  - Special reading events will be offered through the library.
  - Book groups with the principal will be conducted once a week during lunch.
  - Pictures of adults (parents and teachers) with their favorite children's book will be posted for students to see.
- Parent workshops will be offered on the reading process and how to read with children at home.
- Reading assessment sessions and classes will be offered to parents and teachers to include: Book Handling, Print Awareness, Miscue Analysis.
- Teachers will assess the reading needs of students at the beginning and end of the school year. Reading assessment data will be collected during the school year and placed in the student's portfolio. A system will be developed for carrying reading assessment data forward to the next teacher.
- Teachers will be offered release time to attend a 1-day Margaret Mooney workshop and to attend the Alaska State Literacy Association Conference in October 1996.
- Teachers will develop and teach reading strategy lessons designed to increase student understanding and personal response to literature.

<u>GOAL 2</u>—Students in grades K–6 will establish and meet a home or school reading goal as documented by parents and compiled by the classroom teacher.

EXPECTATION—Ninety percent of the students who attend Muldoon for the full school year will meet their home or school reading goal as demonstrated by the numbers of books read from October 1996 to May 1997.

ACTION PLAN
- A schoolwide reading incentive program will be implemented by teachers and parents for October 1996–May 1997, including:
  - All students will set a personal reading goal.
  - Book-It Program with Pizza Hut will be implemented in October.
  - Reading Is Fundamental distributions will occur throughout the year.
  - Monthly Family Storytime in the library will be conducted throughout the school year.
  - Schoolwide silent reading periods will be established in each classroom for 20–30 minutes daily.
  - Special reading events will be offered through the library.
  - Book groups with the principal will be conducted once a week during lunch.
  - Pictures of adults (parents and teachers) with their favorite children's book will be posted for students to see.

GOAL 3—To develop socially responsible students and reduce violence in the school.

EXPECTATION—Student out-of-school suspensions will be reduced by 10% from last year's rate.

ACTION PLAN
- RCCP and social skills lessons will be taught by teachers and the counselor weekly throughout the school year, and the mediator program will continue to operate during the lunch period and other needed times during the school day.
- RCCP training will be provided to students and parents through the RCCP grant.
- New classroom teachers will be encouraged to take the RCCP class offered by the district.
- The staff will continue to develop and implement the schoolwide discipline plan.
- On-the-job training will be provided to new teachers and parent workers.
- Conduct regular Monday morning assemblies at least twice a month to celebrate peaceful practices and learning occurring in the school.

GOAL 4—To continue to increase parent and community awareness and involvement in school and community issues.

EXPECTATION—To foster greater coordination of activities among PTA, community, business partners and school staff.

To increase parent involvement in the school discipline policy, in planning for health, safety and emergencies, and visibility of parents in the school.

ACTION PLAN
- To continue to involve parent and community volunteers in a significant way in the school, including:
  - Parent workshops
  - School events like concerts, field trips, carnivals, conferences, and book fairs
  - Family nights
  - Parent workers in the school
  - Joint planning for school and community events that include all the groups
  - At least one Saturday workshop for parents and children conducted at the school by staff and other volunteers
- To continue to conduct a public relations campaign in the community to get the word out that it takes an entire community to raise a child.

17 Principles for Best Practice

(Adapted from Zemelman, Daniels, & Hyde, 1993)

● ●

CHILD-CENTERED. The best starting point for schooling is kids' real interests; all across the curriculum, investigating students' own questions should always take precedence over studying arbitrarily and distantly selected "content."

EXPERIENTIAL. Active, hands-on, concrete experience is the most powerful and natural form of learning. Students should be immersed in the most direct possible experience of the content of every subject.

REFLECTIVE. Balancing the immersion in direct experience must be opportunities for learners to look back, to reflect, to debrief, to abstract from their experiences what they have felt and thought and learned.

AUTHENTIC. Real, rich, complex ideas and materials are at the heart of the curriculum. Lessons or textbooks that water down, control, or oversimplify content ultimately disempower students.

HOLISTIC. Children learn best when they encounter whole, real ideas, events, and materials in purposeful contexts, and not by studying subparts isolated from actual use.

SOCIAL. Learning is always socially constructed and often interactional; teachers need to create classroom interactions that "scaffold" learning.

FLEXIBLE GROUPING. Flexible grouping rather than ability grouping meets needs of learners and avoids long-term labeling.

MULTIAGE GROUPING. Promotes prosocial behavior, provides modeling, helps build self-esteem, capitalizes on "zone of proximal development," and more.

COLLABORATIVE. Cooperative learning activities tap the social power of learning better than competitive and individualistic approaches.

DEMOCRATIC. The classroom is a model community; students learn what they live as citizens of the school.

COGNITIVE. The most powerful learning for children comes from developing true understanding of concepts and high order thinking associated with various fields of inquiry and self-monitoring of their thinking.

DEVELOPMENTAL. Children grow through a series of definable but not rigid stages, and schooling should fit its activities to the developmental level of students.

CONSTRUCTIVIST.   Children do not just receive content; in a very real sense, they recreate and reinvent every cognitive system they encounter, including language, literacy, and mathematics.

PSYCHOLINGUISTIC.   The process of young children's natural oral language acquisition provides our best model of complex human learning, and once learned, language itself becomes the primary tool for more learning, whatever the subject matter.

CHALLENGING.   Students learn best when faced with genuine challenges, choices, and responsibility in their own learning.

NONGRADED.   Enhances continuous progress of students through curriculum at learner's pace; eliminates artificial separations of grade levels based on factory model.

AUTHENTICALLY ASSESSED.   In order to fulfill objectives of assessment, authentic assessments need to be part of student assessment. Standard assessments are inappropriate for younger learners and not suitable for making instructional or placement decisions.

Science Content Standards, K–12

Unifying Concepts and Processes

Standard: As a result of activities in grades K–12, all students should develop understanding and abilities aligned with the following concepts and processes:
- Systems, order, and organization
- Evidence, models, and explanation
- Constancy, change, and measurement
- Evolution and equilibrium
- Form and function

Content Standards: K–4

Science as Inquiry

Content Standard A: As a result of activities in grades K–4, all students should develop:
- Abilities necessary to do scientific inquiry
- Understanding about scientific inquiry

Life Science

Content Standard C: As a result of activities in grades K–4, all students should develop understanding of:
- The characteristics of organisms
- Life cycles of organisms
- Organisms and environments

Earth and Space Science

Content Standard D: As a result of their activities in grades K–4, all students should develop an understanding of:
- Properties of Earth materials
- Objects in the sky
- Changes in Earth and sky

Science and Technology

Content Standard E: As a result of activities in grades K–4, all students should develop:
- Abilities of technological design
- Understanding about science and technology
- Abilities to distinguish between natural objects and objects made by humans

Science in Personal and Social Perspectives

Content Standard F: As a result of activities in grades K–4, all students should develop understanding of:
- Personal health
- Characteristics and changes in populations
- Types of resources
- Changes in environment
- Science and technology in local challenges

History and Nature of Science

Content Standard G: As a result of activities in grades K–4, all students should develop understanding of:
- Science as human endeavor

Content Standards: 5–8

Science as Inquiry

Content Standard A: As a result of activities in grades 5–8, all students should develop:
- Abilities necessary to do scientific inquiry
- Understanding about scientific inquiry

Physical Science

Content Standard B: As a result of their activities in grades 5–8, all students should develop an understanding of:
- Properties and changes of properties in matter
- Motions and forces
- Transfer of energy

Life Science

Content Standard C: As a result of their activities in grades 5–8, all students should develop understanding of:
- Structure and function in living systems
- Reproduction and heredity
- Regulation and behavior
- Populations and ecosystems
- Diversity and adaptations of organisms

Earth and Space Science

Content Standard D: As a result of their activities in grades 5–8, all students should develop an understanding of:
- Structure of Earth's system
- Earth's history
- Earth in the solar system

Science and Technology

Content Standard E: As a result of activities in grades 5–8, all students should develop:
- Abilities of technological design
- Understanding about science and technology

Science in Personal and Social Perspectives

Content Standard F: As a result of activities in grades 5–8, all students should develop understanding of:
- Personal health
- Populations, resources, and environments
- Natural hazards
- Risks and benefits
- Science and technology in society

History and Nature of Science

Content Standard G: As a result of activities in grades 5–8, all students should develop understanding of:
- Science as human endeavor
- Nature of science
- History of science

IRA/NCTE Standards for the English Language Arts

The vision guiding these standards is that all students must have the opportunities and resources to develop the language skills they need to pursue life's goals and to participate fully as informed, productive members of society. These standards assume that literacy growth begins before children enter school as they experience and experiment with literacy activities—reading and writing and associating spoken words with their graphic representations. Recognizing this fact, these standards encourage the development of curriculum and instruction that makes productive use of the emerging literacy abilities that children bring to school. Furthermore, the standards provide ample room for the innovation and creativity essential to teaching and learning. They are not prescriptions for particular curriculum and instruction. Although we present these standards as a list, we want to emphasize that they are not distinct and separable. They are, in fact, interrelated and should be considered as a whole.

1. Students read a wide variety of print and nonprint texts to build understanding of texts, of themselves, and of the cultures of the United States and the world; to acquire new information; to respond to the needs and demands of society and the workplace; and for personal fulfillment. Among these texts are fiction and nonfiction, classic and contemporary works.

2. Students read a wide range of literature from many periods in many genres to build an understanding of the many dimensions (e.g., philosophical, ethical, aesthetic) of human experience.

3. Students apply a wide range of strategies to comprehend, interpret, evaluate, and appreciate texts. They draw on their prior experiences, their interactions with other readers and writers, their knowledge of word meanings and of other texts, their word identification strategies, and their understanding of textual features (e.g., sound-letter correspondence, sentence structure, context, graphics).

4. Students adjust their use of spoken, written, and visual language (e.g., conventions, style, vocabulary) to communicate effectively with a variety of audiences for a variety of purposes.

5. Students employ a wide range of strategies as they write and use different writing process elements appropriately to communicate with different audiences and for a variety of purposes.

6. Students apply knowledge of language structure, language conventions (e.g., spelling and punctuation), media techniques, figurative language, and genre to create, critique, and discuss print and nonprint texts.

7. Students conduct research on issues and interests by generating ideas and questions and by posing problems. They gather, evaluate, and synthesize data from a variety of sources (e.g., print and nonprint texts, artifacts, people) to communicate their discoveries in ways that suit their purpose and audience.

8. Students use a variety of technological and informational resources (e.g., libraries, databases, computer networks, videos) to gather and synthesize information and to create and communicate knowledge.

9. Students develop an understanding of and respect for diversity in language use, patterns, and dialects across cultures, ethnic groups, geographic regions, and social roles.

10. Students whose first language is not English make use of their first language to develop competency in the English language arts and to develop understanding of content across the curriculum.

11. Students participate as knowledgeable, reflective, creative, and critical members of a variety of literacy communities.

12. Students use spoken, written, and visual language to accomplish their own purposes (e.g., learning, enjoyment, persuasion, and exchange of information).

National Council for Social Studies Standards

APPENDIX Q

The 10 Themes

The 10 themes that form the framework of the social studies standards are:

Culture. The study of culture prepares students to answer questions such as: What are the common characteristics of different cultures? How do belief systems, such as religion or political ideals, influence other parts of the culture? How does the culture change to accommodate different ideas and beliefs? What does language tell us about the culture? In schools, this theme typically appears in units and courses dealing with geography, history, sociology, and anthropology, as well as multicultural topics across the curriculum.

Time, Continuity, and Change. Human beings seek to understand their historical roots and to locate themselves in time. Knowing how to read and reconstruct the past allows one to develop a historical perspective and to answer questions such as: Who am I? What happened in the past? How am I connected to those in the past? How has the world changed, and how might it change in the future? Why does our personal sense of relatedness to the past change? This theme typically appears in courses in history and others that draw upon historical knowledge and habits.

People, Place, and Environments. The study of people, places, and human-environment interactions assists students as they create their spatial views and geographic perspectives of the world beyond their personal locations. Students need the knowledge, skills, and understanding to answer questions such as: Where are things located? Why are they located where they are? What do they mean by "region"? How do landforms change? What implications do these changes have for people? In schools, this theme typically appears in units and courses dealing with area studies and geography.

Individual Development and Identity. Personal identity is shaped by one's culture, by groups, and by institutional influences. Students should consider such questions as: How do people learn? Why do people behave as they do? What influences how people learn, perceive, and grow? How do people meet their basic needs in a variety of contexts? How do individuals develop from youth to adulthood? In schools, this theme typically appears in units and courses dealing with psychology and anthropology.

Individuals, Groups, and Institutions. Institutions such as schools, churches, families, government agencies, and the courts play an integral role in people's lives. It is important that students learn how institutions are formed, what controls and influences them, how they influence individuals and culture, and how

282

they are maintained or changed. Students may address questions such as: What is the role of institutions in this and other societies? How am I influenced by institutions? How do institutions change? What is my role in institutional change? In schools this theme typically appears in units and courses dealing with sociology, anthropology, psychology, political science, and history.

VI **Power, Authority, and Governance.** Understanding the historical development of structures of power, authority, and governance and their evolving functions in contemporary U.S. society and other parts of the world is essential for developing civic competence. In exploring this theme, students confront questions such as: What is power? What forms does it take? Who holds it? How is it gained, used, and justified? What is legitimate authority? How are governments created, structured, maintained, and changed? How can individual rights be protected within the context of majority rule? In schools, this theme typically appears in units and courses dealing with government, politics, political science, history, law, and other social sciences.

VII **Production, Distribution, and Consumption.** Because people have wants that often exceed resources available to them, a variety of ways have evolved to answer such questions as: What is to be produced? How is production to be organized? How are goods and services to be distributed? What is the most effective allocation of the factors of production (land, labor, capital, and management)? In schools, this theme typically appears in units and courses dealing with economic concepts and issues.

VIII **Science, Technology, and Society.** Modern life as we know it would be impossible without technology and the science that supports it. But technology brings with it many questions: Is new technology always better than old? What can we learn from the past about how new technologies result in broader social change, some of which is unanticipated? How can we cope with the ever-increasing pace of change? How can we manage technology so that the greatest number of people benefit from it? How can we preserve our fundamental values and beliefs in the midst of technological change? This theme draws upon the natural and physical sciences, social sciences, and the humanities, and appears in a variety of social studies courses, including history, geography, economics, civics, and government.

IX **Global Connections.** The realities of global interdependence require understanding the increasingly important and diverse global connections among world societies and the frequent tension between national interests and global priorities. Students will need to be able to address such international issues as health care, the environment, human rights, economic competition and interdependence, age-old ethnic enmities, and political and military alliances. This theme typically appears in units or courses dealing with geography, culture, and economics but may also draw upon the natural and physical sciences and the humanities.

X **Civic Ideals and Practices.** An understanding of civic ideals and practices of citizenship is critical to full participation in society and is a central purpose of social studies. Students confront such questions as: What is civic participation and how can I be involved? How has the meaning of citizenship evolved? What is the balance between rights and responsibilities? What is the role of the citizen in the community? How can I make a positive difference? In schools, this theme typically appears in units or courses dealing with history, political science, cultural anthropology, and fields such as global studies, law-related education, and the humanities.

Glossary

Ability Grouping   The placement of students according to similar levels of intelligence or achievement in some skill or subject, either within or among classes or schools; also called *tracking* or *homogeneous grouping*. (Harris & Hodges, 1995)

Authentic Assessment   A type of assessment that seeks to address widespread concerns about standardized, norm-referenced testing by representing "literacy behavior of the community and workplace" and reflecting the "actual learning and instructional activities of the classroom and out-of-school worlds" (Hiebert, et al., 1994 In Harris & Hodges, 1995) as with the use of portfolios; naturalistic assessment. (Harris & Hodges, 1995)

Basics   A term referring to the more traditionally taught subjects when the curriculum is stripped of arts, health, and physical education, and the focus is limited to language arts and reading along with mathematics and some content study. Cries of "back to basics" can be a backlash against changes.

Buddy Reading   A holistic strategy in which children of either similar or slightly different reading abilities read aloud back and forth to each other informally.

Combined Class or **Combination Class**   A classroom that consists of children of two traditional grade levels, such as half second graders and half third graders; created due to a lack of enough students to create complete units of each grade and treated as two separate groups sharing the same teacher and room with different daily work and routines.

Composite Multiage   A multiage class that encompasses two traditional grade levels, such as kindergarten and grade 1, grades 2 and 3, or grades 4 and 5, which is created deliberately and as a single learning community.

Concept Unit   A unit taught in school that is centered around a concept rather than a topic, such as *cycles*, and in which content study as well as math and literacy is embedded for an emphasis on authentic, integrated learning.

Consensus Decision Making   A process by which members of a group come to an agreement on a solution or idea or a decision made after a great deal of communication and productive argument.

Continuous Progress (CP)   A plan in which students advance at their own individual rates rather than at a rate set by age or grade-level standards. (Harris & Hodges, 1995)

Core Knowledge or **Core Curriculum**   Curriculum organized on the basis of subjects or topics deemed essential for all students regardless of subjects taken; curriculum organized on the basis of student problems or societal needs and that draws on the content of subjects and can contribute to understanding or resolving them. (Harris & Hodges, 1995)

Cross-Age Tutoring   Instruction of a student by a knowledgeable student of another age group, usually older. (Harris & Hodges, 1995)

Curriculum   The overall plan or design of institutionalized education; the actual opportunities for learning provided at a particular place and time; all the educational experiences planned and provided for by a school (Harris & Hodges, 1995); that which students have the opportunity to learn under the auspices of schools. (McCutcheon, 1995)

Cycling   *See* Looping.

Developmental Grouping   Grouping that meets developmental needs for a short period of time. Developmental grouping is teacher-initiated to accomplish the objectives for small groups of learners in any subject area. Teachers pull together a small group whose members share a need for at least one session.

Developmentally Appropriate Practice (DAP)   A cluster of practices based on research aimed at advocating cutting-edge practices, especially with young children. These practices, first proposed by the National Association for the Education of Young Children in Washington, D.C., include those that are both age-appropriate and individually appropriate and are elaborated here in Appendix A and in other publications. (Bredekamp, 1987; Kostelnik, Soderman, & Whiren, 1993; Walmsley, Camp, & Walmsley, 1992)

Early Reading   In the New Zealand model of reading (Mooney, 1988; Renwick & Department of Education, 1985), early reading is the stage following emergent reading and preceding fluent reading. During this stage, children are "becoming readers" and are encouraged to draw meaning from the text and increase their confidence by using their background experience; taking risks and making approximations; using text and illustrations to predict, sample, and confirm; using letter-sound associations to confirm predictions; using knowledge of print conventions; rereading when they have lost meaning; self-correcting; and integrating strategies in a self-improving system.

Emergent Reading   In the New Zealand model of reading, emergent reading is "making a start." The emergent reader learns that books are a special way of telling a story or information, that words stay the same, that pictures help readers to understand the story, and that books are written by authors. During this stage, children show an interest in books and attempt to read unaided, consider what is read with what is already known, discuss what is happening and likely to happen, recognize some words within context, and interact with favorite books repeatedly. This term differs philosophically from *reading readiness*, which implies a sequential model with activities and skills that are prerequisites to reading; emergent reading implies immersion in real reading activities with others, even before independent reading occurs.

Factory Model   A model by which factories have generally been set up, historically speaking, with a supervisor, assembly line production, and types of quality-control checks. Schools were initiated on the same model and largely still operate with the language and value system of this model (as demonstrated by promotion and retention policies).

Family Grouping   A term synonymous with multiage grouping because of its family-like atmosphere.

Fluent Reading   In the New Zealand model of reading, fluent reading refers to the final stage of reading development, when students are "going it alone." This stage continues through lifetime reading development and includes readers integrating cues, reducing attention to print detail, maintaining meaning through longer and increasingly complex texts, and adjusting reading to suit different purposes and difficulties. Fluent reading also refers to a quality of reading that includes proficiency in decoding words smoothly, meaningfully, and effortlessly so that readers use their full mental resources to engage in the more important task of making sense of and responding to texts. (Rasinski & Padak, 1996)

Guided Reading   In the New Zealand model of reading, guided reading refers to lessons designed for a small group of readers to talk, read, and think their way purposefully through a text, making possible an early introduction to silent reading. The steps to guided reading include choosing a text appropriate for the children, introducing the reading, setting purposes and asking questions, reading together (teacher reading aloud or children reading chorally) in short sections and then increasing the amount of text that children read silently, and discussion led by the teacher with open-ended questions. Guided reading also refers to the process during a reading lesson in which a teacher provides the structure and purpose for reading and responding to material. (Harris & Hodges, 1995)

Inclusion   The placement of students with all abilities in a classroom, including those with disabilities, no matter how severe. (Harris & Hodges, 1995)

Industrial Model   *See* Factory Model.

Instruction   The act of instructing; teaching; education.

Intermediate House   A deliberate multiage configuration, with one teacher or team taught, in which all or nearly all intermediate grades are included, such as 3–5, 3–6, or 4–6.

Learning Center   A setting in which students of any age complete meaning-centered work in small groups, such as at a table or other predetermined place in a classroom that contains all the directions and materials needed for a specific task or type of task. Learning centers do not usually generate a product, except on a long-term basis, and they do not have a teacher present during the time that students are there. Learning centers can be short-term (e.g., to complete an art project related to a theme) or long-term (like a listening center, but listening materials change periodically) and can either be student-selected, teacher-assigned, or both, depending on the circumstances.

Learning Station   *See* Learning Center.

Literature-Based Reading   A curricular practice in which literary works, usually trade books, are the dominant materials for instruction (Harris & Hodges, 1995). Literature-based reading as a practice is consistent with whole language philosophy.

Looping   The practice in which a teacher moves with a class to a subsequent grade level for the purpose of continuity of instruction and relationship, such as a first-grade teacher remaining with a group of children when they become second graders. Also called *cycling*.

Mission   The charge or purpose of a school, district, or organization.

Multiage Grouping   The deliberate grouping of students across grade levels instead of segregating them by age or grade level, forming a single learning community; the community in which most children reside for longer than 1 academic year (Kasten & Clarke, 1993). Configurations of multiage grouping vary, such as *composite* (two grade levels, traditionally speaking, such as K–1, 1–2, 2–3, 3–4, or 4–5), *triple* (three grade levels, traditionally, such as K–2, 1–3, 3–5, or 4–6), or *spectrum* (more than triple, such as K–5).

Nongradedness   A set of principles—including goals for schooling, organizational structures, curriculum, instruction, materials, and assessment for educational reform—based on a strong body of research about best practices for schools. (Anderson & Pavan, 1993)

Peer Tutoring   Students teaching other students, directly or indirectly, who are of similar ages and abilities but more experienced in the concept being taught.

Primary House   A multiage classroom, whether self-contained or team taught, that encompasses most or all primary-age children. Configurations vary somewhat, such as K–2, K–3, or 1–3. In most cases, a primary house also qualifies as a triple or spectrum multiage grouping.

Reader's Workshop   A period of time in the instructional day set aside to focus on the process of reading (although reading will likely be related in various ways to theme study in the classroom) that consists of several components, which include (but are not limited to) opportunities for students' independent reading, book sharing, book discussions in groups, and minilessons by the teacher for skill instruction.

Rubric   An assessment tool that is constructed for a particular project or situation that describes the criteria for the most desirable outcome and assigns a value (such as a number or letter) to the best examples, with lesser criteria for each decreasing level of desirability. Rubrics are like the ratings given to motels and restaurants (three-star, four-star, five-star) based on established criteria that include facilities and services. In education, rubrics are used widely for writing proficiency tests but can also be constructed by a teacher for the evaluation of a report, project, or presentation.

Shared Book Experience   First developed by Holdaway (1979), an instructional format in which teachers use predictable (usually) big books with enlarged text, have students read chorally while the teacher points to the text, and teach extension activities and skill lessons within this story-reading format.

Shared Reading Experience   *See* Shared Book Experience.

Spectrum Multiage   A multiage grouping of more than three traditional grade levels, such as K–3, K–5, K–8.

Split Class   A classroom made up of students from more than one grade level (usually two), placed together for economic or practical staffing considerations (e.g., not enough students to afford a teacher for each group or to constitute two separate classes). In such a case, students are treated as separate groups in most curricula and sometimes even in lunch periods, physical education, and so on. Also called *combined* or *combination class*.

Standardized Test   A group-administered test based on psychometric principles of reliability, objectivity, and validity that employs mostly or solely multiple-choice items and has been normed based on a sample test group. The results were designed to track trends and can take the form of achievement tests or other forms. Standardized tests reward the ability to think quickly, convergently, and superficially but cannot measure the ability to think deeply, divergently, or creatively (Darling-Hammond et al., 1995; Kamii, 1990). They are consistent with a factory model of learning and education (Hart, 1994) and are especially inappropriate for primary-age children (Kamii, 1990).

Teamed Multiage Classroom   A deliberate class structure and grouping pattern in which two or more teachers create a larger multiage learning community in a larger classroom, accomplishing planning and teaching together in some fashion. Grouping patterns might be composite (two traditional grade levels), primary house (all primary grades, K–2, or K–3), or intermediate house (3–5 or 4–6). Classrooms are still heterogeneous in ability and achievement and balanced for gender and ethnicity.

Thematic Teaching   A curriculum designed to integrate all or nearly all subjects into a theme, such as *Our Changing World* or *Peoples of the Earth*. Thematic teaching includes large- and small-group instruction, independent study, and learning centers or stations.

Thematic Unit   The plan for thematic teaching.

Topical Unit   Similar to a thematic unit but based on a more specific topic, such as *trees, wolves, penguins,* or *Japan,* which is then taught for a period of time and includes some integration of subject areas. Topical units are generally more teacher planned and implemented than thematic or concept units, but they still might include large- and small-group instruction, independent study, and learning stations or centers.

Transmission-Style Teaching   Teaching characterized by lectures or limited to whole-group instruction that is entirely teacher-centered. Knowledge is transmitted to learners and assessed by one method, such as tests.

Triad Multiage   A multiage grouping of three traditional grade levels, such as 1–3, or 4–6.

Vertical Grouping   Another term for multiage grouping or family grouping, in which students are grouped across age and grade levels instead of by them.

Vision   A dream or concept shared within an organization that represents the ideal toward which the group is working.

Whole Language   A set of principles based on research in which language learning and literacy are viewed as dynamic, including a holistic approach to the acquisition and development of literacy and a positive view of all learners. It includes the beliefs that language is central to human learning; that learning is easiest when it proceeds from whole to part, is in authentic contexts, and is functional for learners; that learners and teachers are empowered to make choices and decisions in the context of the classroom; that learning is both personal and social; that educational settings need to be learning communities; that all learners and their languages, cultures, and experiences should be accepted; that learning is both joyous and fulfilling; and that learning is developmental in nature and builds on prior experiences and knowledge. (Whole Language Umbrella brochure, 1996)

Whole Language Umbrella   An international confederation of teachers and other educators dedicated to meaning-centered education that was founded in 1987.

Writer's Workshop   Growing out of the New Hampshire writing research and seminars, writer's workshop is a classroom curricular context that devotes blocks of time to writing several times a week and consists of student writers working on long-term, self-selected, multiple-draft pieces of writing; short minilessons or related mechanical or style issues by the teacher; teacher modeling of writing; sharing of writing; and teacher checks on the status of manuscripts with class members (Atwell, 1987). Adapted to suit the youngest writers (ages 5 or 6) through adult classes, these practices are consistent with current writing research.

References

Aardema, V. (1977). *Who's in rabbit's house?* New York: Dial Books.

Aardema, V. (1991). *Traveling to Tondo.* New York: Knopf.

Anderson, R. H., & Pavan, B. N. (1993). *Nongradedness: Helping it to happen.* Lancaster, PA: Technomic Press.

Anthony, R. J., Johnson, T. D., Mickelson, N. I., & Preece, A. (1991). *Evaluating literacy: A perspective for change.* Portsmouth, NH: Heinemann.

Armstrong, T. (1987). *In their own way.* Los Angeles: Teacher.

Armstrong, T. (1994). *Multiple intelligences in the classroom.* Alexandria, VA: Association for Supervision and Curriculum Development.

Armstrong, W. H. (1969). *Sounder.* New York: HarperTrophy.

Atwell, N. (1987). *In the middle: Writing, reading, and learning with adolescents.* Portsmouth, NH: Heinemann.

Avi. (1990). *The true confessions of Charlotte Doyle.* New York: Avon Books.

Barell, J. (1995). *Teaching for thoughtfulness: Classroom strategies to enhance intellectual development* (2nd ed.). New York: Harper & Row.

Barth, R. S. (1990). *Improving schools from within.* San Francisco: Jossey-Bass.

Baskwill, J. (1989). *Parents and teachers: Partners in learning.* New York: Scholastic.

Bertrand, J. (1991). Assessment and evaluation. In B. Harp (Ed.), *Assessment and evaluation in whole language programs.* Norwood, MA: Christopher-Gordon.

Bickmore-Brand, J. (Ed.). (1990). *Language in mathematics.* Portsmouth, NH: Heinemann.

Bizman, A., Yinon, Y., Mivtzari, E., & Shavit, R. (1978). Effects of the age structure of the kindergarten on altruistic behavior. *The Journal of School Psychology 16*(2), 154–160.

Bonila, J.W. (1991). *Response journals.* New York: Scholastic.

Borders, S., & Naylor, A. (1993). *Children talking about books.* Phoenix, AZ: Oryx Press.

Bornstein, M. H., & Bruner, J. S. (Eds.). (1989). *Interaction in human development*. Hillsdale, NJ: Erlbaum.

Bredekamp, S. (1987). *Developmentally appropriate practice in early childhood programs serving children from birth through age 8*. Washington, DC: National Association for the Education of Young Children.

Bromley, K. (1993). *Journaling*. New York: Scholastic.

Brooks, J. G., & Brooks, M. G. (1993). *The case for constructivist classrooms*. Alexandria, VA: Association for Supervision and Curriculum Development.

Bruner, J. S. (1963). *The process of education*. Cambridge, MA: Harvard University Press.

Bruner, J. S. (1966). *Toward a theory of instruction*. New York: Norton.

Bruner, J. S. (1979). Notes on a theory of instruction. In A. Floyd (Ed.), *Cognitive development in the school years*. New York: Wiley.

Bruner, J.S. (1990). *Acts of meaning*. Cambridge, MA: Harvard University Press.

Buffie, E. G. (1963). A comparison of mental health and academic achievement: The nongraded school vs. the graded school. *Dissertation Abstracts International 23*, A4255.

Bunting, J. R. (1974). Egocentrism: The effects of social interactions through multi-age grouping. (Doctoral dissertation, State University of New York, Buffalo.) *Dissertation Abstracts International 35*(10), 6356A.

Burns, P. C., & Roe, B. D. (1993). *Burns-Roe informal reading inventory*. Princeton, NJ: Houghton Mifflin.

Caldwell, S. D. (Ed.). (1989). *Staff development: A handbook of effective practices*. Oxford, OH: National Staff Development Council.

Calkins, L. M. (1994). *The art of teaching writing*. Portsmouth, NH: Heinemann.

Cambourne, B., Turbill, J., & Dal Santo, D. (1994). Interpreting data: How to make sense of what we collect. In B. Cambourne & J. Turbill (Eds.), *Responsive evaluation: Making valid judgments about student literacy*. Portsmouth, NH: Heinemann.

Canfield, J., & Wells, H. C. (1976). *100 ways to enhance self-concept in the classroom: A handbook for teachers and parents*. Englewood Cliffs, NJ: Prentice-Hall.

Carbone, R. F. (1961). A comparison of graded and nongraded elementary schools. *Elementary School Journal 62*(2), 82–88.

Cazden, C. (1992). *Whole language plus: Essays on literacy in the United States and New Zealand*. New York: Teachers College Press.

Clay, M. (1979). *Concepts about print test*. Portsmouth, NH: Heinemann. (Original work published 1972.)

Clemmons, J., Laase, L., Cooper, D., Areglado, N., & Dill, M. (1993). *Portfolios in the classroom: A teacher's sourcebook*. New York: Scholastic.

Clyde, J. A. (1994). From multiage to multiple ways of knowing: Discovering the strengths of our children. In P. Chase & J. Doan (Eds.), *Full circle: A new look at multiage education*. Portsmouth, NH: Heinemann.

Cordeiro, P. (1992). *Whole learning: Whole language and content in the upper elementary grades*. Katonah, NY: Owen.

Countryman, J. (1992). *Writing to learn mathematics: Strategies that work, K–12*. Portsmouth, NH: Heinemann.

Crafton, L. (1991). *Whole language: Getting started, moving forward*. Katonah, NY: Owen.

Cuban, L. (1988). *The managerial imperative and the practice of leadership in schools*. Albany, NY: State University of New York Press.

Curwin, R. L., & Mendler, A. N. (1988). *Discipline with dignity*. Alexandria, VA: Association for Supervision and Curriculum Development.

Cushman, K. (1990). The whys & hows of the multi-age primary classroom. *American Educator 14*(2), 28–32, 39.

Damon, W. (1984). Peer education: The untapped potential. *Journal of Applied Developmental Psychology 5*, 331–343.

Daniels, H. (1994). *Literature circles: Voice and choice in the student-centered classroom*. Norwood, MA: Christopher-Gordon.

Darling-Hammond, L. (1994). Performance-based assessment and educational equity. *Harvard Educational Review, 64* (1), 5–30.

Darling-Hammond, L., Ancess, J., & Falk., B. (1995). *Authentic assessment in action: Studies of schools and students at work*. New York: Teachers College Press.

Day, B., & Hunt, G. H. (1975). Multi-age classrooms: An analysis of verbal communication. *Elementary School Journal 75* (7), 458–464.

DeFina, A. A. (1992). *Portfolio assessment: Getting started*. New York: Scholastic.

Dewey, J. (1897). *My pedagogic creed*. Kellogg.

DiLorenzo, L. T., & Salter, R. (1965). Co-operative research on the nongraded primary. *Elementary School Journal 65* (5), 269–277.

Doise, W., & Mugny, G. (1984). *The social development of the intellect*. Elmsford, NY: Pergamon Press.

Drake, J. (1993). Daniel and Collis: At-risk students growing towards literacy through college age tutoring. *Ohio Reading Teacher 27* (3), 3–6.

Edelsky, C., Altwerger, B., & Flores, B. (1991). *Whole language: What's the difference?* Portsmouth, NH: Heinemann.

Eisner, E. W. (1994). *Cognition and curriculum reconsidered*. New York: Teachers College Press.

Emig, J. (1981). Writing as a mode of learning. In G. Tate & E. Corbett (Eds.), *The writing teacher's sourcebook*. New York: Oxford University Press.

Epstein, J. (1995). School, family, community partnerships: Caring for children we share. *Phi Delta Kappan 76* (9), 705–707.

Farr, R., & Tone, B. (1994). *Portfolio and performance assessment: Helping students evaluate their progress as readers and writers*. New York: Harcourt Brace Jovanovich.

Flower, L., & Hayes, J. R. (1981). A cognitive process theory of writing. *College Composition and Communication 32* (4), 365–387.

Ford, B. E. (1977). Multiage grouping in the elementary school and children's affective development: A review of recent research. *Elementary School Journal 78* (2), 149–160.

Forester, A. D., & Reinhard, M. (1989). *The learner's way.* Winnipeg, Manitoba, Canada: Peguis.

Freeman, M. S. (1995). *Building a writing community: A practical guide.* Gainesville, FL: Maupin.

Fullan, M. (1993). *Change forces: Probing the depths of educational reform.* Bristol, PA: Falmer Press.

Fulwiler, T. (Ed.). (1987). *The journal book.* Portsmouth, NH: Heinemann.

Gajadharsingh, J. (1991). *The multi-age classroom: Myth and reality.* Toronto, Ontario, Canada: Canadian Education Association.

Gardner, H. (1991a). *The unschooled mind.* NY: Basic Books.

Gardner, H. (1991b). The school of the future. In J. Brockman (Ed.), *Ways of knowing.* New York: Prentice-Hall.

Gardner, H. (1993). *Multiple intelligences: The theory in practice.* New York: Basic Books.

Gartner, A., Kohler, M. C., & Riessmon, F. (1971). *Children teach children: Learning by teaching.* New York: Harper & Row.

Gawned, S. (1990). An emerging model of the language of mathematics. In J. Bickmore-Brand (Ed.), *Language in mathematics.* Portsmouth, NH: Heinemann.

Gayfer, M. (Ed.). (1991). *The multigrade classroom: Myth and reality.* Toronto, Ontario, Canada: Canadian Education Association.

Genishi, C. (Ed.). (1992). *Ways of assessing children and curriculum: Stories of early childhood practice.* New York: Teachers College Press.

Gibbs, J. (1995). *Tribes: A new way of learning and being together.* Sausalito, CA: CenterSource Systems.

Ginsburg, H., & Opper, S. (1969). *Piaget's theory of intellectual development: An introduction.* Englewood Cliffs, NJ: Prentice-Hall.

Gipps, C., & Murphy, P. (1994). *A fair test? Assessment, achievement, and equity.* Philadelphia: Open University Press.

Glatthorn, A. A. (1994). *Developing a quality curriculum.* Alexandria, VA: Association for Supervision and Curriculum Development.

Goldman, J. A. (1981). Social participation of preschool children in same versus mixed age groups. *Child Development 52* (2), 644–650.

Goodlad, J. I. (1966). *School, curriculum, and the individual.* Waltham, MA: Blaisdell.

Goodlad, J. I. (1984). *A place called school.* New York: McGraw-Hill.

Goodlad, J. I., & Anderson, R. H. (1987). *The nongraded elementary school*. New York: Teachers College Press.

Goodman, K. (1986). *What's whole in whole language?* Portsmouth, NH: Heinemann.

Goodman, K., Bird, L. B., & Goodman, Y. (1992). *The whole language catalog supplement on authentic assessment*. Santa Rosa, CA: American School.

Goodman, K., Goodman, Y., & Bird, L. (1991). *The whole language catalog*. Santa Rosa, CA: American School.

Goodman, K., Goodman, Y., & Hood, W. (1989). *The whole language evaluation book*. Portsmouth, NH: Heinemann.

Goodman, Y., & Altwerger, B. (1981). *Print awareness in preschool children: A study of the development of literacy in preschool children* (Occasional Paper No. 4). Tucson, AZ: University of Arizona Program in Language and Literacy.

Goodman, Y., Hood, W., & Goodman, K. (1991). *Organizing for whole language*. Portsmouth, NH: Heinemann.

Goodman, Y., Watson, D., & Burke, C. (1987). *The reading miscue inventory: Alternative procedures*. New York: Owen.

Graves, D. H. (1983). *Writing: Teachers and children at work*. Portsmouth, NH: Heinemann.

Graves, D. H. (1991). *Build a literature classroom*. Portsmouth, NH: Heinemann.

Graziano, W., French, D., Brownell, C. A., & Hartup, W. W. (1976). Peer interaction in same and mixed age triads in relation to chronological age and incentive condition. *Child Development 47* (3), 707–714.

Griffin, P., Smith, P., & Burrill, L. (1995). *The American literacy profiles: A framework for authentic assessment*. Portsmouth, NH: Heinemann.

Halliwell, J. W. (1963). A comparison of pupil achievement in graded and non-graded primary classrooms. *Journal of Experimental Education 32* (1), 59–66.

Hammack, B. G. (1974). *Self-concept: Evaluation of preschool children in single and multiage classroom settings*. Unpublished doctoral dissertation, Texas Women's University, Denton.

Harp, B. (1991). Principles of assessment and evaluation in whole language classrooms. In B. Harp (Ed.), *Assessment and evaluation in whole language programs*. Norwood, MA: Christopher-Gordon.

Harp, B. (Ed.). (1994). *Assessment and evaluation for student centered learning* (2nd ed.). Norwood, MA: Christopher-Gordon.

Harris, T. L., & Hodges, R. E. (Eds.). (1995). *The literacy dictionary: The vocabulary of reading and writing*. Newark, DE: International Reading Association.

Hart, D. (1994). *Authentic assessment: A handbook for educators*. Menlo Park, CA: Addison-Wesley.

Hart, L. A. (1983). *Human brain and human learning*. White Plains, NY: Longman.

Hartup, W. (1976). Cross-age versus same-age peer interaction: Ethnological and cross-cultural perspectives. In V. L. Allen (Ed.), *Children as teachers: Theory and research on tutoring* (pp. 41–45). New York: Academic Press.

Hartup, W. (1977). Developmental implications and interactions in same and mixed age situations. *Young Children 32* (3), 4–13.

Hartup, W. (1979). The social worlds of childhood. *American Psychologist 34* (10), 944–950.

Heald-Taylor, G. (1989). *The administrator's guide to whole language.* Katonah, NY: Owen.

Healy, J. M. (1987). *Your child's growing mind.* New York: Doubleday.

Hedin, D. (1987). Students as teachers: A tool for improving school. *Social Policy 17,* 42–47.

Herman, J. L., Aschbacher, P. R., & Winters, L. (1992). *A practical guide to alternative assessment.* Alexandria, VA: Association for Supervision and Curriculum Development.

Hester, J. P. (1994). *Teaching for thinking: A program for school improvement through teaching critical thinking across the curriculum.* Durham, NC: Carolina Academic Press.

Hillson, M., Jones, J. C., Moore, J. W., & Van Devender, F. (1965). A controlled experiment evaluating the effects of a non-graded organization on pupil achievement. In M. Hillson (Ed.), *Change and innovation in elementary school organization.* New York: Holt Rinehart & Winston.

Holdaway, D. (1979). *The foundations of literacy.* Sydney, Australia: Ashton Scholastic.

Hooper, F. H. (1968). Piagetian research and education. In I. E. Sigel & F. H. Hooper (Eds.), *Logical thinking in children: Research based on Piaget's theory.* New York: Holt Rinehart & Winston.

Hunt, I. (1964). *Across five Aprils.* New York: Grosset & Dunlap.

Hunt, I. (1976). *The lottery rose.* New York: Tempo Books.

Hunter, M. (1992). *How to change to a nongraded school.* Alexandria, VA: Association for Supervision and Curriculum Development.

Jalongo, M. R. (1991). *Creating learning communities.* Bloomington, IN: National Educational Service.

Jensen, E. (1996). *Brain-based learning.* Del Mar, CA: Turning Point.

Johnson, D. W., & Johnson, R. T. (1987). *Learning together and alone.* Englewood Cliffs, NJ: Prentice-Hall.

Johnson, D. W., Johnson, R. T., Holubec, E. J., & Roy, P. (1984). *Circles of learning.* Alexandria, VA: Association for Supervision and Curriculum Development.

Joyce, B., Wolf, J., & Calhoun, E. (1993). *The self-renewing school.* Alexandria, VA: Association for Supervision and Curriculum Development.

Juel, C. (1991). Cross-age tutoring between student athletes and at-risk children. *Reading Teacher 45* (3), 178–186.

Kamii, C. (1990). *Achievement testing in the early grades: The games grown-ups play*. Washington, DC: National Association for the Education of Young Children.

Kasten, W. C. (1991). Books beget books. In Y. Goodman, L. Bird, and K. Goodman (Eds.), *The whole language catalog*. Santa Rosa, CA: American School.

Kasten, W. C. (1995). Literature circles for the teaching of literature-based reading. In M. C. Radencich & L. J. McKay (Eds.), *Flexible grouping for literacy in the elementary grades*. Boston: Allyn & Bacon.

Kasten, W. C., & Clarke, B. K. (1993). *The multi-age classroom: A family of learners*. Katonah, NY: Owen.

Kasten, W. C., Clarke, B. K., & Nations, R. O. (1988). Reading/writing readiness for preschool and kindergarten children: A whole language approach. *Research Bulletin, 21* (1).

Klein, D. (1985). Some notes on the dynamics of resistance to change: The defender role. In W. G. Bennis, K. D. Benne, & R. Chin (Eds.), *The planning of change* (pp. 98–105). New York: Holt Rinehart & Winston.

Klitgaard, R. E. (1974). *Achievement scores and educational objectives*. Santa Monica, CA: Rand.

Kohn, A. (1996). *Beyond discipline*. Alexandria, VA: Association for Supervision and Curriculum Development.

Kostelnik, M. J., Soderman, A. K., & Whiren, A. P. (1993). *Developmentally appropriate programs in early childhood education*. New York: Macmillan.

Kotter, J. P. (1996). *Leading change*. Boston: Harvard Business School Press.

Laughlin, M. K., & Latrobe, K. H. (1990). *Readers' theatre for children*. Englewood, CO: Teachers Ideas Press.

Leland, C., & Fitzpatrick, R. (1994). Cross-age interaction builds enthusiasm for reading and writing. *Reading Teacher 47* (4), 292–301.

Leland, C. H., & Harste, J. C. (1994). Multiple ways of knowing: Curriculum in a new key. *Language Arts 71* (5), 337–345.

Lewin, K. (1947). Frontiers in group dynamics. *Human Relations 1*, 5–41.

Little, N., & Allan, J. (1988). *Student-led teacher parent conferences*. Toronto, Ontario, Canada: Lugus.

Lolli, E. M. (1994). *An examination of a nongraded, multiage school from the perspective of the participants: A case study*. Unpublished doctoral dissertation, Miami University, Oxford, Ohio.

Lougee, M. D., Grueneich, R., & Hartup, W. W. (1977). Social interaction in same- and mixed-age dyads of preschool children. *Child Development 48* (3), 1353–1361.

Lowry, L. (1989). *Number the stars*. Boston: Houghton Mifflin.

MacLachlan, P. (1985). *Sarah, plain and tall*. New York: Harper & Row.

Manning, G., & Manning, M. (Eds.). (1989). *Whole language: Beliefs and practices K–8*. Washington, DC: National Education Association.

Martin, B., Jr. (1967). *Brown bear, brown bear, what do you see?* New York: Holt Rinehart & Winston.

Matlin, M. L., & Short, K. G. (1991). How our teacher study group sparks change. *Educational Leadership 49* (3), 86.

Mayer, M. (1973). *What do you do with a kangaroo?* New York: Four Winds Press.

McCutcheon, G. (1995). *Developing the curriculum: Solo and group deliberation.* White Plains, NY: Longman.

McKenna, M. C., & Kear, D. J. (1990). Measuring attitudes toward reading: A new tool for teachers. *Reading Teacher 43* (9), 626–639.

McLoughlin, W. P. (1969). *Evaluation of the non-graded primary.* Jamaica, NY: St. John's University.

Milburn, D. (1981). A study of multi-age or family grouped classrooms. *Phi Delta Kappan 62* (7), 513–514.

Miles, M. B. (Ed.). (1964). *Innovation in education.* New York: Teachers College Press.

Mills, H., O'Keefe, T., & Whitin, D. (1996). *Mathematics in the making: Authoring ideas in primary classrooms.* Portsmouth, NH: Heinemann.

Mitchell, J. (1991, April). Two grades are better than one. *Teacher,* pp. 62–63.

Mooney, M. (1988). *Developing life-long readers.* Wellington, New Zealand: Department of Education.

Morris, V., Proger, B., & Morrell, J. (1971). Pupil achievement in a nongraded primary plan after 3 and 5 years of instruction. *Educational Leadership 4* (5), 621–625.

Most, B. (1996). *If the dinosaurs came back.* Boston: Houghton Mifflin.

Muir, M. (1970). How children take responsibility for their learning. In V. Rogers (Ed.), *Teaching in the British primary school.* London: Macmillan.

Nanus, B. (1992). *Visionary leadership.* San Francisco: Jossey-Bass.

Nelson, J. (1987). *Positive discipline.* New York: Ballantine Books.

Nessel, D. D., & Jones, M. B. (1981). *The language experience approach to reading.* New York: Teachers College Press.

Noguera, P. A. (1995). Preventing and producing violence: A critical analysis of responses to school violence. *Harvard Educational Review 65* (2), 189–212.

Oakes, J. (1985). *Keeping track.* New Haven, CT: Yale University Press.

Oja, S. N. (1980). Adult development is implicit in staff development. *Journal of Staff Development 1,* 7–56.

Ostrow, J. (1995). *A room with a different view: First through third graders build community and create curriculum.* York, ME: Stenhouse.

Otto, H. J. (1969). *Nongradedness: An elementary school evaluation.* Austin, TX: University of Texas.

Owens, R. G. (1981). *Organizational behavior in education.* Englewood Cliffs, NJ: Prentice-Hall.

Papay, J. P., Costello, R. J., Hedl, J. J., & Speilberger, C. D. (1975). Effects of trait and state anxiety on the performance of elementary school children in traditional and individualized multiage classrooms. *Journal of Educational Psychology 67* (6), 840–846.

Parker, R. E. (1993). *Mathematical power: Lessons from a classroom.* Portsmouth, NH: Heinemann.

Paterson, K. (1977). *Bridge to Terabithia.* New York: Avon Camelot.

Pavan, B. N. (1973). Good news: Research in the nongraded elementary school. *Elementary School Journal 73* (6), 233–242.

Pavan, B. N. (1995). The waxing and waning of nongradedness. In R. Fogerty, *Think about . . . multiage classrooms: An anthology of original essays.* Palatine, IL: IRI/Skylight Training.

Pengelly, H. (1990). Acquiring the language of mathematics. In J. Bickmore-Brand (Ed.), *Language in mathematics* (pp. 10–26). Portsmouth, NH: Heinemann.

Perl, S. (1980). Understanding composing. *College Composition and Communication 31* (4), 363–369.

Perrone, V. (1990). How did we get here? In C. Kamii (Ed.), *Achievement testing in the early grades.* Washington, DC: National Association for the Education of Young Children.

Perrone, V. (Ed.). (1991). *Expanding student assessment.* Alexandria, VA: Association for Supervision and Curriculum Development.

Peterson, R. (1992). *Life in a crowded place.* New York: Scholastic.

Peterson, R., & Eeds, M. (1990). *Grand conversations.* New York: Scholastic.

Piaget, J. (1977). Logique genetique et sociologie [Genetic logic and sociology]. In *Etudes sociologiques* (pp. 203-239). Geneva, Switzerland : Librairie Droz. (Original work published 1928)

Pontecorvo, C., & Zucchermaglio, C. (1990). A passage to literacy: Learning in a social context. In Y. Goodman (Ed.), *How children construct literacy: Piagetian perspectives* (pp. 59–98). Newark, DE: International Reading Association.

Pratt, D. (1986). On the merits of multiage classrooms. *Research in Rural Education 3* (3), 111–115.

Raines, S. (1995). *Whole language across the curriculum.* New York: Teachers College Press.

Raines, S., & Canaday, R. (1990). *The whole language kindergarten.* New York: Teachers College Press.

Rasinksi, T., & Padak, N. (1996a). Five lessons to increase reading fluency. In L. Putnam (Ed.), *How to become a better reading teacher: Strategies for assessment and intervention.* Englewood Cliffs, NJ: Merrill.

Rasinski, T., & Padak, N. (1996b). *Holistic reading strategies: Teaching children who find reading difficult.* Englewood Cliffs, NJ: Merrill.

Renwick, W. L. & Department of Education. (1985). *Reading in junior classes.* Wellington, New Zealand: Department of Education.

Resnick, L. (Ed.). (1976). *The nature of intelligence.* Hillsdale, NJ: Erlbaum.

Resnick, L. (1987). *Education and learning to think.* Washington, DC: National Academy Press.

Resnick, L., & Klopfer, L. (1989). Toward the thinking curriculum: An overview. In *Toward the thinking curriculum: Current cognitive research.* Alexandria, VA: Association for Supervision and Curriculum Development.

Rhodes, L. (Ed.). (1993). *Literacy assessment: A handbook of instruments.* Portsmouth, NH: Heinemann.

Rich, D. (1992). *Megaskills.* New York: Houghton Mifflin.

Ridgway, L., & Lawton, I. (1965). *Family grouping in the primary school.* London: Redwood Press.

Rogers, V. (1970). *Teaching in the British primary school.* London: Macmillan.

Roser, N. L., & Martinez, M. G. (Eds.). (1995). *Book talk and beyond: Children and teachers respond to literature.* Newark, DE: International Reading Association.

Rowan, T. E., & Bourne, B. (1994). *Thinking like mathematicians: Putting the K–4 NCTM standards into practice.* Portsmouth, NH: Heinemann.

Schmoker, M. (1996). *Results: The key to continuous school improvement.* Alexandria, VA: Association for Supervision and Curriculum Development.

Schrankler, W. J. (1976). Family groupings and the affective domain. *Elementary School Journal 16* (7), 432–439.

Scieszka, J. (1989). *The true story of the three little pigs.* New York: Viking.

Seeger, P. (1986). *Abiyoyo.* New York: Macmillan.

Sendak, M. (1963). *Where the wild things are.* New York: Harper & Row.

Shaklee, B., Barbour, N., Ambrose, R., & Hansford, S. (1997). *Designing and using portfolios.* Boston: Allyn & Bacon.

Shearer, C. B. (1996). *The MIDAS: A guide to assessment in education for the multiple intelligences.* Columbus, OH: Greyden Press.

Sherblom, S. A., Tchascha, J. D., & Szulc, P. M. (1995). A dialogue with Noam Chomsky. *Harvard Educational Review 65* (2), 127–144.

Slavin, R. (1988). Synthesis on research on grouping in elementary and secondary schools. *Educational Leadership 46* (1), 67–77.

Slavin, R. (1989). *School and classroom organization.* Hillsdale, NJ: Erlbaum.

Smith, J. W. A., & Elley, W. B. (1994). *Learning to read in New Zealand.* Katonah, NY: Owen.

Steere, B. F. (1972). Non-gradedness: Relevant research for decision making. *Educational Leadership 29* (8), 709–711.

Steig, W. (1969). *Sylvester and the magic pebble.* New York: Prentice-Hall.

Sylvester, R. (1995). *A celebration of neurons: An educator's guide to the human brain.* Alexandria, VA: Association for Supervision and Curriculum Development.

Teale, W. H., & Labbo, L. D. (1990). Cross-age reading: A strategy for helping poor readers. *Reading Teacher 43*, 363–369.

Tierney, R. T., Carter, M. A., & Desai, L.E. (1991). *Portfolio assessment in the reading-writing classroom.* Norwood, MA: Christopher-Gordon.

Trelease, J. (1995). *The read aloud handbook* (4th ed.). New York: Penguin Books.

Trudge, J., & Rogoff, B. (1989). Peer influences on cognitive development: Piagetian and Vygotskian perspectives. In M. H. Bornstein & J. S. Bruner (Eds.), *Interaction in Human Development*. Hillsdale, NJ: Erlbaum.

Trussell-Cullen, A. (1996). *Inside New Zealand classrooms*. Katonah, NY: Owen.

Vacca, J. L., Vacca, R. T., & Gove, M. K. (1995). *Reading and learning to read*. New York: HarperCollins.

Valdes, G., & Figueroa, R. A. (1994). *Bilingualism and testing: A special case of bias*. Norwood, NJ: Ablex.

Valletutti, P. J., & Dummett, L. (1992). *Cognitive development: A functional approach*. San Diego, CA: Singular.

Veenman, S. (1995). Cognitive and noncognitive effects of multigrade and multi-age classes: A best evidence synthesis. *Review of Educational Research* 65 (4), 319–382.

Villa, R. A., & Thousand, J. S. (Eds.). (1995). *Creating an inclusive school*. Alexandria, VA: Association for Supervision and Curriculum Development.

Vygotsky, L. (1978). *Mind in society*. Cambridge, MA: Harvard University Press.

Vygotsky, L. (1981). The genesis of higher mental functions. In J. V. Wertsch (Ed.), *The concept of activity in Soviet psychology* (pp. 144–188). Armond, NY: Sharpe.

Wakefield, A. P. (1979). Multiage grouping in day care. *Children Today* 8 (3), 26–28.

Walmsley, B. B., Camp, A. M., & Walmsley, S. A. (1992). *Teaching kindergarten: A developmentally appropriate approach*. Portsmouth, NH: Heinemann.

Ward, G. (1988). *I've got a project on*. Roselle, New South Wales: Primary English Teaching Association.

Watson, D. J. (Ed.). (1987). *Ideas and insights: Language arts in the elementary school*. Urbana, IL: National Council of Teachers of English.

Way, J. W. (1979). Verbal interaction in multi-age classrooms. *Elementary School Journal* 79 (3), 178–186.

Weaver, C. (1990). *Understanding whole language*. Portsmouth, NH: Heinemann.

Webb, R. A. (Ed.). (1977). *Social development in childhood: Day care programs and research*. Baltimore: Johns Hopkins University Press.

Weber, L. (1971). *The English infant school and informal education*. Englewood Cliffs, NJ: Prentice-Hall.

Wheelock, A. (1994). *Alternatives to tracking and ability grouping*. Arlington, VA: American Association of School Administrators.

Whitin, D. J., & Wilde, S. (1992). *Read any good math lately?: Children's books for mathematical learning, K–6*. Portsmouth, NH: Heinemann.

Whitin, D. J., & Wilde, S. (1995). *It's the story that counts: More children's books for mathematical learning, K–6*. Portsmouth, NH: Heinemann.

Whole Language Umbrella. (1997). York, Ontario, Canada: York University.

Wing, R. L. (1979). *The I Ching workbook*. Garden City, NY: Doubleday.

Wolfson, B. J. (1967). The promise of multi-age grouping for individualizing instruction. *Elementary School Journal* 67 (7), 354–363.

Wood, D. (1988). *How children think and learn.* Cambridge, MA: Basil Blackwell.

Wood, D. (1989). Social interaction as tutoring. In M. H. Bornstein & J. S. Bruner (Eds.), *Interaction in human development.* Hillsdale, NJ: Erlbaum.

Zajonc, R. B., & Markus, G. B. (1975). Birth order and intellectual development. *Psychological Review 82* (1), 74–88.

Zemelman, S., Daniels, H., & Hyde, A. (1993). *Best practice: New standards for teaching and learning in America's schools.* Portsmouth, NH: Heinemann.

About the Authors

Wendy C. Kasten taught fourth and sixth grades in Maine, along with Title I reading and math, before beginning graduate study. She received her Ph.D. in Language and Literacy at the University of Arizona. She has taught at the University of Maine, University of South Florida, at Deakin University in Australia, and is currently an associate professor of Curriculum and Instruction-Literacy at Kent State University in Kent, Ohio. She teaches courses in reading, writing, action research, and integrated curriculum at undergraduate and graduate levels. Kasten is active in the International Reading Association, the National Reading Conference, the Whole Language Umbrella, and is the 1997–1998 president of the Center for the Expansion of Language and Thinking. She researches in the areas of whole language, multiage education, emergent literacy, multicultural issues in education, teacher reflection and action research. She has published (with B. K. Clarke), *The Multiage Classroom: A Family of Learners* (1993, Owen) as well as other articles. She consults with multiage classrooms in the United States, Canada, Australia, and New Zealand.

Elizabeth Lolli was the founding principal of Central Academy Nongraded, Ohio's Best Elementary School, 1995 as determined by *Redbook's* America's Top 50 Schools. She received her Ph.D. from Miami University of Ohio. Lolli has taught in elementary schools, been an assistant principal, principal, and curriculum coordinator. She currently is Director of Curriculum and Instruction in Northfield, Ohio. She has been published in *Principal* Magazine, the *ERS Spectrum, Reading Today, Primary Voices* and the *OASCD Journal.* She is a national education consultant in multiage and school reform, having consulted in numerous schools in 25 states and at national conferences such as ASCD, IRA, AASA, and NCTE. In addition to working with public schools, Lolli served as an assistant professor of educational administration at Kent State University. Currently she is an adjunct professor for Kent State and the University of Akron.

Author Index

Subject Index

I

Inclusion, 4, 68, 74, 147, 216
Inservice training, 53–54, 89, 111
Instruction. *See also* Teaching
  definition of, 130–131
  student-led, 211

J

Joachim, Judy, 120
Journaling, 199–200; *see also*
  Writing

K

Kinner, Jodi, 137, 213, 217
Kittelberger, Diane, 110

L

Language
  experience approach, 198
  math as, 226–227, 228
  whole, 12, 15, 20, 21, 27, 52, 69,
    76, 92, 111, 132, 192, 198,
    205, 226
Learning centers, 113, 167, 180,
  181, 182, 195, 198, 203, 208,
  234
Library, 64, 77, 137, 155, 156, 157,
  196, 201
Literacy, 20, 69
  strategies, 186–206
  teaching, compared to math,
    228–229, 231
Literature
  -based board games, 194–195
  circles, 192–194
  -extending activities, 195–196
  and math, 232

M

Mailboxes, student, 202
Mann, Horace, 7

Math, 17, 33, 38, 119, 143, 149,
  151, 152, 204, 210, 225–241
  assessment, 68
  center, 167, 237
  fractions, 18
  grouping for, 181, 213
  at home, 108
  in inquiry-based classroom,
    159, 161, 166, 167
  journals, 199, 228, 235–236,
    240
  manipulatives, 36, 37, 52, 68,
    92–93, 156, 237, 239
  real-life, 234–235, 238–239, 240
  scheduling, 215, 217, 220
  test scores, 22, 202
  in topical units, 168
  workshops, 239–240
Minilessons, definition of, 202
Modeling, 140, 226, 236
Multiage
  benefits of, 13–14, 17, 22–23
  and child rearing, 12
  comparative research on, 21–23
  definition of, 3–5
  foundations of, 61–65
  history of, 7, 9, 61, 64
  implementing, 36, 49–50, 52,
    114–115, 117, 120
  materials for, 64, 77, 129, 153–159
  sabotage attempts, 44–45, 114,
    115–116, 120
Multiple intelligences, 147, 152–
  153, 161, 162, 165, 203, 208,
  248
Music. *See* Teachers, special

N

National Association of Education for Young Children
  (NAEYC), 92